rheka

1990

North America

Arctic Ocean

Greenland

(9) Alaska

Hudson Bay

Canada

Pacific Ocean

(6) Oregon Country

Great Lakes

A 530

United States

(2) Treaty of Paris

(7) Mexican Cession

(3) Louisiana Purchase

(1) Original Colonies

(5) Texas Annexation

(8) Gadsden Purchase

(4) Florida Cession

Atlantic Ocean

(10) Hawaii

Mexico

Gulf of Mexico

Cuba

ARCTIC OCEAN

Greenland

Bering Strait

Alaska

Yukon River

HUDSON BAY

ROCKY MOUNTAINS

Canada

St. Lawrence R.

GREAT LAKES

Ottawa R.

United States

SIERRA NEVADA

Colorado R.

GREAT PLAINS

Mississippi R.

Ohio River

Appalachian Mts.

PACIFIC OCEAN

ATLANTIC OCEAN

Rio Grande

GULF OF MEXICO

Florida

Mexico

Yucatán Peninsula

West Indies

CARIBBEAN SEA

Central America

Amazon River

American Heritage Series

★ My America
★★ Our America
★★★ Our American Heritage
★★★★ The History of Our United States
★★★★★ Old World History and Geography
★★★★★★ New World History and Geography

South America

ANDES MOUNTAINS

Atacama Desert

Strait of Magellan

Cape Horn

The History of Our United States

Judy Hull Moore and **Laurel Hicks**

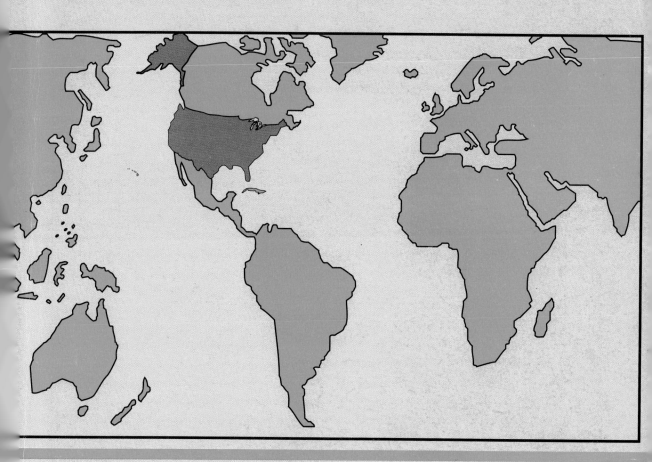

A Beka Book®
A MINISTRY OF
PENSACOLA CHRISTIAN COLLEGE
PENSACOLA, FLORIDA 32523-9160

Pronunciation Key

A pronunciation guide with diacritical marks follows some of the more difficult words and names in the text. The following key will help you to pronounce these words.

ā	ate, they	oi	oil
a	fat	ou	out
ä	father, hot	ū	use, few
â	air, where, their	u	up, oven
ē	eat, people	ə	ago, moment, sanity, comply, circus
e	ten, says, any	ur	urge, earth, first
ī	ice, height, buy	ər	liar, mother, honor
i	it, women, busy	ch	child
ō	open, sew, soul	sh	she
ô	order, all, bought	th	thin
o͞o	brood, rule, move	th	then
oo	book, put, wolf	zh	azure, leisure, pleasure

Revised 1990

Contents

INTRODUCTION:
ONE NATION UNDER GOD

I Pledge Allegiance

I pledge allegiance to the flag of the United States of America and to the Republic for which it stands, one nation under God, indivisible, with liberty and justice for all.

Every school morning, students all over our land rise, face the flag of the United States and with hand over heart, pledge allegiance to the flag. *A* **pledge** *is a promise to do something.* **Allegiance** *means devotion or loyalty.* When you repeat the Pledge, you are promising to be faithful and loyal to your country, the United States of America. You are also saying, "I believe that the flag stands for my country. I believe in a republic where the people choose those who govern them. I believe that our Union of fifty states is united, not divided. I believe that God wants liberty and justice for all people."

This year as you study the history of our United States, you will learn why we promise to be faithful and loyal to our country. You will learn how God has blessed America because of the principles (truths) for which America

1

stands. You will learn to love these wonderful truths that our Declaration of Independence proclaims:

Principles of American Government

1. God has given all men the right to life, liberty, and the pursuit of happiness.
2. It is the job of governments to make sure that these rights are not taken away from the people.
3. The government should not be so powerful that it could take away from the people these God-given rights of life, liberty, and the pursuit of happiness.

One Nation under God

In the beginning, God told men to spread out over the whole earth. He wants people to live and work together as separate **nations.**

People want to do their best when they are serving their nation. In time of war, people even die for their nation. By being willing to die for a noble cause, they show how very different people are from animals. They value not just life, but a noble life. *Next to our love of God and family, nothing should be more dear to us than the love and respect we have for our nation.*

Each nation has its own government. This way it is easier for people to keep governments in control and serving the purposes for which God set up governments.

Each nation has a language that all the people speak. People cannot live well together in a nation unless they speak a common language. It needs to be a language with rules that everyone knows and follows. This is why we study English grammar in school—so we can learn the rules of our language in order to work with the people in our nation. People come to love their own language very much, and their common language helps them to become attached to their neighbors who speak the same language.

This book is the story of one nation, our nation, the United States of America. You will learn how America came to be a nation, who its famous people have been, and what important events have taken place in America. You will learn some of America's great **documents** *(writings),* and you will learn how the truths of the Bible made America the greatest nation on the face of the earth. This year you will learn how America became "one nation under God, indivisible, with liberty and justice for all."

All through history men have struggled for freedom and justice and the right to govern themselves. In many countries people have never seen these wonderful ideas come true for them. But the government of America was founded on the wonderful principles that all men are created equal and are equally deserving of liberty and justice. The people who founded our country, our Founding Fathers, said that these truths were so obvious and clear that everyone who heard them would naturally believe and understand them. This is why they said, in the Declaration of Independence, that all men are created equal.

All Men Are Created Equal

Our Founding Fathers believed that God has created us all. Because God has created us all, we are all of equal value to God, they said. All men belong to God, not to any other man or any government. Everyone is not as strong or smart or talented as everyone else. But everyone belongs to God, and everyone is equally responsible to God to do his duty. No man or government has a right to selfishly take away the rights that God has given to all men equally.

> We hold these truths to be self-evident [open and
>   obvious],
> that all men are created equal;
> that they are endowed by their Creator
> with certain unalienable rights;
> that among these are
>   life,
>   liberty, and
>   the pursuit of happiness.

Life, Liberty, and the Pursuit of Happiness

Our Founding Fathers believed that God has given all men the right to **life.**

Our Founding Fathers believed that God has given all men the right to **liberty.** Liberty is *freedom.* It is not freedom to do whatever you want to do, though. We are not free to hurt other people or steal from them. If we were free to do that, we would be taking away *their* freedom. Our country has laws to protect the freedoms of *all* people.

Our Founding Fathers believed that all men should be free to work hard and earn a living for themselves and their families. This is what they called the right to the **pursuit of happiness.**

The Land of the Free

America is often called the Land of the Free. Americans have freedoms that people in many other countries do not have. We should thank God for our freedoms and pray that they will never be taken away from us.

In America we have **freedom of speech.** This means that

we do not have to be afraid to say what we believe. We also have **freedom of the press,** which means that we can print things in books and newspapers for everyone to read and think about. We have **freedom of assembly,** which means that we can freely meet together in churches and other meetings.

The most wonderful freedom in America is **freedom of religion.** Parents in America are free to take their children to any church they want to. Americans are free to read the Bible for themselves and openly worship God the way they think is right. Americans are free to preach the gospel throughout our land. America is a nation in which people are free to spread Christianity as well as other religions. We should especially thank God for our freedom of religion and pray that no one will ever take it away from us.

As you study American history this year, you will meet many people who came to America to be free. You will learn about people who were even willing to die to make our country free. And you will learn about people all over our land who have used their freedoms to make new homes, study, write, teach, invent things, build cities, preach the gospel, and serve the people of our United States. You will learn of many things that *you* can do to be a good citizen of the United States of America.

Check Your Understanding

1. What are you promising when you pledge allegiance to the flag?

2. What are some of the great American documents? (See pages 308–310.)

3. What is liberty? Do we have freedom to do whatever we want to do? Why not?

The United States

Vermont

Maine

New Hampshire

Massachusetts

Rhode Island

Connecticut

New Jersey

Delaware

Maryland

New York

Pennsylvania

Minnesota

Wisconsin

Michigan

Iowa

Illinois

Indiana

Ohio

West Virginia

Virginia

Missouri

Kentucky

North Carolina

Tennessee

South Carolina

Arkansas

Mississippi

Alabama

Georgia

Louisiana

Florida

Map Study: A World to Explore

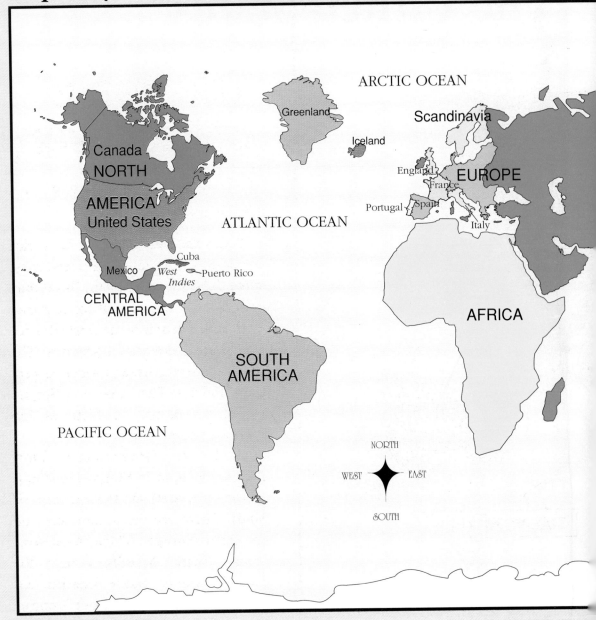

List the seven continents.

_____

_____

ASIA

Japan

China

India

PACIFIC
OCEAN

NDIAN
CEAN

AUSTRALIA

THE WORLD

List the four oceans.

_____

_____

The Years of Discovery

Columbus Discovers America

Today the United States of America is one of the largest, wealthiest, most powerful nations on earth. But it may surprise you to learn that for centuries most of the people in the world did not even know there was an America! The only people who lived in America were a few Indians. There were no cities, no roads, no farms, no factories, no schools, and no churches.

The **history** *of America as we know it actually began in Europe* [yoor'əp]. Europe is a **continent** (a large mass of land). There are seven continents on the earth: **Europe, Africa, Asia, Australia, North America** (where the United States is), **South America,** and **Antarctica.** Although Europe is one of the smallest continents, it has played an important part in history. *Europe is responsible for the settlement of America.* Brave men from Europe set sail five hundred years ago and found two new continents. The two new continents came to be known as **North America** and **South America.** People from Europe came to the new lands to settle them. Most of these people came from the *four countries that are most responsible for the settlement of America:* **England, France, Spain,** *and* **Portugal.**

As you look at the map of the world, you can see the seven continents, including North America and South America. You can also see that much of the earth is covered with water. About three fourths of the earth's surface is covered with water. **Geographers** (*people who study the earth*) call the largest bodies of water **oceans.**

There are four oceans: the **Atlantic** (the most heavily-traveled ocean), the Pacific (the largest ocean), the **Indian,** and the **Arctic.**

Five hundred years ago, Europeans did not have accurate maps like the maps in this book. They did not know how many continents and oceans are on the earth. Many people *thought* they knew what the earth looked like, but they could only guess. Some of them made maps. Many of these ancient maps do not look anything like the true surface of the earth because they were based on incorrect information.

One man who thought he knew what the surface of the earth looked like was **Christopher Columbus.** Columbus was an Italian from **Genoa, Italy,** who had spent much of his life as a sailor. He had read every book he could find about **geography** (*the study of the surface of the earth*).

New Words

1. **continent**—a large mass of land
2. **history**—the story of what has happened in the life of a country or people
3. **geography**—the study of the surface of the earth
4. **Old World**—the name used to refer to Europe
5. **New World**—the name used to refer to America

New Names

6. **Christopher Columbus**—the man who discovered America (but thought it was Asia)
7. **Marco Polo**—an Italian who visited China and described its riches to Europe
8. **Khan**—the ruler of China
9. **Niña, Pinta, Santa Maria**—the three ships used on Columbus's first voyage
10. **Ferdinand and Isabella**—the king and queen of Spain who financed Columbus's voyages
11. **Indians**—the name Columbus gave to the people of the New World
12. **Vikings**—a sea-going Scandinavian people
13. **John Cabot**—the explorer who claimed North America for England
14. **Henry VII**—the king of England who gave Cabot permission to explore America
15. **Amerigo Vespucci**—the explorer who was the first to realize that America was a New World

Christopher Columbus wanted to sail across the ocean to **Asia.** He wanted to visit the land of Cathay (**China**) and Cipangu [si-pang'ōo: **Japan**]. Columbus had read a book by Marco Polo. **Marco Polo** was a merchant who had traveled **east** to China and had visited the Khan [kän: the ruler of China]. After seeing the great wealth of China, Marco Polo went back west to Europe and wrote about the wonders he had seen. Polo's stories were so amazing that some Europeans did not believe them. Others, however, were eager to visit Asia and get some wealth for themselves. Christopher Columbus believed Marco Polo's story and devised a plan to sail across the ocean to China.

Columbus thought that if he sailed **west** *from Europe he would eventually come to Asia.* But if you look at the map, you can easily see what was wrong with his plan: he did not know that two continents and *two* oceans lie between Europe and Asia. Columbus thought that he would have to cross only one ocean, because he did not even know the Pacific Ocean existed.

Ferdinand and **Isabella,** the king and queen of Spain, gave Columbus the funds that he needed. Columbus prepared three ships—the *Nina* [ñē'nyə], the *Pinta* [pēn'tə], and the *Santa Maria* [sän'tə mə-rē'ə]—for the unusual journey.

Finding the ships was not as hard as finding the men to sail the ships. *The fearful and superstitious sailors did not want to go with Columbus into an ocean which no one before them had crossed.* Some of the more ignorant sailors thought that the earth was flat. They were sure that Columbus would

16. **Vasco da Gama**—a Portuguese explorer, the first to sail around the tip of Africa
17. **Balboa**—the Spanish explorer who first saw the Pacific Ocean
18. **Ponce de León**—the explorer who first visited Florida

New Places

19. **Cathay**—an old name for China
20. **Cipangu**—an old name for Japan
21. **San Salvador**—the place where Columbus first landed
22. **Vinland**—the Vikings' name for America

New Dates

23. **1000**—Viking explorers visit North America
24. **1492**—Columbus, seeking a route to Asia, discovers America
25. **1497**—Cabot claims North America for England; da Gama sails around the tip of Africa
26. **1506**—death of Columbus
27. **1507**—the name *America* was first put on a map
28. **1513**—Ponce de Leon searches for the Fountain of Youth in Florida

fall over the edge of the earth if he sailed too far. Even those who knew the earth was round were afraid that the unknown sea was too big to cross. They were afraid that the men would die of starvation and thirst before they reached Asia. And there were also stories about sea monsters which ate ships that had wandered too far into unknown waters.

Finally, Columbus found a crew brave enough to go with him. In August, 1492, Columbus began his first voyage. As the three ships disappeared over the horizon, no one was sure if

This is a portrait of Christopher Columbus, who wanted to find a short route to Asia but instead discovered a New World.

Columbus would ever be seen again.

After two months of sailing west into unknown waters, Columbus's crew began to get nervous. No sign of land had been spotted. They had sailed farther away from land than any crew had before them. The men grew angry and rebellious. They wanted to turn around and head back to Spain. Columbus persuaded them to sail on for three more days.

On the evening of the second day, land was sighted.

Columbus landed on the island of **San Salvador** *on October 12, 1492.* Columbus thought he had reached **India,** which is a part of Asia. Therefore, he referred to the people that he saw on the island as **Indians.** Even though Columbus was thousands of miles away from India, the name he gave to the native Americans remains to this day, and the islands he reached are now called the **West Indies.**

Columbus was interested in the Indians, but he was more interested in gold. He asked the Indians where they had gotten the little gold ornaments that almost all of them wore. One of the places that the Indians mentioned was **Cuba.** We know that Cuba is a large island to the south of Florida, but to Columbus—who thought he was near Asia—the word *Cuba* was the Indians' way of saying the name

Cipangu (Japan).

Columbus visited several islands in the West Indies as he continued his search for gold. On this journey Columbus never actually landed on the coasts of North or South America.

Columbus lost one of his ships, the *Santa Maria,* when it hit a reef and sank. With the two remaining ships, Columbus headed back for Spain. *Despite furious storms along the way, both ships returned safely to Spain.*

Christopher Columbus had accomplished a magnificent feat. His bravery and his skill as a navigator allowed him to explore new lands and new seas. Columbus became an instant hero. The king and queen gave him a royal welcome. *Everyone all over Europe praised Columbus for his bravery,* and everyone waited eagerly to see what Columbus brought back from his journey.

Columbus brought back strange plants, brightly colored birds, carvings, and other interesting items. He even brought back several Indians. But he brought back very little gold. In truth, Columbus's first journey was a disappointment.

Columbus made three more journeys to America. On each one he showed his superior talents as a navigator. Such was his skill that, using only crude maps and instruments, he could always land at the exact point where he landed on his first journey. He was such a good navigator that he could sail around the waters of the New World as though it were his own back yard. But as years passed, people forgot about the excitement they felt when Columbus returned from his first journey. They lost interest in his later journeys. In 1506 Columbus died, a lonely and forgotten man.

According to an old story, Columbus was having dinner with some rich men not long after he had returned from his first voyage. The men, who were jealous of all the attention that Columbus was getting, began to belittle Columbus's achievement by saying that anyone could have done what Columbus did. Columbus picked up an egg and asked the men if they could balance the egg on its end. Each man tried and failed. "It's impossible!" they said. Then Columbus tapped the egg on the table, breaking the shell slightly. When he set the egg on the table, it did not topple over. Columbus looked at the men. "See?" he said. "Even something that is impossible is easy to do—once someone shows you how."

Columbus himself never realized that he had discovered a new world.

Columbus landed on the island of San Salvador on October 12, 1492.

He always insisted that he had really reached Asia. Columbus also thought that he was claiming new lands for the Catholic Church. He wanted the gold he found there to be used by Spain to conquer the world for that church. But God's plans are not always the same as man's plans. The plans that Columbus and the religious leaders of his faith had for America were not God's plans.

Columbus was a great man because he showed others the way to do some-thing that was supposedly impossible —sail across the unknown ocean. Other explorers were quick to realize what Columbus had found.

Soon after Columbus's early voyages other men were sailing west. Columbus led the way for the settlement of the New World, part of which was to become the United States of America. Columbus's daring deeds started a chain of events that would lead to a new country with freedom for all.

Columbus's Journeys to the New World

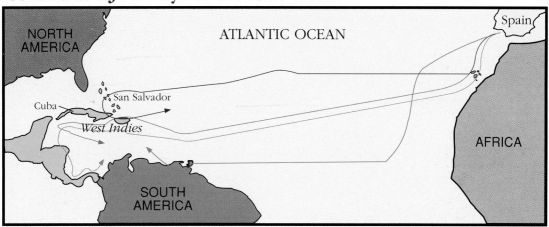

Did You Know?
Christopher Columbus was not actually the first person to discover America, though his discovery was the one that counts. No one realized in 1492 that Europeans had visited America almost 500 years before Columbus.

The **Vikings** were a group of people from **Scandinavia** (a part of northern Europe). The Vikings were always short of two things: land and food. To get food, the Vikings raided the countries around them. People in England, France, and many other countries feared the Vikings. They knew when they saw a Viking ship near their shores that the Vikings had come to rob their food and possessions. The Vikings ran short of land as well as food. As the population grew, the Vikings looked desperately for more lands to settle.

The search for land caused the Vikings to make three interesting discoveries. First they found **Iceland,** a small island between Europe and America. Next they found **Greenland,** the largest island in the world. The Vikings established settlements on both these islands. Then about the year 1000, a ship traveling from Scandinavia to Greenland was blown off course by a storm. When the ship finally arrived in Greenland, the men told of a strange land

15

they had seen to the west. A Viking named **Leif Ericsson** decided to see the new land for himself. Leif Ericsson and his crew became the first Europeans to visit America. They probably landed somewhere in **Canada,** although no one is sure exactly where they landed. Leif Ericsson named the new land **Vinland,** because of all the grape vines the Vikings found there.

Other Vikings went to Vinland and tried to establish a settlement there, but they failed. The Vikings lost interest in Vinland, and Europe had to wait 500 years for the next "discovery" of America.

Why is Columbus more famous than the Vikings? The Vikings kept their discovery a secret; they wanted all the food and land for themselves. But Columbus was eager to share the news with Europe. His voyages led to the settlement of America by Europeans. Columbus's discovery made a difference in history, but the Vikings' discovery did not. The Vikings' discovery of America was a well-kept secret that was almost completely forgotten by history.

Viking explorers landed on the North American continent five hundred years before Columbus reached the New World.

North America Is Claimed for England

There was excitement in the air. News had just reached England that Christopher Columbus's voyage had been successful. Everyone believed what Christopher Columbus himself believed—that he had reached the Far East.

A man by the name of **John Cabot** lived in **England.** He was a mapmaker who liked to sail on the Mediterranean Sea and trade goods. Like everyone else, he was eager to find a sea route to the Indies in order to trade goods for more spices.

"If Columbus had sailed further north, he would have found an even shorter route to the Indies," thought Cabot. "If only I could try myself!"

King Henry VII of England gave Cabot permission. With a crew of only eighteen men, Cabot set sail. No one knows for sure where he landed, but it was most likely in a part of what is now Canada. Thinking that he, too, had reached the lands of the Far East, he claimed the land for England. *This was the first trip an English ship had made to North America.*

Remember John Cabot's claim for England. The year was 1497. *Though many years would pass before it happened, John Cabot's claim would give England the right to begin English colonies in America.* At the time when the English colonies really did get started, the Bible was being read and preached all over England. Englishmen at the time were working hard for self-rule and the right to worship God as they thought the Bible teaches. *The English people who would finally come to America would bring with them ideas about freedom based on the Bible. These ideas would make our country a land of freedom.*

America Gets Its Name

After news of Columbus's discovery spread around, other sea captains lost their fear of sailing across the Atlantic Ocean. They were eager to make their own discoveries.

One such explorer, an Italian named **Amerigo Vespucci** [a-mâr′i-gō ves-pōō′chē], claimed that he had crossed the Atlantic Ocean four times. He wrote a letter saying, "I have found a new world." Like Columbus, he had reached South America, but unlike Columbus, he realized that this could not possibly be part of the Indies.

Although Columbus really found the New World before Vespucci, Vespucci was the first person to call it the

17

"*New World.*" To Europeans, Columbus's discovery and Vespucci's discovery were two different places! From that time on, Europeans spoke of the land Amerigo Vespucci found as the **New World.**

In 1507, a German mapmaker was drawing a map. He did not know what name to give the New World. After reading Vespucci's letters, the mapmaker decided to name the New World "America" in honor of the man he thought had discovered it— **Amerigo** Vespucci.

At first the name "America" meant only South America. With the passing years, as other explorers found out that there were two continents, the name "America" meant both North and South America.

Within thirty years, the **Old World** (Europe) realized that Columbus had discovered the **New World** (America). However, the name "America" remained.

Yet the people of the Old World still believed they could find a faster sea route to the rich Indies from America. To find this route, men tried to get around America. They tried to find a river through America. Little by little, they began to realize the enormous size of the New World. *Columbus's discovery was leading to greater discoveries in the history of America.*

In 1507, a map which looked like this was the first to use the name "America" for the New World. America lies at the left of this map; as you can see, the mapmaker had very little idea of what America actually looked like.

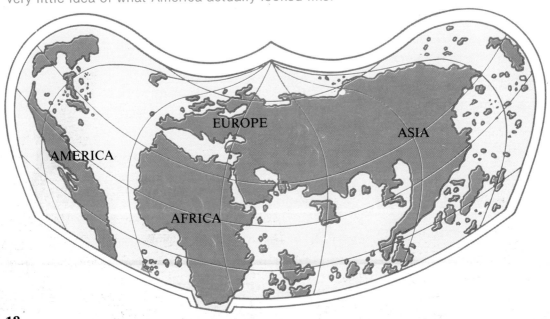

AMERICA

EUROPE

ASIA

AFRICA

Did Anyone Ever Really Find a Sea Route to the Indies?

Before Columbus ever sailed, sea captains from **Portugal** were talking about reaching India by sailing around Africa. Even when Columbus claimed he had reached the Indies in 1492, the Portuguese sea captains went ahead with their plans to sail around Africa.

On July 8, 1497, four ships sailed from Portugal commanded by a Portuguese explorer, **Vasco da Gama** [vas′kō də gä′ma]. The ships sailed south in the Atlantic Ocean, below the tip of Africa, and then north to India.

When Vasco da Gama returned to Portugal, his ships carried the spices and goods from India. Because of da Gama's discovery, Europe found a much cheaper and faster way of getting the spices and goods it had longed for.

Vasco da Gama made a great discovery for Europe by finding a way to sail around Africa to get to India. Although Europe did not realize it yet, Christopher Columbus also made a great discovery for Europe by discovering America. While Portugal interested itself in developing a good trade with the Indies, Spain interested itself in the New World.

A New Ocean Is Found

Spain became very active in the New World. *Many explorers sailed from Spain with the purpose of finding as much gold and wealth as they could.*

After a difficult journey, Balboa looked out over the vast Pacific Ocean.

One of these Spanish explorers was **Vasco Núñez de Balboa** [vas′kō nōōn′yez dā bal-bō′a]. Balboa treated the Spanish men who worked for him fairly. He treated the Indians with kindness and soon won their friendship. The Indians began to tell Balboa wonderful things about their land. They told Balboa that there was another sea to be found if they traveled west.

Taking both Spaniards and Indians, Balboa set out to find the sea. It was not an easy journey. The men had to cut their way through thick jungles and fight sickness as well as the dangers of the jungle in the land in Central America that we now call Panama.

After days of hard work, the Indians pointed to a steep hill. "From there," they said, "you can see the new sea."

Hurriedly, Balboa climbed the hill. From the top, *he saw only a part of the tremendous body of water that would one day be called the* **Pacific Ocean.** *Balboa named it the Great South Sea.*

It took Balboa and his men four more days of walking to reach the shore of the ocean they had seen from that hill. Stepping into the waves of the beautiful blue ocean, *Balboa claimed the ocean and the land for the king of Spain.*

Juan Ponce De León Explores Florida

By now, you must be wondering when an explorer would ever explore land that is now a part of the United States. As far as we know, *the first European to reach what is now the United States was a Spanish explorer by the name of* **Juan Ponce de León** [wän pän′sə dā lā-ôn′].

After Ponce de León sailed with Christopher Columbus on his second voyage to America, he was eager to explore for himself the many islands he saw in the New World. Ponce de León led Spanish soldiers against unfriendly Indians in America. He became the governor of **Puerto Rico,** an island which he had conquered in the West Indies.

One day he heard an Indian say that on the island of Bimini there was a special spring or fountain of water. The Indian's story went on to say that if anyone drank from this fountain, he would become young again.

In 1513, Ponce de León led a group of Spanish explorers to search for the Fountain of Youth, as it came to be called. He found a land that was bright with many wonderful new kinds of flowers. He thought it was an island, but it was really a **peninsula,** *a body of* land with water on three sides of it. He named it **"Florida,"** which is the Spanish name for flowers.

Ponce de León explored the coast of Florida, but he did not find what he was searching for—a Fountain of Youth. He did find many unfriendly Indians who fought against him. Ponce de León decided to return to Puerto Rico.

Several years later, he planned to begin a settlement in Florida. This time, he took about 200 men as well as tools, seeds, and other supplies for the men to begin a new life in Florida. However, the Indians fought fiercely. Most of his men were killed. Ponce de León himself was wounded by an arrow. The men who survived took Ponce de León to the nearby island of **Cuba,** where he died. He never knew the greatness of the land he had found.

Ponce de León explored Florida but never found the Fountain of Youth.

Map Study: Florida and the West Indies

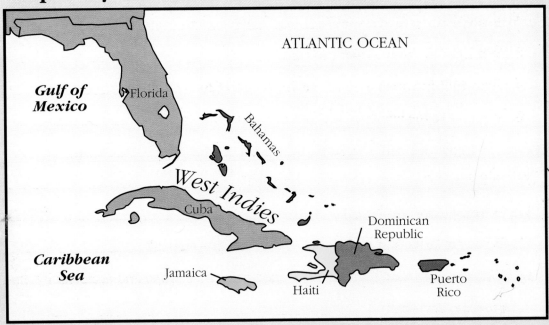

1. What great piece of land did Ponce de León mistake for an island?

   _____

2. Which island did he govern?   3. On which island did he die?

   _____   _____

Facts to Remember

1. What is a continent? _____

2. What are the seven continents? _____

   _____

3. What is the story of what has happened in the life of a country or people

   called? _____

4. What is the study of the surface of the earth called? _____

5. What continent is responsible for the settlement of America? _____

6. What are the four oceans? _____

7. Who discovered America? _____

8. What did Columbus want to find? _____

9. Who told Europeans about his journey to China? _____

10. What were the names of Columbus's three ships? _____

    _____

11. When did Columbus discover America? _____

12. Where did he land? _____

13. What did Columbus call the people he met in America? _____

14. What group from Scandinavia raided parts of Europe and accidentally discovered America? _____

15. When did the Vikings land in America? _____

16. What did the Vikings call America? _____

17. What explorer claimed North America for England in 1497? _____

18. What explorer first called America a "New World"? _____

19. Who first used the name *America?* _____

20. What did the name *America* first stand for? _____

21. What Portuguese explorer first sailed around Africa to get to Asia?

    _____

22. Who was the first Spaniard to reach the Pacific Ocean? _____

23. What did he name the Pacific? _____

24. What explorer wanted to find the Fountain of Youth? _____

25. What land did he explore? _____

The Years of Conquest

The Conquest of Mexico

As we have seen, one man's discovery led to explorations by others. *We will now study the Spanish explorations of Mexico, which soon led to other explorations in what is now the United States.*

The Aztecs

The **Aztecs** *were Indians who had built a large and beautiful city in Mexico.* **Montezuma** [män-tə-zoo′mä] was the name of the Aztecs' ruler. The Aztecs were so rich and powerful that other Indians hundreds of miles away from them had heard of their wealth. The Spanish explorers heard the stories of the Aztecs' wealth from other Indians. Most Spanish explorers were very greedy. More than anything else, the Spanish desired to make these riches their own.

During the years of conquest, European soldiers cruelly conquered the Indians of South America.

Hernando Cortés

In 1519, the Spanish explorer **Hernando Cortés** [âr-nän′do kôr-tez′] *set out to conquer Mexico.* With him, he took a fleet of ships, soldiers, cannons, and horses. When Cortés' ships arrived in Mexico, he gave orders that all ships but one be sunk.

Map Study: Mexico

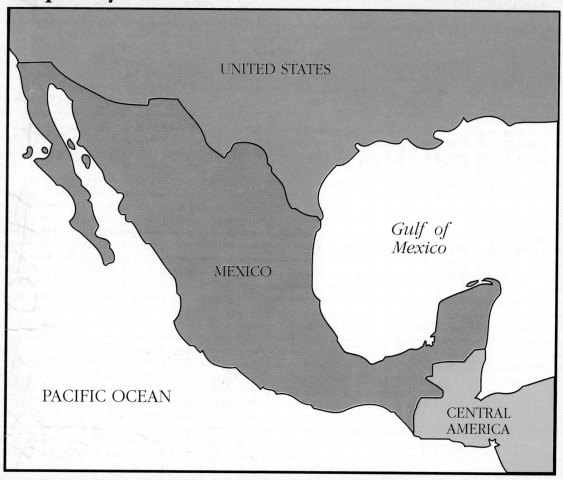

Mexico is in the southwestern part of North America. Of course, this is *not* part of the United States, but it is much closer to the United States than it is to South America. Stories of the great riches found in Mexico led other explorers to search for their share of the riches in other parts of the New World.

The crews watched as one by one, each ship sank below the waves. The one ship that was left was sent back to Spain to give a report to the king.

With the ships gone, every man knew there was no chance to turn back. *Cortés reminded his men of the great wealth yet to be found. To become rich was their goal.* They cared for nothing else. With their cannons and horses, they marched forward.

When they reached the beautiful Az-

When Cortés and his soldiers reached the Aztec capital, Montezuma greeted them with gifts of silver and gold.

tec city, Montezuma himself greeted the Spaniards with gifts of silver and gold. The Spaniards and the Indians were amazed with each other. The Indians had never seen white men, cannons, or horses before. They felt sure that the Spaniards were white gods come to visit them. And the Spaniards had never seen such a wealth of gold and silver before!

The Aztecs were very generous with their gifts of silver and gold, but Cortés was not satisfied. He felt he must have all of the Aztecs' wealth. *After years of cruel, hard fighting in which he killed thousands of Indians, Cortés and his men conquered Mexico.*

Mexico then became a Spanish colony. Ship after ship loaded with gold and silver left for Spain. In the next few years, Mexico as well as other Spanish colonies made Spain the wealthiest country in the world.

Because of Cortés, Spain became rich. The king of Spain was very happy. How happy was Cortés? Sur-

New Words

1. **conquer**—to win by force
2. **fleet**—a number of ships commanded by one man
3. **raid**—a surprise attack

New Names

4. **Aztecs**—an Indian tribe which lived in Mexico
5. **Montezuma**—the ruler of the Aztecs
6. **Cortés**—the Spaniard who conquered the Aztecs

7. **Cartier**—a man who explored the New World for France
8. **Coronado**—the Spanish explorer who traveled throughout the Southwest and discovered the Grand Canyon
9. **De Soto**—the Spanish explorer who discovered the Mississippi
10. **"sea dogs"**—the name given to English pirates who raided Spanish ships
11. **Drake**—the most famous English pirate
12. **Champlain**—the French explorer who founded Quebec

prisingly, he died a poor, lonely man. People became jealous of Cortés. His friends became his enemies. Too late, Cortés realized that gold cannot buy happiness.

People in Spain began to hear how cruelly the Indians of Mexico were being handled. *Catholic priests came from Spain and set up missions.* The purpose of these missions was to teach the Indians their religious beliefs. Sometimes the priests genuinely loved the Indians and treated them well, but sometimes the priests were just as cruel to the Indians as the soldiers were.

France: Cartier Explores the New World

Spain was not the only country interested in what the New World might have to offer. Gold, silver, and furs were powerful riches which drew England and France into the explorations of the New World, too.

But more than the hope of finding gold and silver was the hope of finding a sea route through America which would lead to the even greater riches of the Indies. This was the hope of the French and the English.

If you look on a map of America, you will see that there is no waterway through America. Of course, you must realize that in the 1500's, no one had a true map of America. There was only one way for explorers to find out how big America is. That way was to explore America!

In 1534, a Frenchman named **Jacques Cartier** [zhäk kär-tyā′] *set sail in hopes of finding a waterway through North America to the Pacific Ocean.* Then he planned to sail on to China. If Cartier could find such a route, he would gain wealth for the king of France.

New Places

13. **Seven Cities of Cibola**—fabled cities which Coronado searched for, but never found
14. **Arizona**—the area which Coronado explored while he was searching for the Seven Cities
15. **Mississippi**—the "Father of Waters," the greatest American river, discovered by De Soto
16. **St. Augustine**—the oldest permanent settlement in the United States
17. **New France**—the name first given to Canada
18. **Quebec**—the first French colony in America

New Dates

19. **1519**—Cortés sets out to conquer Mexico and the Aztecs
20. **1534**—Cartier explores the New World for France
21. **1540-1542**—Coronado searches for the Seven Cities of Cibola
22. **1541**—De Soto discovers the Mississippi River
23. **1603**—Champlain arrives in Canada
24. **1608**—Champlain founds Quebec

Many Indians watched as Cartier claimed the land for France. They probably did not understand what he was saying, but they trusted him. *Unlike most of the explorers from Spain, the French explorers were friendly to the Indians.* The Indians had valuable animal furs to trade. Cartier wanted these furs, but he did not *take* them. Instead, he *traded* colorful coats, caps, beads, knives, and other goods for the Indians' furs. The Indians were eager to trade with their new friends, for they had no other way to get these goods.

Cartier was delighted to have the furs to take back to France, but he did not find what he set out to find—a water route through North America to Asia.

However, *Cartier did do three important things for France:*

1. He opened the way for a valuable fur trade between the French and the Indians.

2. He made a lasting and valuable friendship between the French and the Indians.

3. Above all, Cartier's explorations gave France a claim to part of the New World.

Cartier opened the way for a valuable fur trade between the French and the Indians. Here, Cartier's ship is seen exploring the St. Lawrence River.

Map Study: Cartier Finds the St. Lawrence River

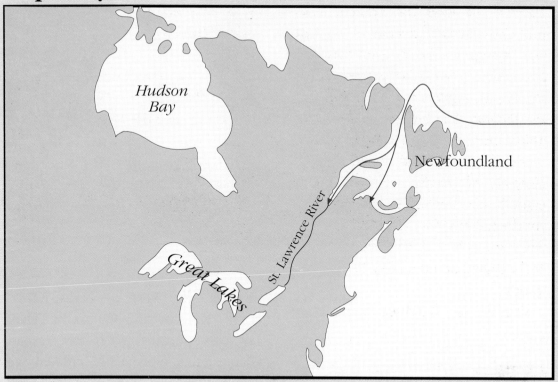

Hudson Bay

Newfoundland

Great Lakes

St. Lawrence River

Cartier sailed around the island of Newfoundland. Then he discovered the mouth of a great river which later was named the St. Lawrence River. Cartier explored this river in hopes of finding a waterway to the Pacific. On the banks of this river, Cartier landed and set up a wooden cross which had these words written upon it: "Long live the king of France." In doing this, he claimed this part of North America for France.

Spain: Coronado's Search for the Seven Cities of Cibola

The year was 1540. *Eager to get rid of the cruel Spanish explorers, the Indians kept telling them stories of golden cities far from their villages of clay.* Perhaps the Indians did this in hopes that the Spanish would wander far away and never bother them again.

The Spanish explorers became excited whenever they heard Indian stories of the Seven Cities of Cibola.

Coronado and his men never found the Seven Cities of Cibola, but they did become the first Europeans to see the Grand Canyon.

"These cities in the country of Cibola are rich in gold and silver," the Indians told the Spanish. "Even the walls of their cities are made of gold."

The Spanish believed these stories and decided they must have this gold too. **Francisco de Coronado** [fran-sis′kō dā kör-ō-nä′dō] was chosen as the captain who would lead three hundred Spaniards as well as several hundred captive Indians in search of the cities.

In his search for the Seven Cities of Cibola, Coronado and his men explored much of what is now the southwestern United States. He marched his men through Arizona, where they discovered the beautiful Grand Canyon. But the Grand Canyon held no interest for Coronado. On they marched through New Mexico, Texas, Oklahoma, Kansas, and Colorado. They saw clay pueblos [pweb′lōz: Indian villages] that glowed like gold in the beautiful sunrise and sunset, but they found no gold.

Finally, Coronado realized that he had been tricked by the Indians. Coronado returned to Mexico in 1542. Only one hundred of the three hundred soldiers he started with returned with him. It had been a long, hard trip. Many men died. Some had been killed by Indians. Some had left Coronado to explore for themselves.

Coronado was brokenhearted. He and his men had marched over 3,000 miles. He had his heart set on finding cities of gold. Instead, he found cities of clay.

Map Study: Coronado in the Southwest

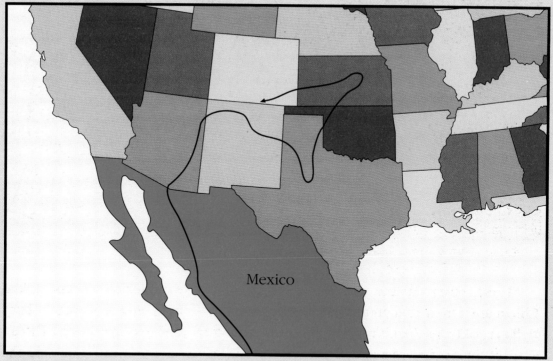

Mexico

Coronado explored much of what is today the southwestern United States. Which states did Coronado explore? See if you can label the states shown on the map. If you need to, refer to the United States map on pages 6 and 7.

De Soto Discovers the Mississippi

Hernando De Soto [âr-nän'dō dā sō'tō] was a very rich Spanish explorer. Although he had all the riches a man could possibly want, he still was not satisfied. Hearing false stories that Florida was a "land of gold," he decided he must have that gold, too.

The true stories of the fierce Indians that killed Ponce de León did not bother De Soto. *He planned to conquer the Indians of Florida.*

De Soto and 600 soldiers sailed to Florida in the hopes of finding gold. Through land that was one day to become Florida, Georgia, South Carolina, North Carolina, and Tennessee, De Soto led his men. Many Indians fought fiercely, for they did not

De Soto and his men discovered the great Mississippi River on their journey.

welcome strangers who came to steal from them.

Though many of his soldiers were being killed by Indians and many more became sick, De Soto would not give up his search for gold. Down through the land that would become Alabama and across Mississippi, De Soto marched his men.

In May, 1541, De Soto and his men discovered a great river. The Indians called it "the Father of Waters." *Later it would become a great highway for boats and would be named the Mississippi River.* It would then become the most valuable river in the United States.

What did De Soto think of this great, wide river that he had discov-ered? To him, it was just a muddy river that stood in his way of finding gold. The river forced him and his men to build boats in which they crossed the Mississippi River and continued their search for gold. Through what is now Arkansas and Louisiana they searched. For all his trouble, De Soto found no gold.

De Soto became sick with a fever and died. Fearing that the Indians would attack them if they knew their leader was dead, the soldiers buried De Soto in the Mississippi River. The remaining soldiers built their own boats and sailed down the Mississippi River until they found safety at a Spanish settlement in Mexico.

Map Study: De Soto in the Southeast

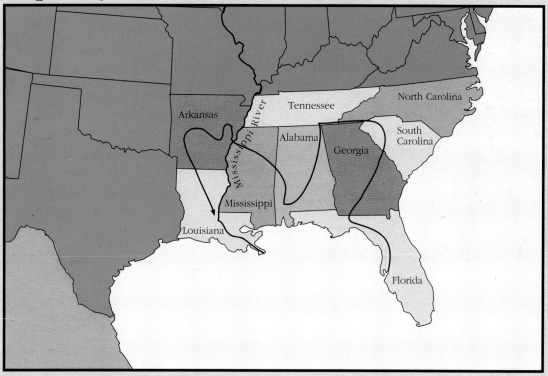

For four years, De Soto and his soldiers had searched what is now the southeastern United States. They discovered the great Mississippi River, but they found no gold.

List the states that De Soto and his men explored.

_____

_____

_____

_____

_____

_____

England: "Drake the Dragon"

Spain had become very wealthy from the explorations of the New World. Her wealth made her a world power. It did not take long for other countries to notice Spain's wealth and power. "Why should Spain have all the riches of the New World?" they asked themselves.

Pirates began to sail where only Spanish ships had sailed before. *At that time, Queen Elizabeth I ruled England. She encouraged English sea captains to raid Spanish boats. These English sea captains who raided Spanish boats were called "sea dogs."*

The most famous sea dog was **Sir Francis Drake.** The queen sent Drake to capture the goods on Spanish ships. After he had taken the goods on board his ship, he often sank the Spanish ship. Then Drake would bring back the Spanish gold, silver, and other treasures to the English queen.

To the Spanish, Drake became the most feared pirate of the time. He was so successful in raiding Spanish ships that the Spanish nicknamed him "Drake the Dragon."

Slowly but surely, Spain lost its great wealth and power. Sir Francis Drake helped England to become more powerful, both on the sea and in the New World.

Queen Elizabeth knighted Francis Drake because he helped England fight against Spain.

St. Augustine, in Florida, is the oldest city in America. This picture shows one of the city's old homes.

France:
The First French Settlement in the New World

The sixteenth century had passed. The seventeenth had begun. Although "Drake the Dragon" had weakened Spain's power, *Spain was the only country that had a settlement in America.* That Spanish settlement in North America was **St. Augustine,** Florida.

The French had discovered that the beautiful animal furs of North America could be sold for high prices in France. Those Frenchmen who were wealthy were willing to pay high prices for beaver hats. Others enjoyed coats made from animal skins. Many Indians were eager to trade their furs with the Frenchmen, who treated them as friends.

In 1603, **Samuel de Champlain** [sam′ū-el dā sham-plān′] *arrived in Canada.* At that time in history, the French called Canada "New France." Champlain and his men explored and traded with the Indians. The French then sailed back to France with a valuable cargo of furs.

Castilio de San Marcos is a fort that was built by the Spanish to defend St. Augustine, our nation's oldest city.

The king of France became interested in starting a settlement in North America. He knew that trading furs with the Indians would be a valuable business. Frenchmen must be sent there to live.

In 1608, Champlain returned to New France (Canada). This time, he also explored the coast line of New England, of which he made good maps. He discovered the beautiful Lake Champlain in what is now New York state. Then he returned to New France, where he helped to build the first important French settlement in the New World. It was named **Quebec** [kwe-bek′].

That meant that three powerful countries now had a claim to land in the New World: England, Spain, and France. Soon you will see how England gained more and more of the land that is now the United States of America, and you will learn about a sea battle that made England one of the most powerful countries in the world. *Because the English people at the time of the settlement of America read and preached the Bible, our country was to become a land of freedom and liberty.*

Facts to Remember

1. What great Indian tribe lived in what is now Mexico? _____

2. Who was their leader? _____

3. What Spanish soldier conquered the Aztecs? _____

4. Who explored North America for France? _____

5. What was Cartier searching for? _____

6. What legendary place did the Indians describe to the greedy Spaniards? ____

_____

7. Who searched for the cities? _____

8. What areas did he explore? _____

_____

9. What natural wonder did Coronado discover on his journey? _____

_____

10. How many soldiers did De Soto take with him on his search for gold? _____

11. What did De Soto discover on his journey? _____

12. What queen permitted British pirates to attack Spanish ships? _____

_____

13. What were the British pirates called? _____

14. Who was the most famous sea dog? _____

15. What was Canada first called? _____

16. What was the first French settlement in America? _____

17. Who helped found it? _____

18. What was the first Spanish settlement in America? _____

19. What were the three powerful countries with claims in the New World during

the years of discovery? _____

_____

The First Americans

The very first Americans did not know anything about the Bible until Europeans brought it to them. Because they did not have the Bible, which tells us about the one true God, they worshiped many false gods. Their worship of false gods kept them from advancing the way the Europeans had.

The Differences in American Indians

When Columbus discovered America, he mistakenly called the people who lived there "Indians" because he thought he was near India. It was a mistake that never was corrected. The original Americans had never called themselves Indians before this. Although each tribe had a name for its own group, as far as we know, no tribe had a name for all the Indians combined. *Each tribe thought of itself as a separate country. Each tribe was*

different from the others in many ways.

Indian Homes

Many people today have the mistaken idea that all Indians lived in *tepees.* This is not true. Few Indians lived in tepees. Pictured are homes of six different groups of Indians. And there were many more.

American Indian Dwellings

A lodge made of earth and wood.

A Sioux teepee.

Iroquois long houses.

A Mandan village.

A hogan.

A pueblo dwelling.

39

Appearance

Some people think that all Indians look alike. As you study the pictures, you will see that this is not true.

These Indians are traveling in birch bark canoes.

Transportation

How did Indians travel? Before the European explorers came, the Indians had no horses or oxen. There was no need for the Indians to have wagons, because they had no animals to pull them.

For most tribes, water was the best way of travel. Therefore, the American Indians built many different kinds of boats.

Indian Games

Indians of all ages loved games. Indian children played much the same as children do today. Little girls often played with dolls made of cornhusks and other dried plants. Boys were given toy bows and arrows with blunt points. With these, they could pretend

New Words

1. **tepee**—a Plains Indian tent made by stretching buffalo skins over poles
2. **bullboat**—a Plains Indian boat made by stretching buffalo skins over a round frame
3. **syllabary**—the name given to the Cherokee alphabet

4. **reservation**—a piece of land that has been set aside by our government for the Indians

New Names

5. **Indians**—the name Columbus gave to the native Americans because he thought he had reached India

to be mighty hunters bringing home deer or buffalo for their family's meat.

And of course, there were always games of skill such as canoe and foot races, fishing, swimming, and target practice. These games not only provided the children with fun; they gave them practice for the day when they would need these skills.

Children were not the only ones who enjoyed games. Both men and women enjoyed sports. Have you ever played the game "Which hand is it in?" in which you tightly close both fists? Inside one fist is an object. The other player then tries to guess which hand holds the object. Nearly all Indians liked to play this game in some form. The most popular way was with moccasins. An object was placed inside each moccasin, but only one object was marked. Each Indian tried to guess which moccasin contained the marked object.

For those Indians who lived in the North, there were winter sports. One popular winter game was snowsnake.

First of all a track was made by dragging a log through the snow. Long sticks were found and made smooth. The end of the stick was carved to look like a snake's head. Each player would try to slide his snowsnake farther than anyone else. When one snowsnake stopped, it was stood upright and stuck in the snow to mark its place. The next person would then try to send his snowsnake even farther.

The Indians' Way of Life Changes

Before the Europeans began exploring America, each Indian tribe took care of all its own needs. They had not yet learned to trade with other tribes, and because of this, they were often very poor.

The Indians were isolated from the gospel and had never seen the Scriptures. Each tribe made its own religion. Some worshiped idols. Some worshiped the sun and moon.

When the white men began to explore and settle America, the In-

6. **John Eliot**—a missionary who translated the Bible into the Indian language
7. **Roger Williams**—a preacher who made friends with the Indians by treating them fairly
8. **David Brainerd**—a missionary who gave his life to take the gospel to the Indians
9. **John Wesley**—a famous preacher from England who preached to the Indians
10. **Jim Thorpe**—a great Indian athlete
11. **Sequoyah**—a Cherokee who developed the only Indian alphabet

41

This picture shows a tribe of Indians doing a "scalping dance." The tribes had no real organized government. Tribes seldom joined together to help each other; they often fought.

dians' way of life slowly changed. They began to trade furs and food for strong iron pots and shiny copper kettles. Making pottery and baskets was no longer necessary for some Indians. They began buying cloth to make clothes instead of using animal skins. Colorful beads took the place of the bones and shells used to make Indian jewelry. Guns and knives began to take the place of arrows.

As the white men built more homes and killed more game animals, there was less meat for the Indians to eat. Indians were forced to farm more by planting crops to grow food. This improved their way of life.

With the white men came horses, oxen, and cattle. The horse especially changed the Indians' way of living.

Even their ways of building homes improved. In the 1800's, some Indians built log cabins.

The Indians' way of life changed when the white man came to America. Here, some Indians are seen displaying the furs they have brought to trade with the Europeans.

Missionaries to the Indians

The biggest change of all came when the Indians heard about the one true God. The Indians had been locked into a system of false religion. They had no Bible to read, and they often offered prayers and sacrifices to the "god of the sky," the "god of the forest," the "god of the river," and many other false gods. Then, white men came from Europe. They brought with them the Bible, which tells about the one true God. Some Europeans simply forced the Indians to be baptized without knowing anything about how to be saved.

Some Indians did come to understand the truths of the Bible, however. There were a few white men who loved the Indians and who wanted to see the Indians accept Christ.

John Eliot

One such man was **John Eliot,** who came over to America in 1631. While he was preaching in the colony of Massachusetts, Eliot learned the language of the Massachusetts Indians and began to translate the Bible into their tongue. It took him nearly thirty years of patient work to do this, and all that time he was preaching and teaching as well. His Bible was one of the first books printed in America, and many of his "praying Indians," as his Indian followers were called, learned to read in it.

Eliot was a sweet, simple, and very generous man. Once, when giving him his salary, the church secretary tied the money up in a handkerchief with several knots so Mr. Eliot would not give it all away before he got home. Eliot met a poor woman and tried to give her some money, but he could not untie the knots. That did not stop John Eliot from helping someone in need. He gave her the handkerchief, with *all* the money in it! "Here, my dear, take it," he said. "I believe the Lord designs it all for you." Eliot also showed his kindness by speaking up when people tried to sell the Indians as slaves. Because of Eliot's kindness and Bible teaching, many Indians were kept from fighting against the English during times of Indian wars.

Roger Williams

Roger Williams, whom you will read more about later, was another missionary to the Indians. Roger Williams left a large colony in 1636 to set up his own colony. Usually the Indians would kill a white man who lived by himself, because the white men often stole the Indians' land. But this man was different.

Roger Williams soon became the Indians' friend because he was willing to treat the Indians fairly. He offered to buy land from them instead of merely taking it. More important, he truly loved the Indians. He saw that Indians were men just like himself, that they were sinners like all men, and that they needed to be saved. So for many years he taught Indians the Bible and witnessed to them about Christ.

David Brainerd

A third man who wanted the Indians to know more about Christ was **David Brainerd** [brā′nərd]. He lived in the early 1700's. David Brainerd was a brilliant Bible scholar who had completed his education and who could have become the pastor of a large New England church. But instead he left the comfort and security of New England to spend his life preaching to the Indians in the wilderness. He knew that winning lost souls to Christ was more important than living in comfort.

His hard work and the poor conditions where he lived caused him to die when he was only twenty-nine. Many people felt that David Brainerd had thrown his life away, but some knew that he had given his life to bring the message of salvation to the Indians whom he loved.

John Wesley

John Wesley also brought the good news of salvation to the Indians. Wesley was one of the most famous preachers of his day. When he came from England to preach in America in 1735, he desired to go out among the Indians and preach to them. He was amazed at the Indians' desire to learn more about the Word of God. One Indian told him, "We would not be made Christians as the Spaniards make Christians: we would be taught before we are baptized." The Indians wanted to understand what they were doing so they could accept Christ.

John Wesley preached to the Indians when he came to America from England.

Wesley preached to as many Indians as he could during his visit to America.

The Word of God is far more valuable than anything else that the Europeans brought to America. The Europeans who truly preached the Bible to the Indian tribes did more good than kettles, horses, and farming methods could ever do. Influenced by the Bible, Indians, like other Americans, would in the future have the opportunity to enjoy freedom and liberty and play their role in building the country.

People Worth Knowing More About

Sequoyah was the man who developed the syllabary, or Cherokee alphabet.

Sequoyah

Do you know where the tall sequoia trees of California got their name? They are named after a famous Cherokee Indian, **Sequoyah** [si-kwoi′ə], who lived in North Carolina.

Sequoyah often wished his people could read and write the way white men could. After twelve years of hard work, he created the only known Indian alphabet of this time.

Other Indian tribes had only spoken languages. If they did write, they wrote in pictures. Sequoyah created eighty-six symbols. Each symbol stood for a sound in the Cherokee language. After the Cherokee alphabet, which is called the **syllabary** [sil′ə-bâr-ē], was completed, the Cherokee Indians quickly learned how to read and write in their own language. The New Testament was translated. And soon, the Cherokees were printing their own newspaper!

Jim Thorpe

Who was the greatest athlete that ever lived? To most people, the answer to that question would be **Jim Thorpe** (1888–1953), an Indian from Oklahoma.

Jim Thorpe was the great-great grandson of the Indian chief Black Hawk. As a boy, Jim loved to run across the fields of Oklahoma and wrestle with his brothers. Later, when he went to a small Indian college in Pennsylvania, Jim's love for sports continued to grow. His incredible

The Indian athlete Jim Thorpe was one of the greatest sportsmen of all time.

abilities in several different sports amazed his coaches. Jim was a talented baseball pitcher; he set world records in track and field; and he played football so well that his school was soon beating the best college teams in the nation.

Jim went to the Olympics in 1912. After the Olympics were over, everyone knew that Jim Thorpe was the world's best athlete. When Jim returned to America, he was given a hero's welcome.

After college Jim played professional baseball *and* professional football for many years. Most football players are ready to retire when they near the age of forty, but not Jim Thorpe. He kept playing as a kicker even when he was past forty, amazing his fans with seventy-yard punts and fifty-yard field goals.

In 1950 sports writers were asked to name the greatest athlete of the century. The man they named was Jim Thorpe, who was chosen above sports heroes such as Babe Ruth, Jack Dempsey, Ty Cobb, and Lou Gehrig. Everyone across America agreed with the sports writers: Jim Thorpe, an Indian who had learned to love sports by racing his brothers across the Oklahoma fields, was the greatest athlete who ever lived. No one so far has been able to take that title away from him.

Something Worth Finding Out

How many tribes of Indians can you name? If you made a study of the names of states, towns, lakes, and rivers in our country, you would find many names of Indian tribes. Following is a list of states, towns, lakes, and rivers that were named for Indian tribes. If the tribe's name is a state, put an *S* beside it. If it is a town or a city, put a *T* beside it. If it is a river, put an *R* beside it. If it is a lake, put an *L*. You may have to look in an encyclopedia or a dictionary. Note: Some of the names have two answers.

Illinois____   Kansas____   Delaware____   Cheyenne____

Wichita____   Iowa____   Susquehanna____   Erie____

Huron____   Massachusetts____   Omaha____

Facts to Remember

1. Who gave Indians their name? _____

2. Why did he call them *Indians*? _____

_____

3. What is a tepee? _____

4. Did all Indians live in tepees? _____

5. What is a bullboat? _____

_____

6. Did the Indians enjoy playing games? _____

7. What game did many Northern Indians play? _____

8. Did the Indians often cooperate in war, agriculture, etc.? _____

9. What caused the greatest change in the Indians' way of life? _____

_____

10. Who are four missionaries who took the gospel to the Indians? _____

_____

11. Who developed the Cherokee alphabet? _____

What was the alphabet called? _____

12. What Indian was named the greatest athlete of this century in 1950? _____

_____

The English Come to America

The Pilgrims were the most famous group of English settlers to come to America.

The year was 1585, and the English people were ready to begin a very difficult task. They were going to plant a colony in the wilderness. A **wilderness** *is a wild, empty land that has not been settled and taken care of by people.* America was that wilderness. There were some Indians in America, of course, but the Indians left the land wild and did not take care of it, and so America was still a wilderness—a wild, unsettled land.

England and the Bible

Nearly one hundred years had passed since 1497, when John Cabot claimed North America for England. By this time, an important change had taken place in England. England had become a Protestant country, and all the people in England were free to read the Bible for themselves. This had an important effect on the kind of people who came to America from England and the kind of government they would set up.

The Lost Colony

Queen Elizabeth I *was the ruler of England in 1585.* She was proud of England. She wanted all Englishmen to be proud of England, too. A successful English colony in the New World would boost her people's pride.

Walter Raleigh [rä′lē] was a good friend of the queen. When he asked for permission to begin a colony, Queen Elizabeth gave it to him without hesitation. But the queen told him that he himself could not go to America—he had to choose someone else to go!

How strange it seems that the man who was to plan the first English colony in America never went to America himself! The queen had very good reasons.

Queen Elizabeth was a powerful ruler of England during the 1500's.

Sir Walter Raleigh planned the first colony in America, but he never went to America himself.

England was having trouble with Spain. If a war broke out, she knew she could trust Raleigh's judgment to help England.

Raleigh sent two sea captains to find a good place in America for an English colony. When they returned, they reported finding an island called **Roanoke** [rō′ə-nōk] that would be a good place to begin a colony.

Queen Elizabeth was as delighted as Raleigh. For his excellent plans, the queen added a title to his name. From now on, he would be called Sir Walter Raleigh. And the land the sea captains explored was given a name. *This part of the New World would be called* **Virginia,** *after Elizabeth, who was called the "Virgin Queen."*

Raleigh sent about one hundred men and five ships to begin a colony on Roanoke Island. However, these men were more interested in becoming rich and returning to England than they were in beginning a colony and living in the New World. They probably did not realize how dangerous the American wilderness was, and how much work it would take to live there. More interested in searching for gold than in planting gardens, they soon ran out of food. Trying to force the Indians to give them their food only made more trouble. Tired and hungry, the men returned to England. The colony had failed. Would Raleigh try again?

Again, Raleigh made plans for a colony. Starting a colony in the wild lands of America was a dangerous task, but he would try again. *In 1587 another group of colonists sailed for Roanoke Island.* This time, a group of brave men, women, and children were sent. Raleigh reasoned that families would be more interested in building houses, planting gardens, and settling down than single men who desired only wealth and adventure.

The colonists arrived safely at Roanoke and began repairing houses that the first colony had left. A little girl was born and named **Virginia Dare.** She was the first English child born in America.

Soon afterwards, John White, the governor of the colony, decided to return to England for supplies which the colony badly needed.

"If you have to leave this island, carve a message on a tree to tell me where you are when I return," John White told the people of the colony. "And if you are in trouble, carve a cross over the message."

John White sailed back to England, but unfortunately, he found England ready to go to war with Spain. The queen gave orders that every English ship was to be used to fight Spain. Even Sir Walter Raleigh could not get a ship to help John White. *In 1588 England won the war with Spain in what is called the defeat of the Spanish Armada. England was becoming the most powerful country in the world.*

Three years passed before John White could return to Roanoke. When he returned, there was no one to greet him. It seemed as if everyone had vanished! Carved on a tree was the word *Croatoan,* which was the name of another island where friendly Indians lived. Since there was no cross over the message, they were not in trouble when

New Words

1. **wilderness**—a wild, empty land that has not been settled and taken care of by people
2. **Spanish Armada**—a navy defeated by the English
3. **merchants**—businessmen
4. **charter**—an official permit to start a settlement
5. **peninsula**—a strip of land that is surrounded on three sides by water
6. **swamp**—an area where the ground is wet and spongy and where the land cannot be farmed
7. **Common House**—a combination house, fort, and church
8. **treaty**—a written promise or agreement

New Names

9. **Elizabeth I**—a powerful queen of England
10. **Walter Raleigh**—an Englishman who tried to start a colony in America
11. **Virginia Dare**—the first English child born in America
12. **James I**—the English king who wanted to have a colony in America
13. **The London Company**—the group of merchants who headed up the founding of Jamestown
14. *Susan Constant, Godspeed, Discovery*—three ships which brought the Jamestown settlers to America
15. **John Smith**—the leader of the Jamestown Colony
16. **Separatists**—those Englishmen who wanted to separate from the Church of England
17. *Mayflower*—the ship which brought the Pilgrims to America
18. **Strangers**—those on the *Mayflower* who were not Separatists
19. **Pilgrims**—those who traveled on the *May-*

The only clue left behind by the settlers of Roanoke was the word *Croatoan* carved on a tree. No other trace of the settlers has ever been found.

they carved the message. *However, no trace of the settlers could be found.*

What happened to the colony at Roanoke? No one knows. The first English colony in America had failed. John White returned to England. Sir Walter Raleigh sent several ships in search of the colonists, but the settlers were never found. Today Roanoke is known as "The Lost Colony." It has become a great mystery to all who study history, and it shows us what a dangerous task the English had ahead of them in settling the New World.

flower to America to make it their new home

20. **Mayflower Compact**—the first written agreement for self-government in America, written by the Pilgrim leaders

21. **John Carver**—the first governor of Plymouth

22. **Elder Brewster**—the Pilgrims' minister

23. **Miles Standish**—the soldier chosen by the Pilgrims to protect them

24. **Samoset, Squanto, Massasoit**—friendly Indians who helped the Plymouth settlers

25. **William Bradford**—the governor of Plymouth for thirty-six years

26. *Of Plymouth Plantation*—a history of Plymouth written by William Bradford

New Places

27. **Roanoke**—an early English colony in America that disappeared

28. **Virginia**—the name given to England's land in America

29. **Jamestown**—England's first permanent colony in the New World

30. **Chesapeake Bay**—the bay on which Jamestown was built

31. **Massachusetts**—the area where the Pilgrims settled

32. **Plymouth**—the first American settlement of the Pilgrims

New Dates

33. **1584**—Raleigh offers to establish an English colony in America

34. **1587**—founding of Roanoke, "the Lost Colony"

35. **1588**—England defeats the Spanish Armada

36. **1607**—Jamestown is founded

37. **1609–1610**—the "starving time"

38. **1619**—the first women arrived in Jamestown

39. **1620**—Plymouth is founded

Jamestown—The First Lasting English Colony

Twenty years had passed since England had tried and failed to begin a colony at Roanoke. Queen Elizabeth I was dead. **King James I** *was England's new ruler.* It was his desire to have a successful English colony in the New World.

By beginning a colony, King James hoped to

1. **find a sea passage through America to the riches of the Indies;**
2. **find gold, silver, and valuable minerals;**
3. **find the people of the Lost Colony of Roanoke; and**
4. **teach the Indians Christianity.**

The London Company

A group of **merchants** (*businessmen*) made a plan to begin a new colony in Virginia. Each businessman would pay part of the cost of sending ships of colonists to the New World. The colonists would repay these merchants by sending back furs, lumber, and, perhaps, gold and silver from the New World. And of course, if one of the colonists happened to find a sea passage to the Indies, the merchants would be rich. This group of merchants called themselves the **London Company.** King

James was delighted with their plans.

The London Company obtained a **charter;** that is, an official permit to start settlements in America. Then it busied itself with finding ships and colonists and buying supplies.

To make this voyage to Virginia, 101 men and 4 boys were chosen. What kind of men would you have chosen to begin a new colony? Let's see what was needed. A new colony in a wilderness would need hard-working men to clear the land and farmers to farm the land for food to eat. It would need carpenters to build houses and a fort for protection against unfriendly Indians. Since one of King James's purposes was to teach the Indians Christianity, missionaries would be needed. And a new colony would need men of good character who were willing to do whatever work needed to be done.

Those are the kinds of men a successful colony would need, but unfortunately the London Company did not choose such men. Half of the men that were chosen were wealthy men who could afford to have servants do most of their work for them. They were not used to doing manual labor themselves. Wealthy men are often hard workers, but *these* wealthy men were lazy.

Why, then, would such men come to the New World to begin a colony? The

London Company was eager to send people to Virginia. They, who had never been to the New World, spread stories around that in Virginia, nuggets of gold lay on the beaches, just waiting to be picked up. They said that food was plentiful. However, they did not say anything about the unfriendly Indians.

Is it any wonder then that these wealthy gentlemen pictured themselves strolling along the beaches, picking up nuggets of gold? These men were thinking only of becoming even richer and then returning to England. They had no thoughts of building a colony. This laziness would cause them some real problems.

The Founding of Jamestown

In April of **1607,** *three small wooden ships sailed into the* **Chesapeake Bay.** *The names of the three small ships were the* **Susan Constant,** *the* **Godspeed,** *and the* **Discovery.** *From the mouth of the Chesapeake Bay, they sailed into a river. They named it the* **James River,** *in honor of their king.*

It was springtime. Sweet clover blossomed in fields. Wild flowers gave a colorful appearance and sweet perfume to the fields and green forests.

The men on board the ships thought they must make a quick settlement and begin to explore Virginia. Instead of taking time to search out the land and plan wisely for the future, they quickly decided on a place to settle. They chose a **peninsula** *(a strip of land that is surrounded on three sides by water).* They did not realize that this was the hunting grounds of a tribe of Indians.

Jamestown was the first permanent English colony in America.

53

This alone would mean trouble, but it was not the only danger.

The land was swampy. They would have trouble finding fresh drinking water. In the summer, sickness would spread from the mosquitoes that lived in the **swamp** *(a swamp is an area where the ground is wet and spongy and where the land cannot be farmed)*. But their thoughts of the future were thoughts only of finding gold. *Again, in honor of their king, the new settlement was named* **Jamestown.**

Spring does not last forever. Soon it became too late to plant gardens. The summer heat dried up their water supply. Mosquitoes swarmed in from the swamps, bringing fever and sickness with them. Before the summer was over, half of the colonists had died.

Winter was coming. Because few gardens had been planted, there was little food to see them through. Even though they faced starvation, only a few of the colonists would work.

A Hard Worker

Fortunately for Jamestown, one colonist was a hard worker. His name was **Captain John Smith.** With his help, huts were built to house the colonists. He managed to trade with the nearby Indians for food to help the colonists through the winter.

John Smith saved the Jamestown colony by making everyone do a fair share of the work.

In 1608, Captain Smith took control of Jamestown. He knew that unless every colonist, including the gentlemen, worked hard, they would starve again that winter. *Wisely, he made a new rule: "He that does not work shall not eat."*

At first the gentlemen did not believe him, but when dinnertime came and they were refused food, the men knew Smith meant business. Grumbling, they picked up their tools and began working. How much better it would have been if they had been the kind of men who could make *themselves* work!

To be sure, life was not easy that second winter in Jamestown. The London Company had sent several hundred new colonists to Jamestown, and very little food to feed them.

The Starving Time

Again, Jamestown faced failure when Captain Smith was badly burned in an accident. He had to return to England where he could be helped. With their leader gone, the gentlemen again refused to work. *The winter of 1609–1610 was so bad that the colonists called it "the starving time." When Captain Smith left, Jamestown had 500 colonists. In the spring, only about 60 were still alive.*

The few who did not die were weak from hunger and sickness. What was there to do, but to make plans to return to England? Was this colony doomed to failure, too?

With all the strength they had, they packed their few belongings on boats and began sailing back. Suddenly, they saw a sail of a ship. The London Company was sending more colonists, more supplies, and more food! The sixty colonists turned their boats around and sailed back to Jamestown.

Successful at Last

Jamestown would not fail. Slowly and painfully *it became the first successful English colony in America.* When the colonists saw that there was no gold there, they began to look for other ways of making a living.

In 1619, ninety women arrived in Jamestown. Having families to take care of, the colonists were eager to build stronger houses. They were more eager to earn a living to provide for the needs of their families. Tobacco became the most important money-making crop. At one time, the colonists even grew tobacco in the streets of Jamestown. The money they made from tobacco may have saved Jamestown from failing.

King James I had hoped to accomplish four things by beginning an English colony in America, but

1. **no sea passage through America to the Indies was found;**
2. **no gold or silver was found;**
3. **no one from the Lost Colony of Roanoke was found; and**
4. **the Indians were taught very little about Christianity.**

Yet Jamestown was successful in becoming the first lasting English settlement. Because of it, other English people would have the courage to come to America and begin other colonies.

As these and other men found out in time to come, the greatest wealth of America was not gold or silver. *The greatest wealth was the happiness to be found in building their own homes and working in freedom in a wonderful new land.*

The Pilgrims: Lovers of Religious Freedom

We have seen that the men who first settled Jamestown were lovers of gold. They only became successful when a man strong enough to *make* them work became their leader. They did not have the strength of character to govern (rule) themselves. *Now we will study the real heroes of America's beginning: the* **Pilgrims.**

The Pilgrims *were* able to govern themselves, because they loved religious freedom and strove for the glory of God. Their love for God and freedom came from their understanding of the Bible and from their English heritage.

There was a lack of freedom in England at this time, even though the English were a freedom-loving people. James I was still the king of England. He said that he was head of the church as well as the head of the government. Because the king forced everyone to attend his church, the **Church of England,** the people of England were not free to worship as they thought they should.

The **Separatists** believed that the Church of England was not being true

The Pilgrims searched for religious freedom and found it in America.

to the Bible. Because the Separatists wanted to preach and do what the Bible really teaches, these brave people held secret meetings to study the Bible. When the king heard of these meetings, he sent men to spy on the Separatists. When the Separatists were caught, they were often put in jail for their beliefs.

The Move to Holland

The Separatists wanted to form their own churches. But they could not do this in England.

The Separatists loved England, but they loved God and religious freedom more. When they heard that in Holland there was freedom of worship, they gave up their homes in England and moved to the country of Holland.

However, they were not happy in Holland. In England, they had been farmers. In Holland, they had no money to buy farms, and they had to work in factories. Although they left England, they missed being among English people. With time, their children were beginning to speak Dutch. They were forgetting the English ways which their parents wanted them to remember. More important, the children were starting to copy their Dutch friends and do things that the Bible says not to do.

The Separatists had heard of the settlement in Jamestown. Perhaps the king of England would allow them to make their own settlement in America. There they could build an English colony and yet worship in their own way. *Their dream was to build their own churches in their own land so they could have freedom of worship.* They asked permission from King James to found a colony in America, where they would remain loyal subjects of King James but be able to worship God in their own churches. King James gave them permission to go to America.

Aboard the Mayflower

In September of **1620,** a group of Separatists boarded a little ship known as the *Mayflower.* On board were 102 passengers. Not every passenger was a Separatist. Some were people who wanted a chance to work in the New World, and some went for adventure.

The Separatists called these people **Strangers.** Most of the Strangers were content with the Church of England. The Separatists did not try to force the Strangers to believe as they did, though they probably witnessed to them about God's truth in the Bible. The Separatists were not at all like King James. They believed that they should have the freedom to worship God as they thought best, and they were willing for other people to have the same freedom.

The *Mayflower* brought the Pilgrims to America.

The Separatists and the Strangers were two groups of people with different beliefs. Yet both were wanderers to the New World. Together, they became known as the **Pilgrims.**

The group on board the *Mayflower* in 1620 reminds us of what the United States of America would be like over 150 years later. There were different kinds of people aboard with different ideas, different backgrounds, different goals, different beliefs. But all were lovers of freedom—not just for themselves, but for others as well. They followed the words of Jesus, Who said, "Therefore all things whatsoever ye would that men should do to you, do ye even so to them" (Matthew 7:12). They knew that if they were to have freedom for themselves they must let others have freedom, too.

There were probably some arguments during the sixty-five days that it took the *Mayflower* to cross the storm-tossed Atlantic Ocean, but because the Separatists and Strangers respected each other and had good character they were able to work things out.

It is the American way for different kinds of people to get along together in one country because they respect the rights of others. This little ship, the *Mayflower,* was like a picture of what America was to become.

Surprising News

When land was finally sighted, the *Mayflower's* captain, **Captain Chris-**

topher Jones, had some surprising news for the Pilgrims. He had planned to sail the *Mayflower* closer to Jamestown, but storms had blown the ship far off its course.

"We are off the coast of **Massachusetts,**" Captain Jones told the Pilgrims. "You had planned to settle on land owned by the London Company. You are too far north. If you settle here, you will have no government."

Planning a Government

A few men on board said that when they got off this ship they would be free to do whatever they wanted, and nobody could tell them what to do. The wise Pilgrims knew that this is not true freedom. They knew that if people are left to do anything they want, then bad people will take away the freedom and safety of other people.

In order to protect themselves and

The Mayflower Compact declared that the Pilgrims would be free to govern themselves.

others, and in order to protect their right to worship God the way they felt was best, they knew that they must set up a government. They wanted a government by laws rather than a government by men only. That way a bad man could not come in and take away their freedoms. They wanted to set up the best kind of laws that would help them to govern themselves.

The Pilgrim leaders met together in the cabin of the *Mayflower.* Here they wrote what is known as the **Mayflower Compact.** *It is an important part of American history, because it is the first written agreement for self-government in America.* The Mayflower Compact says many things that the Declaration of Independence and the Constitution of the United States would say later.

The colonists of Jamestown were not self-governing; they had a governor given to them by England.

The Pilgrims chose their own governor, a man named **John Carver.** *They made their own plans for their own government. This is what is meant by* **self-government.** It takes a certain kind of people to be able to make self-government work. It takes the kind of people who are able to control themselves. This is the kind of people that God wants us to be. This is the kind of people the Pilgrims were.

In the Mayflower Compact, the Pilgrims promised to make just laws. Here is what they wrote:

In the name of God, Amen. We whose names are under-written, the loyal subjects of our dread sovereign Lord, King James, by the grace of God, of Great Britain, France, and Ireland king, defender of the faith, etc. Having undertaken, for the glory of God, and advancement of the Christian faith, and honour of our king and country, a voyage to plant the first colony in the Northern parts of Virginia, do by these presents solemnly and mutually in the presence of God, and one of another, covenant and combine ourselves together into a civil body politic, for our better ordering and preservation and furtherance of the ends aforesaid; and by virtue hereof to enact, constitute, and frame such just and equal laws, ordinances, acts, constitutions, and offices, from time to time, as shall be thought most meet and convenient for the general good of the colony, unto which we promise all due submission and obedience.

The Pilgrims read the agreement. Then the Mayflower Compact was signed. Later on, they would choose a governor and make laws. Each man who signed the Mayflower Compact was promising to obey those laws when they were made.

The Mayflower Compact was signed on Saturday, November 21, 1620. The Pilgrims spent the next day, Sunday, as they always did—praying and listening to the preaching of their minister, **Elder Brewster.** Then on Monday the men left the *Mayflower* and went ashore to find a good place for the group to settle.

The Pilgrims knew that it is important to have laws. They knew that the Bible says, ''For all have sinned and come short of the glory of God'' (Romans 3:23). We need laws to protect us from those who would do wrong. We need a government to make laws and punish those who break the law.

Settling in Plymouth

How different were the attitudes of the Pilgrims compared to those of Jamestown! The men of Jamestown had been eager to settle anywhere, but the Pilgrims knew they must search for a place where they had

1. **a good supply of drinking water,**
2. **a good harbor for ships to sail into, and**
3. **a place free from unfriendly Indians.**

The Pilgrims realized the importance of listening to their captain. Even before they left England, the Pilgrims realized they would need a soldier to guide them in dealing with the Indians and in building a settlement. For this job, they hired **Captain Miles Standish,** a very wise and brave man. Captain Standish was not a

Separatist himself, but he did much to protect these people, and they were thankful for his wise guidance. They obeyed him and respected his authority.

The men of Jamestown had not relied upon God nor given Him thanks, but the Pilgrims daily prayed and thanked God.

For several weeks, Captain Standish led a group of men exploring the area where the *Mayflower* landed. At last they found a place which filled all their requirements. The men sailed the *Mayflower* to this new area, which was called **Plymouth.** It was now December.

New England winters are cold and snowy. The Pilgrims had little food, but they would have to wait until spring to plant crops. Even the wild animals take shelter from the cold, so there were few deer or wild turkeys to be found by hunters.

On Christmas Day, the men began chopping down trees in the snow to build what they called a **Common House.** It would be a house, fort, and church to all the Pilgrims that winter.

The Pilgrims grew very weak from lack of food. Most became sick from the cold. At one time, only seven were strong enough to be up taking care of the sick. By spring, half of the Pilgrims had died. Yet there was no thought of giving up. No one ever complained about being sick and cold and hungry. They were confident that God would help them.

Making Friends with the Indians

Imagine the Pilgrims' surprise when one day an Indian walked into their settlement and said, "Welcome, Englishmen!" This friendly Indian's name was **Samoset.**

The colony at Plymouth was very small and simple, but the Pilgrims were willing to face great hardships so that they could be free.

Are you surprised that an Indian knew how to speak English? *The Pilgrims were not the first Englishmen to visit New England.* Captain John Smith (the same person who had helped Jamestown) had explored and made a map of New England. In fact, the Pilgrims were using John Smith's map of New England. The Indians had met and traded with Englishmen and even learned a few words of English. Thus, Samoset greeted the Pilgrims in English.

Samoset left and brought back **Squanto** [skwän′tō], an Indian who had been to England and who spoke English well. He also brought **Chief Massasoit** [mas-ə-soit′] and other Indians.

Chief Massasoit came to make peace with the Pilgrims. Together, Massasoit and the Pilgrims made a **treaty.** A treaty is a promise or agreement. They promised to help each other. They promised never to fight. The promises they made were never broken as long as Chief Massasoit lived.

Afterwards, the Indians returned to their home, but Squanto chose to stay with the Pilgrims. The Pilgrims soon realized that God had sent Squanto to them. *Without Squanto's help the Pilgrims may not have survived.*

Although Chief Massasoit's tribe was friendly, there were other tribes that were unfriendly. Yet through the courage of Captain Standish and the help of Chief Massasoit, the Pilgrims had little to fear.

Hard Times

In April, 1621, the *Mayflower* sailed back to England. It must have been a temptation to some of the Pilgrims, who had suffered so much already in this new land, to give up and go back on the ship. But not one of them asked to go back to England, and they all wrote brave letters to their friends at home. *After the* Mayflower *had sailed away,*

Chief Massasoit promised to help the Plymouth settlers.

Governor Carver became ill and died, and **William Bradford** *was elected to take his place.* Governor Bradford was such a good leader that the people elected him again and again, and during the next thirty-six years he was head of the colony nearly all the time. He wrote a book, *Of Plymouth Plantation,* which tells us much of what we know about the Pilgrims.

Squanto became a great favorite of the Pilgrims. He played with the children, taught the boys to trap game, and told the settlers to plant their corn as soon as the leaves of the white oak were as large as a mouse's ear. He also taught them to put a fat fish in each hill to fertilize the growing grain, because the ground was very sandy.

The colonists now worked diligently, planting their fields and gardens over the graves of their dead companions so that no hostile Indian could find out how many had died or dig up their bones. Once the crops were all planted, the Pilgrims built their homes, made friends with nine Indian chiefs, and traded with the Indians for furs.

But every day they had to use up more of the food they had brought from England, and finally they saw with dismay that they would be completely out of food long before their corn was ripe. To make the food last,

they put themselves on a strict diet. It is said that sometimes they had only six grains of corn for a meal! As they were not good hunters or experienced fishermen, they lived almost entirely on shellfish. But rather than complaining about what they did not have, they thanked God for what they did have. Elder Brewster offered thanks to God for supplying them with "the abundance of the seas and the treasures hid in the sand."

The winter had been very damp, but this summer was just the opposite. It was so dry that it soon seemed as if the Pilgrims' crops would perish for lack of rain. A special day was set aside for prayer and fasting, and for nine hours the Pilgrims prayed to God for help. Some Indians, hearing that the Pilgrims were going to pray for rain, watched the sky anxiously. When the sky finally clouded over and a gentle rain began to fall, the Indians remarked in awe-stricken tones that the God of the white man had heard the white man's prayers.

The First Thanksgiving

Ten days of rain followed this day of prayer, and the crops were saved. The Pilgrims were so grateful for God's mercy that they set aside a special time of thanksgiving (giving thanks) and feasting. Men went out to hunt deer and turkeys. Pumpkin, corn, and beans were cooked. Nuts were gathered from the woods.

Ninety Indians came with Chief Massasoit to join the feast. That first time of Thanksgiving lasted three days. The Indians listened as the Bible was read and prayers of thanksgiving were raised to God. It was a special time to thank God, but we must remember that the Pilgrims thanked God at *all* times, when they had plenty of food and even when they had none.

Everyone had fun that first Thanksgiving. The Indians ran races with the Pilgrims. Captain Standish showed how his men could march. Then everyone ate and ate and ate! It was with happy hearts and full stomachs that everyone returned home.

Plymouth Grows

Soon after the first Thanksgiving, a ship arrived from England. It brought newcomers who would be staying. The Pilgrims were glad to see old friends and hear news from England, but they

The Pilgrims and the Indians joined together to give thanks to God for His blessings.

were disappointed to hear that the newcomers had brought no food for the winter. With not a second thought, the Pilgrims would share their homes and their food with the new settlers. Because of the unexpected extra people they had to feed, there would be less food than they thought. There would be many days when they would go hungry. But there would be no starving time during their second cold New England winter.

These brave people, the Pilgrims, who had such a deep faith in God, were the true heroes of our country's beginnings. *We remember them for their courage, for their love of religious freedom, for their establishment of self-government, and for their faith in God and thankfulness to Him.* They set up a free government in the New World—a government in which the leaders were selected by the people and in which people could vote no matter what religion they were.

Map Study: Jamestown and Plymouth

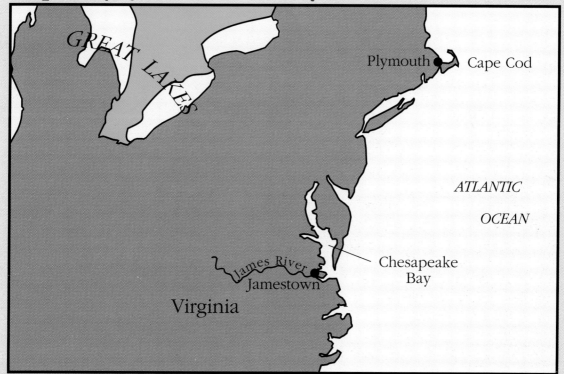

The first two English colonies in America were Jamestown and Plymouth.

Facts to Remember

1. What is a wilderness?_____

    _____

2. To whom did Queen Elizabeth give permission to start a colony in America?

    _____

3. What was Raleigh's colony called? _____

4. What was the name given to England's land in America?_____

5. Who was the first English child born in America? _____

6. What happened to Roanoke? _____

7. What event caused England to win the war against Spain? _____

    _____

8. What king reopened England's efforts to establish a colony in America?

    _____

9. What group of merchants agreed to finance the founding of a colony?

    _____

10. What is a charter? _____

11. What kind of men were sent to America by the London Company? _____

    _____

12. What were the names of the three ships which brought the men to Virginia?

    _____

13. Where was Jamestown built? _____

14. What is a peninsula? _____

    _____

15. On what bay was Jamestown built? _____

16. What is a swamp? _____

_____

17. What leader of Jamestown demanded that men work for their food?

_____

18. What was the winter of 1609–1610 called, during which over four hundred

people died? _____

19. When did the first women arrive in Jamestown? _____

20. What became Jamestown's main "money crop"? _____

21. Did James I's plans for Jamestown succeed? _____

22. What religious group wanted to separate from the Church of England?

_____

23. Where did the Separatists go before coming to America? _____

24. What boat brought the Separatists to America? _____

25. Passengers of the *Mayflower* who were *not* Separatists were called what?

_____

26. Together, the Separatists and Strangers were called what? _____

27. What document was the first charter of self-government written in America?

_____

28. What was the name of the Pilgrim's colony? _____

29. Who was the first governor of Plymouth? _____

30. Who was the minister in Plymouth? _____

New England Colonies

The population of America grew very slowly. For many years America remained a vast, empty land dotted here and there with tiny villages. But as time went by, more and more people from England and other countries in Europe journeyed to America, hoping to find a better life. You have learned of **Jamestown,** the first lasting settlement in Virginia, which was started in **1607.** You have also learned of **Plymouth,** which

was settled in **1620** in the colony of Massachusetts. By 1735 there were thirteen colonies in America.

The **thirteen original colonies** *were Virginia, Massachusetts, Rhode Island, New Hampshire, New York, Connecticut, Maryland, Delaware, New Jersey, Pennsylvania, North Carolina, South Carolina, and Georgia.* We often divide the colonies into three regions: the **New England Colonies,** the **Middle Colonies,** and the **Southern Colonies.** In this chapter you will learn how the colonies in New England were founded. *The* **New England Colonies** *are Massachusetts, Rhode Island, Connecticut, and New Hampshire.*

Massachusetts Bay Colony

As you have read, Plymouth was one of the first colonies in America. The Pilgrims of Plymouth were happy in their new land, even though life there was very hard. They loved the religious freedom they found in America. The Separatists in Plymouth knew that they could worship God in the way they felt was right.

The Puritans

Back in England, there was another unhappy group called the **Puritans.** The Puritans wanted to belong to the Church of England, but they wanted to change it. *The Puritans wanted to "purify" the Church of England, remove all the things that they thought were bad from the Church of England.* Of course, the king of England would not permit this. He wanted everyone to believe and worship as he did. Anyone who disobeyed was thrown into jail.

The Puritans' unhappiness led them to thoughts of going to America. "If the Separatists can build a colony in the New World, so can we," they said.

Sailing to America

In the spring of 1630, eleven ships with nearly 1,000 men, women, and children on board sailed to New England. Later that same year, more ships followed them until there were 2,000 Puritans in the New World. They called their colony the **Massachusetts Bay Colony.** The biggest town in that colony was named **Boston.** Later, Plymouth would become a part of the colony, and the colony would be called simply **Massachusetts.**

Many of the Puritans were wealthier than their neighbors in Plymouth. Massachusetts quickly became a prosperous center of trade and commerce. *Boston grew to be one of the most important cities in America.*

Boston, which was one of the most important colonial cities, has preserved many of its historical buildings. At the left is a picture of the Boston state house early in the colonial period; at the right is a modern photograph of the same building. The surroundings have changed, but the building itself has changed very little over the last three hundred years.

New Names

1. **Puritans**—people who wanted to purify the Church of England. One group of Puritans founded Massachusetts, but there were also many other groups of Puritans.

2. **John Winthrop**—the governor of Massachusetts

3. **Obadiah Holmes**—a man who was persecuted in Massachusetts for preaching the gospel

4. **Roger Williams**—the man who founded Rhode Island

5. **John Clarke**—the man who went to England to get Rhode Island's charter

6. **The *Jonathon***—the ship which brought the first settlers to New Hampshire

7. **John Mason**—the man who gave New Hampshire its name

8. **Thomas Hooker**—the man who built the first major settlement in Connecticut

9. **The Fundamental Orders of Connecticut**—the document which established Connecticut's system of government and said that it should be ruled by the people

New Places

10. **The New England Colonies**—Massachusetts,

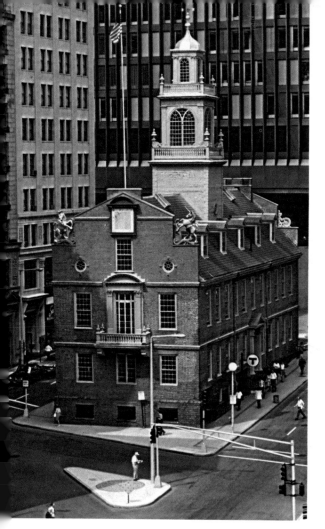

Governor John Winthrop

The Puritans are remembered today for their trust in God, their willingness to work hard, their high standards, their strict discipline, and their belief that everyone should have a good education. One of their most famous leaders was Governor John Winthrop, who was elected governor twelve times. One of the other leaders praised Governor Winthrop for his "piety, liberality, wisdom, and gravity." The Indians recognized Winthrop's good character, too. They called him "Single Tongue" because he was a truthful man.

Governor Winthrop was also a generous man. The first winter in Boston was very cold, and some people could not get enough fuel. One man was caught stealing wood from Governor Winthrop's yard. The Puritans considered stealing almost as bad as murder, and if

Rhode Island, Connecticut, New Hampshire

11. **Massachusetts Bay Colony**—the first colony founded by the Puritans
12. **Boston**—the largest city in the Massachusetts Bay Colony
13. **Providence**—the first city in Rhode Island
14. **Rhode Island**—the colony founded by Roger Williams
15. **Quinnequktucut**—the river along which the cities of Connecticut were built
16. **Hartford**—the city in Connecticut settled by Thomas Hooker

New Dates

17. **1623**—the first settlers came to New Hampshire
18. **1630**—Massachusetts Bay Colony settled
19. **1630**—the settlement of Connecticut began
20. **1638**—Obadiah Holmes arrived in Massachusetts
21. **1638**—Hooker's sermon about government by the people
22. **1639**—Roger Williams founded America's first Baptist church
23. **1639**—the Fundamental Orders of Connecticut were written

John Winthrop, governor of Massachusetts, was an honest and generous leader.

who had reported the theft. "Find him stealing if you can!"

Like the Plymouth colonists, the Puritans were threatened with starvation long before their ships could return from England with provisions. Governor Winthrop generously gave people food from his own storehouse, and he actually gave the last flour he had in his house to a poor man who came to beg. But the good governor did not suffer on account of his generosity, for that very day the returning ships sailed into port, bringing plenty of provisions for all.

Massachusetts Grows

During the next ten years, more than twenty thousand English-speaking persons came over to New England. There, in time, they formed fifty villages, connected by roads and bridges. A governor was elected to rule over the colony, and each town ruled itself. But the people also sent representatives to the General Court, or Assembly, where public matters were discussed and laws were made for the good of the whole colony.

Freedom for Some

There were many good things about the Puritan colony of Massachusetts, and there were many good people there. Some people, however, were unhappy

the man had been brought to trial, he might have been put to death. When Governor Winthrop was told about the thief, he cried, "I'll put a stop to that!" Then he turned to the thief and said, "Friend, I fear that you have not wood enough for this winter. Help yourself from my pile whenever you choose."

"Didn't I tell you I would put a stop to it?" the Governor said to the man because of something that Massachusetts did *not* have. There was religious freedom in Massachusetts for the Puritans, but not for anyone else! That sounds strange, because the Puritans had come to Massachusetts *seeking* religious freedom. They were so firm in their beliefs, however, that once they had control of the colony they expected *everyone* to worship God exactly as they did. Once they got away from the king of England, they started acting like him! What the Puritans did was not unusual for their times. Almost every country in Europe at that time had a state church, and very few people thought of separating religion and government. Because religion and government were ruled by the same people, the only people in Massachusetts who could vote were the Puritans. Puritans were the only ones with religious and political freedom.

Problems for Others

Christians in Massachusetts who did not belong to a Puritan church could not start a church of their own. The Puritan leaders said, "You must come to our church, even if you don't belong to our church. You must pay money to our church and you must obey the laws made by our church. And you cannot vote unless you are a member of our church." The Puritans knew it was right to attend church. But they seemed to believe that by forcing people to go to their church, they could make everyone become Christians.

Obadiah Holmes came to Massachusetts in 1638. Because he was a Baptist, he did not worship God exactly the way the other Puritans did. He moved away from Massachusetts so he could have religious liberty, but one day he went back with his pastor and another man to visit a very old, blind man who was also a Baptist. They had a church service in the man's house and preached, baptized, and held communion. The leaders did not like this, and they sent two policemen to arrest the three strangers. The three men were tried in Boston and Obadiah Holmes was beaten with a whip for his preaching. This is just one sad thing that happened because of the lack of religious freedom in Massachusetts Colony.

The Puritans were intelligent people, however, and they eventually learned that *everyone* ought to have religious freedom, for if everyone doesn't, then no one will for long. *The Puritans of Massachusetts came to learn what the Pilgrims already knew: that when one man's freedom is taken away, everyone's freedom is threatened.*

The Pilgrims were not the only people who saw this truth about religious freedom very early. A Puritan named **Roger Williams,** whom you have already met as a missionary to the Indians, saw it, too. Roger Williams and preachers like Obadiah Holmes have gone down in history as champions in the cause of liberty for all.

Rhode Island

Roger Williams was a Puritan preacher in Massachusetts. He did much to bring about religious freedom in America. Because Williams believed in salvation by faith alone, he knew that no person could ever be forced to become a Christian. *He told his neighbors that it is wrong to punish people for not believing exactly as they themselves believe, since punishment can never make a person believe on Jesus in his heart.* In 1639, Roger Williams founded America's first Baptist church.

Roger Williams's teaching upset some of the leaders of Massachusetts. The leaders told Williams that he must either change his ways or leave Massachusetts.

Williams's ideas about the Indians also upset some people. He traded with them fairly and never tried to cheat them. After they finished trading, he would tell them about God.

At times, the Massachusetts settlers were unfair to the Indians. They believed that since the Indians were not Christians, they had a right to take their land from them. Roger Williams asked the Puritan leaders, "How do you expect the Indians to become Christians when you as Christians do not treat them fairly? The Indians should be paid for their land."

The Puritan leaders became very angry. They ordered a ship to take Roger Williams back to England. Learning of their plans, Williams escaped into the wilderness. It was wintertime and he became very sick. Friendly Indians found him and took care of him until spring.

In the spring he moved further on. Williams tried to buy some land from the Indians, but the Indians would not hear of it. They liked him too much!

"Take the land. You are our friend," they said.

"I shall call this place **Providence,** for surely God has directed me here," said Williams.

Freedom of Religion

Soon other people from the Massachusetts Bay Colony joined Williams. Three cities besides Providence were

Roger Williams escaped from Massachusetts and founded his own colony. Friendly Indians took care of Williams during the harsh winter.

settled. More and more settlers wanted to come to Roger Williams's colony, for it offered something very special: complete religious freedom. The people of Providence could worship as they chose.

Rhode Island Becomes a Colony

As the colony grew larger, Roger Williams decided that it should have a government and that it should become an official British colony. Thus it was that the colony of **Rhode Island** came into being.

Many people who had been persecuted for their beliefs helped Roger Williams set up Rhode Island. These people decided that Providence and the three other cities should band together and form one large government for the common good of Rhode Island. Years later, the thirteen colonies would do very much the same thing when they banded together to form the United States of America.

Rhode Island Gets a Charter

Next, the people of Rhode Island needed to get a charter. The **charter** was the "plan" that the colony followed. When the king approved the charter, the colony had a legal right to exist. Rhode Island's charter was far different from other charters. Here is the most important part of Rhode Island's charter:

> No person within the said Colony, at any time hereafter, shall be in any wise molested, punished, disquieted, or called in question, for any differences in opinions in matters of religion, and do not actually disturb the civil peace of our said Colony.

The charter was saying that the government of Rhode Island could not bother a man whose religious beliefs were different from others, as long as that man did not disturb the peace. The charter went on to say:

> All may, at all times hereafter, freely and fully have and enjoy their own judgments and consciences, in matters of religious concernments...not using this liberty to licentiousness and profaneness, nor to the civil injury or outward disturbance of others.

In other words, Rhode Islanders could worship God however they chose. The government was not to get involved in religion—church and state were separate. This did not mean, of course, that people could do whatever they chose to do. Those who did wrong things to others would be punished by the law.

The people of Rhode Island believed strongly in religious freedom. They sent a minister, Dr. John Clarke, to England to get the charter. Even though he had to stay in England for twelve years, he did not come home until he had the charter! With the charter from England, they were assured that they were legally a colony and that they had religious freedom.

Freedom for All

Because of Roger Williams and a small group of brave men, Rhode Island was the first colony to offer complete religious freedom. Because of its religious freedom, Rhode Island had political freedom, too. When Roger Williams began his colony, he could have forced everyone to do what he wanted. But he loved religious freedom and wanted everyone to be free to accept Christ by faith alone. He knew that God's truth about spiritual matters can stand alone, without being forced by a government. Roger Williams's little colony of Rhode Island offered religious freedom and political freedom—the two important freedoms that all Americans would someday know. George Washington, our first President, said of Rhode Island:

> While the Baptists have always defended the principles of religious liberty, they have never violated them. They have had but one opportunity of forming a system of civil government, and they so formed it as to create an era in the history of civilization. In the Little Baptist State of Rhode Island was the experiment first attempted of leaving religion wholly to herself, unprotected and unsustained by the civil arm. The principles which were here first planted have taken root in other lands, and have borne abundant fruit.

New Hampshire

In 1623, an English ship named the *Jonathon* sailed near the coast of what is now New Hampshire. Only a few men were on board. What was the purpose of their visit to the New World? They came because they were hired to fish and cut down trees for lumber. They did not consider themselves colonists, for a company had hired them to do this. The fish and lumber were to be taken back to be sold in England.

These men needed a place to live while they worked in the New World, and so they built a settlement. Small settlements such as this one, scattered here and there, gave new settlers a place to live. These settlements began to grow.

A few years later, the land was given to **John Mason,** who was an early English explorer of New England. He named the land given to him in the New World **New Hampshire,** after Hampshire County, where he had lived in England.

Meanwhile, some Puritans had settled in New Hampshire. In the early 1640's, the Puritans made New Hampshire a part of Massachusetts. However, the king of England later decided to make New Hampshire a separate colony once again.

Connecticut

One day some Indians appeared in Plymouth. They came to the colony to invite the white men to come and live on their land. "Our land is rich," the Indians said. "Beaver live in our woods. Our woods are thick with trees. The white man could trap furs and cut lumber for a living."

The Indians went on to say why they wanted the white men to come. "A fierce tribe lives on each side of our tribe. We are peaceful. Our enemies are afraid of the white man's guns. If you

Thomas Hooker took his people to Connecticut and built a new colony there.

come, we will all live in peace.

In 1630 one man from Plymouth went into the area and built a trading post on a river which the Indians called **Quinnequktucut** ("long river"). He reported that the Indians were telling the truth—the area was a good place to live. Soon other settlers were flocking to Connecticut, the white man's name for the area.

The most famous of the settlers was **Thomas Hooker,** a Puritan preacher from the Massachusetts Bay Colony. He and about 100 of his church members built the first major settlement in Connecticut. They named the settlement **Hartford.** Hartford and several smaller towns joined together to form the colony of Connecticut.

In 1638 Thomas Hooker preached an important sermon. *In the sermon Hooker stated that the people should control the government rather than the government ruling the people. He said that people should have the right to elect the officials who run the government.* In 1639 Connecticut put these ideas into the **Fundamental Orders of Connecticut,** the document which established Connecticut's system of government. *Later, the Fundamental Orders would provide a good pattern for the Constitution of the United States.*

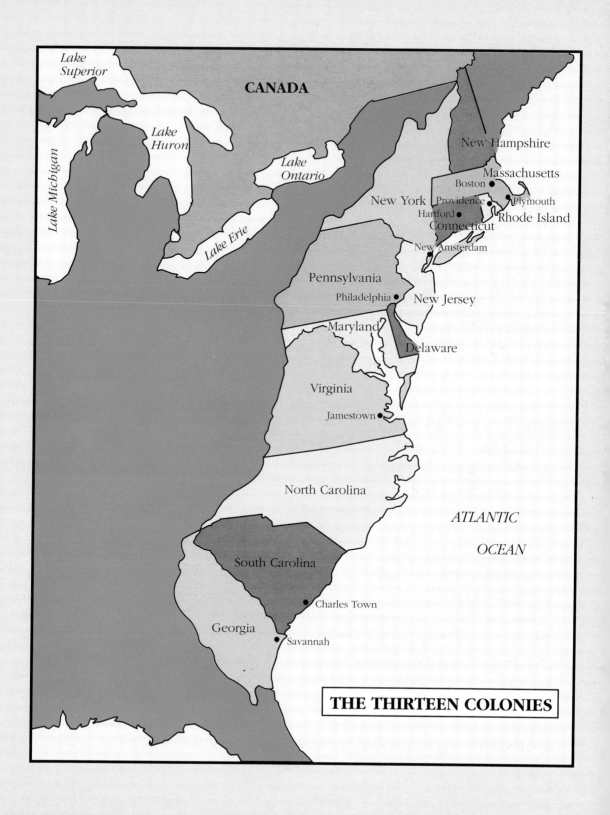

THE THIRTEEN COLONIES

Facts to Remember

1. How many colonies were there in America by 1735? _____

2. What are the New England colonies? _____

   _____

3. Which religious group wanted to purify the Church of England? _____

   _____

4. Which colony did the Puritans settle in 1630? _____

   _____

5. What became the largest city in Massachusetts? _____

6. What governor of Massachusetts was known for his honesty, fairness, and

   generosity? _____

7. What man was beaten with a whip for preaching in Massachusetts?

   _____

8. Who had to leave Massachusetts because of his religious beliefs?

   _____

9. What kind of church did Roger Williams establish in 1639? _____

10. Why did the Indians like Roger Williams? _____

    _____

11. What colony did Roger Williams establish? _____

12. What was the largest city in the colony of Rhode Island? _____

13. What did Rhode Island's charter guarantee? _____

    _____

14. Who went to England to get a charter for Rhode Island? _____

_____

15. Which ship brought the first settlers to New Hampshire? _____

_____

16. Who obtained New Hampshire and gave it its name? _____

17. New Hampshire was forced to become a part of what colony for several

years? _____

18. What river gave Connecticut its name? _____

19. Which preacher settled the city of Hartford? _____

20. Which plan of government was based upon a sermon by Thomas Hooker?

_____

21. The Fundamental Orders of Connecticut later served as a pattern for what

important document? _____

The Middle and Southern Colonies

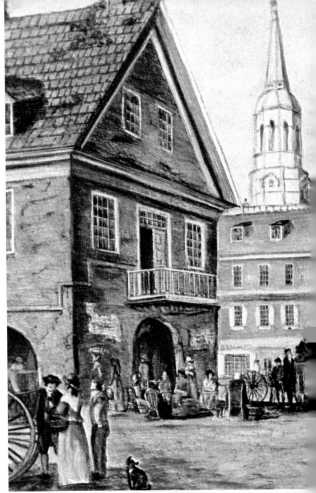

While the New England colonies were being settled in the north, other colonies were being started along the rest of the Atlantic coast. They were the **Middle Colonies:** *New York, Delaware, New Jersey, and Pennsylvania,* and the **Southern Colonies:** *Virginia, Maryland, North Carolina, South Carolina, and Georgia.*

New York

New York was an unusual colony, because three countries claimed to own it at the same time.

The **Dutch** are people who live in the **Netherlands** (also called **Holland**). In 1609, the Dutch sent a man named **Henry Hudson** to find a shortcut to Asia. Instead, Hudson found an area containing friendly Indians and plenty

The Dutch sent Henry Hudson to find a shortcut to Asia.

Philadelphia was the largest and most important city in the Middle Colonies during colonial times.

of beaver. Since beaver skins were very valuable, the Dutch quickly claimed the area that Hudson explored. This area is now the southern part of New York.

However, during the same year (1609), a Frenchman named **Samuel de Champlain** sailed down from Quebec and explored what is now the northern part of New York. So France became the second country to claim New York.

You will remember that in 1497 John Cabot discovered North America and claimed it for England. Since New York is a part of North America, England also claimed New York.

Even though three countries claimed New York, only one began to build settlements there. The Dutch built a small village there which they called Fort Orange. Later the Dutch bought Manhattan Island from the Indians and built a village there. The Dutch called this city **New Amsterdam,** since Amsterdam was the capital of the Netherlands. The Dutch named the whole colony **New Netherland.**

New Netherland had rich farm land. Men were getting wealthy from beaver furs. New Amsterdam had one of the best harbors in America. Now England decided it was time to take control of what she claimed was hers. English ships sailed into the harbor; English soldiers told the people that England was going to take control of New Netherland.

New Amsterdam quickly became an important settlement in America.

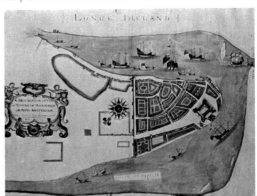

Even though he wanted to fight, Peter Stuyvesant was finally forced to surrender New Amsterdam to the British.

The brave and fearless **Peter Stuyvesant** [stī′və-sənt], the governor of the colony, at first refused to surrender to the British. But the British promised to treat the Dutch fairly, and the Dutch saw that they could never defeat the British. The Dutch people refused to fight. Brokenhearted, the governor surrendered.

The British did indeed treat the Dutch fairly. The Dutch were allowed to keep their farms, and most of them stayed on after the British took over. But the British *changed a few names —New Amsterdam became* **New York City;** *New Netherland was now called* **New York.**

New Words

1. **admiral**—a chief commander in the navy
2. **indigo**—a plant from which the colonists got a blue dye
3. **plantation**—a very large southern colonial farm

New Names

4. **The Dutch**—the people who live in the Netherlands
5. **Henry Hudson**—the man who explored what is now New York and claimed it for the Netherlands
6. **Samuel de Champlain**—the man who explored northern New York and claimed it for France
7. **Peter Stuyvesant**—the Dutch governor of New Netherland who surrendered to the British
8. **Carteret and Berkeley**—the founders of the New Jersey Colony

The British now owned another colony in America. *Eventually, England would control all thirteen American colonies.*

Delaware

The Dutch were the first to begin a

9. **Quakers**—a religious group which settled in Pennsylvania
10. **William Penn**—the founder of Pennsylvania
11. **George Calvert (Lord Baltimore)**—the man who formulated the idea of settling Maryland and making it a refuge for Roman Catholics
12. **George Whitefield**—the preacher who established the first orphanage in America

New Places

13. **Middle Colonies**—New York, New Jersey, Delaware, Pennsylvania
14. **Southern Colonies**—Virginia, Maryland, North Carolina, South Carolina, Georgia
15. **The Netherlands**—a country in Europe, also called Holland
16. **New Amsterdam**—the Dutch name for what is now New York City

settlement in Delaware, but there was much trouble between the settlers and the Indians. The settlement failed.

Then Sweden became interested in beginning a colony in the New World. However, it seems as though the people of Sweden were content to stay in Sweden. In 1638, only about fifty settlers arrived on the two ships that Sweden sent to Delaware. They may have been few in number, but theirs was the first successful settlement in Delaware.

The Swedes were peaceful farmers and hard workers. So were the Indians that lived around them. Though the Indians did not get along with the Dutch, they became friends with the Swedes.

Nevertheless, the Swedes believed in protecting themselves. They built a fort which they named "Fort Christina" in honor of the young queen of Sweden. (Today this area is the city of Wilmington, Delaware.) They named their settlement New Sweden.

New Sweden never grew large. The country of Sweden was having its own

17. **New Netherland**—the Dutch name for what is now New York

18. **Fort Christina**—Swedish settlement which eventually became Wilmington, Delaware

19. **New Sweden**—the settlement which eventually became the colony of Delaware

20. **Chester**—the oldest settlement in Pennsylvania

21. **Philadelphia**—the city in Pennsylvania specially designed by William Penn

22. **St. Mary's**—the first settlement in Maryland

23. **Carolana**—the original name for what became North and South Carolina

24. **Charles Town**—the largest settlement in Carolana

25. **Savannah**—the first settlement in Georgia

New Dates

26. 1609—Henry Hudson sailed to America for the Dutch

27. 1624—the Dutch settled New Netherland (New York)

28. 1634—the *Ark* and the *Dove* brought the first settlers to Maryland

29. 1638—Delaware settled

30. 1643—the settling of Pennsylvania began

31. 1650—the settlement of Carolana began

32. 1655—the Dutch took over New Sweden (Delaware)

33. 1670—Charles Town was built

34. 1681—the Quakers began their settlement of Pennsylvania

35. 1733—Savannah was settled

36. 1737—George Whitefield began the first orphanage in America

37. 1752—Oglethorpe gave Georgia to the king and went back to England

problems and could not help the colony. As a result, the Dutch took over all of New Sweden in 1655. And the Dutch had Delaware for only ten years when the English took it away from them.

New Jersey

Across the Hudson River from New York is **New Jersey.** At one time, the Dutch claimed New Jersey as part of New Netherland as they once did Delaware.

The Dutch settled New Netherland (New York) in 1624. However, they did very little to send settlers across the river to settle New Jersey. So a few Swedish settlers from Delaware began to wander into New Jersey. This angered the Dutch, who forced the Swedes to leave. Then in 1660, the Dutch began the first permanent settlement in New Jersey.

Now it was England's turn to be angry. New Netherland was in the middle of English colonies. England considered the Dutch a threat to English colonies. The English claimed the Dutch were living on land that belonged to England.

You will remember that in 1664, English warships sailed to New Amsterdam. Without even a shot, the English took over New Amsterdam. No longer did the Dutch rule in any colony of the New World.

The king's brother, the duke of York, received not only New Netherland, but also the land that would become New Jersey. The duke of York in turn gave New Jersey to two of his friends, Sir George Carteret and Lord John Berkeley. These are the men that gave New Jersey its name. These men offered to sell land at low prices to colonists. *They also offered any colonist the freedom of religion. These offers brought many colonists seeking religious freedom to New Jersey, and a number of Presbyterians and Baptists who would become famous at the time of our Declaration of Independence lived there.*

Pennsylvania

In 1643, Swedish settlers wandering from Delaware began a small settlement in what is now Pennsylvania. This was the first settlement in Pennsylvania. The settlement was later named Chester.

However, the settlement for which we most remember Pennsylvania began in 1681. For the story of this settlement, we must first go back to England. You will remember that England did not offer freedom of religion at that time.

For this reason, many Separatists, Puritans, and Catholics had settled in the New World. However, there was one group of people whose beliefs seemed so strange to others that they were not even welcome in the new American colonies! *This group called themselves* **Quakers** *or Friends.*

Quaker Beliefs

Now, let's look at some of the Quakers' beliefs that made them so unpopular.

- The Quakers did not believe that one person could be more important than another. Therefore, they would not show more respect for one person than another. They would not take off their hat to

show respect for someone. Neither would they bow before anyone, not even the king of England.

- The Quakers did not believe in any kind of fighting. Therefore, they would not fight to protect themselves or their country, even in time of war.

As you can see, the Quakers' beliefs were quite different from those of other groups who lived at that time. *Although the Quakers were a very peaceful group of people, no other groups welcomed them.* They were arrested for their beliefs in England. Those Quakers who did go to the colonies were often beaten and treated worse than they had been in England.

A Quaker meeting, 1682.

William Penn

A young man named William Penn became curious about the Quakers' beliefs. Wanting to find out more about these people, he attended their meetings. William Penn liked what he heard. It was not long before he became a Quaker, too.

William Penn's father was an *admiral* in the British navy and a good friend of the king of England. You can imagine how angry he was when his son told him that he had become a Quaker. His father had hoped that his son would become an important officer in the British navy as he had done, but a Quaker would not fight. His father was well liked by the king, but William, being a Quaker, would not show respect for the king. His father was also a very wealthy man, but Quakers did not feel wealth was important.

Try as he did, William Penn's father could not change his son's mind. After his father died, Penn remembered that the king had borrowed a large sum of money from his father and had never paid it back. Penn knew that the king would never give him, a Quaker, the money. But perhaps the king would give him land in America to begin a colony for the Quakers.

The king was pleased with Penn's idea. Not only could he easily repay the debt by giving Penn land in far-away America, but he would also rid England of the troublesome Quakers. The king named the new colony **Pennsylvania,** which means "Penn's Woods."

A New Colony—Pennsylvania

In 1681, William Penn sent a group of settlers to choose a good place to build a town. The next year, Penn went with a group of colonists to Pennsylvania.

Penn himself went to the Indians and asked them to sell land to him. His conscience told him it was wrong to take land from the Indians. The Indians agreed to sell land to their new white friend. Then William Penn told the Indians that Quakers did not believe in fighting. They would never carry guns or knives to hurt the Indians. In return, the Indians promised peace to the white men. As a result, Quaker children played with Indian children. The Indians paid the Quakers neighborly visits. There was no fear of Indian wars for many years.

"The City of Brotherly Love"

Penn began making plans for a beautiful city with gardens and trees between houses, and straight, wide roads leading through the town. The name Penn chose for his city was **Philadelphia,**

William Penn, the founder of Pennsylvania, always treated the Indians fairly.

which means "the city of brotherly love."

Who would be allowed to live in Pennsylvania? Philadelphia means "brotherly love." Penn believed that no one should be forced to believe the Quakers' beliefs. *People of all faiths would be welcome in Pennsylvania.*

Pennsylvania had much to offer new colonists. It had good farm land, peaceful neighbors, good government, and freedom of religion. Settlers came from many different European countries seeking the peace and freedoms that Pennsylvania had to offer. *Before long,* *Pennsylvania grew to become a very important colony.*

Maryland

In England, the Catholics, like the Separatists and Puritans before them, could not worship as they pleased. They were forced to attend the Church of England.

George Calvert (whose title was Lord Baltimore) was a Catholic man who worked as a secretary to the king. He did his work well and became the king's friend. Realizing how unhappy his

Catholic friends were, he asked a favor of the king. He asked the king for land in America where he could begin his own colony.

"Who could you take there?" asked the king.

"I want to take those who are Catholics, yet I would take anyone who claims to be a Christian, as long as he is willing to work together with the rest," replied Lord Baltimore. "The people of the Maryland colony will be free to build and go to a Christian church of their choice."

The king granted him his wish. While plans were still being made for the new colony, Lord Baltimore died. His son, **Cecil Calvert,** became the second Lord Baltimore. He continued his father's plans for Maryland. Because he had much work to do in England, Cecil Calvert could not go to Maryland. Instead, he chose to send his brother, Leonard Calvert, who was to become the first governor of Maryland.

Two small ships named the **Ark** and the **Dove** set sail from England. On board the ships were about 200 passengers who were coming to the New World for religious freedom.

In 1634, the *Ark* and the *Dove* sailed up the Chesapeake Bay. The colonists and the governor bought land from friendly Indians who were planning to move anyway. The Indians were delighted with the hoes, axes, hatchets, and the knives they received. These tools were far better than the ones they had for planting seed, building, and chopping trees.

The new colonists named the first settlement in Maryland **St. Mary's.** The new colonists had many blessings to be thankful for. They had arrived in early spring. So they busied themselves with planting gardens. Friendly Indians taught them how to plant corn. The rivers were full of crabs, oysters, and fish. The forests had plenty of deer and other animals. They would not go hungry.

The Indians whom they had bought their land from left their huts for the colonists to live in until they had time to build their own houses.

The founding of Maryland is important because it showed that in America Catholics would be able to worship freely. This is an important part of religious freedom—to let people worship in their own way whether you agree with them or not.

The Carolinas

Many years had passed since Sir Walter Raleigh had tried and failed to begin a colony on Roanoke Island off the coast of what is now North Carolina. As time went on, both North and South Carolina became known as one large piece of land called **Carolana.**

By 1650 Virginia had many colonists. Some of the Virginia colonists began to wander down into what is now North Carolina. So the first settlers of North Carolina did not come from across the ocean. They came from Virginia.

Meanwhile, in 1663, King Charles II of England was asked a favor by eight of his favorite workers. They wanted land to begin a colony in America. Willingly, King Charles gave them the land known as **Carolana.**

The Settlement of Charles Town

These eight men became the owners of Carolana. They could make their own laws for the settlers to obey. Their main interest was making money from their new colony. In 1670 the little village of Charles Town was built. Then Charles Town was moved to a better location. (Charles Town became the city of **Charleston,** South Carolina.) The better location had a good harbor from which English ships could sail in and out.

Ships brought settlers from Europe and goods which the settlers could buy. As a result, Charles Town, South Carolina, grew rapidly. It was *South Carolina's first permanent settlement.*

Problems Arise

The eight rulers of Carolana did not set up a good government for their settlers. There were many quarrels about

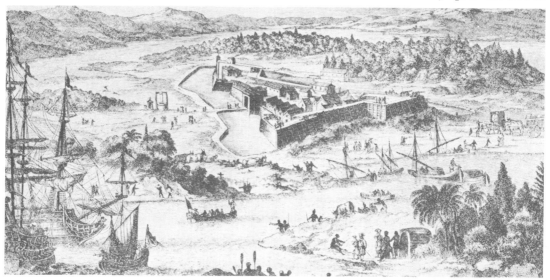

Charles Town as it appeared in 1672.

the laws. They took land unfairly from the Indians. Angered, the Indians fought against the settlers. After many years, the eight owners sold their land back to the king of England.

The Carolinas

The king then divided the land into two colonies, North Carolina and South Carolina. Then he appointed two men to be governors of the two colonies.

South Carolina grew quickly. The colonists found that rice, cotton, and **indigo** grew very well there. Soon many large farms called **plantations** were built to grow large fields of these valuable crops. All three of these crops required much work to grow and harvest. Since there were not enough white set-tlers to work in the fields, the planta-tion owners began buying slaves from Africa to do their work.

North Carolina did not grow as quickly as South Carolina. The people who settled North Carolina were mostly poor and lived simple, hard-working lives. Many built log cabins on small farms. Most planted and worked their own fields. Because of this, there were fewer slaves in North Carolina.

Georgia, England's Last Colony

England, 1732

The people of London, England, were excited. Over a hundred years had

A Southern plantation.

passed since England had begun its first successful colony in the New World. Since then eleven other colonies had struggled to success.

And now, news was spreading that England was about to begin its thirteenth colony. The reason for beginning this colony was completely different from the others. The thought of it made many people in England willing to donate food, supplies, and money to send colonists on their way to the new colony.

At that time, there were many poor people in England who were willing to work, but who could not find jobs. If a person was too poor to pay his bills, he was placed in prison. Of course, he could do nothing to pay back his bill once he was in jail. Unless he was fortunate enough to know someone who was willing to pay his bill for him, he would spend the rest of his life in prison.

In the 1700's, England's prisons were crowded with poor people. Prisons in those days were dark, dirty, cold, and wet. Diseases spread quickly, and many prisoners died. The jailers, whose job it was to look after the prisoners, would often beat their prisoners and rob them of what little they did have, even their food. Many prisoners starved to death. Indeed, English prisons were dreadful and hopeless places.

James Oglethorpe, the founder of Georgia.

James Oglethorpe

James Oglethorpe, *a member of the English government, studied the problems of the poor people.* Through his help, many were released from prison. Yet they faced the struggle of finding jobs.

"If only these people could go to America!" thought James Oglethorpe. "There would be plenty of work for them to do there."

However, there was one problem with that idea. How could these poor people earn enough money to pay their way on a ship to America?

The king of England heard Oglethorpe's idea, and he liked it.

"The land below South Carolina is unsettled," thought the king. "Spain has a colony in Florida. If England does not settle the land between Florida and South Carolina, Spain will!"

The king made some decisions. "I will appoint twenty-one men who will work without pay. They will choose the people who will go to the new colony. They will plan a set of laws for the new colony to follow, and they will govern the new colony."

The English government gave this group of men $50,000 to use in sending the colonists to the New World. When the people of England heard, many donated food and supplies for the colonists. Churches gave money.

A New Colony—Georgia

The new colony would be named **Georgia,** in honor of King George II.

James Oglethorpe went with the 114 colonists who were chosen to go on the first ship sent to Georgia. He became a great friend to the colonists. On board the ship, he visited the sick. He helped the colonists in whatever way he could.

In February, 1733, Oglethorpe and his colonists arrived in Georgia. He became the first governor of Georgia. In many ways, he was a wise, brave, and kind governor. He made lasting friendships with the Indians of that section, from whom he bought the land. In exchange for his gifts, they presented him with a buffalo robe lined with eagle feathers, saying: "The eagle signifies swiftness, and the buffalo strength. The English are swift as a bird to fly over the vast seas, and as strong as a beast before their enemies. The eagle's feathers are soft, and signify love; the buffalo's skin is warm, and means protection: therefore, love and protect our families."

James Oglethorpe planned and directed the building of the first settlement, which was named **Savannah.** When Spain tried to destroy the new colony, Oglethorpe successfully led the colonists against them. Without his aid, Georgia would probably have been destroyed. And often, he would use his own money to see that the needs of the colonists were met.

The Georgia colonists tried to grow olive trees and breed silkworms, but these attempts failed. Soon rice became an important crop in the colony, and the first fine cotton was raised there with seed brought from India. Oglethorpe, wanting to give his colony a good start, said that neither rum nor slaves should be allowed there. He and John Wesley, who was in Georgia at that time preaching to the colonists and the Indians, both tried to persuade the colonists that they would be far better off if they did their own work and stayed sober. The people listened for a while, but later they decided that they wanted both rum and slavery in their

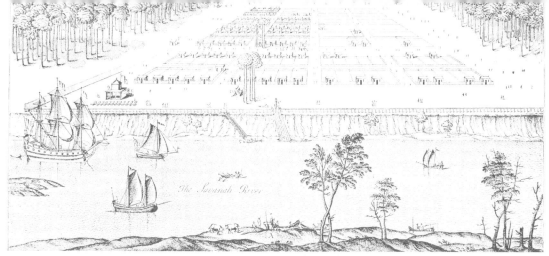

Savannah was the first settlement in Georgia.

colony.

George Whitefield, the great preacher of colonial America, came to visit the Georgia colony in 1738, where he started the first orphanage in America near Savannah.

Oglethorpe gave up Georgia to the king in 1752 and went back to England. He was always interested in the settlement he had founded, and as he lived to be very old, he saw it join the other colonies in 1776 to become a part of the United States of America.

Many People—One Land

We have seen how each of the thirteen original colonies was founded. It took 125 years in all for the colonies to be formed. This seems like a long time, but then it takes time for a new nation to get started in a wilderness. Such an important event does not happen often in history!

Many different kinds of people were in America now. There were people of all different religions—Separatists, Puritans, Quakers, Baptists, Lutherans, Mennonites, Episcopalians, Catholics, and others. *These people were learning to get along with each other and were developing the important ideas of freedom of religion and separation of church and state.* These ideas were new to most of the world, and they would help to make America the kind of country where the Bible could be preached freely and have a great influence on the lives of the people.

Many people came to America looking for a chance to work hard and do their best at jobs of their choice. This is an important part of the American way of life.

Most of the original settlers were English, but America soon became home for people from Germany, Holland, France, Ireland, Switzerland, Scotland, and other countries as well. All of these different kinds of people would learn to respect each other and look upon themselves as one people—the people of America.

Did You Know? When the king gave Carolana to his eight friends, the boundaries of Carolana stretched from the Atlantic Ocean all the way across to the Pacific Ocean! At that time, no one had any way of knowing the size of America. The great size of our land was discovered by explorers and pioneers in the years ahead.

Facts to Remember

1. What were the Middle Colonies? _____

   _____

2. What were the Southern Colonies? _____

   _____

3. What explorer was hired to explore New York for the Dutch? _____

4. What three countries claimed New York? _____

   _____

5. Who explored northern New York for France? _____

6. What man claimed all of North America for England? _____

7. What was New York City originally called? _____

8. What fiery Dutch governor did not want to surrender to the British? _____

   _____

9. Who settled Delaware? _____

10. What was Delaware originally called? _____

11. Who settled New Jersey? _____

12. Who gave New Jersey its name? _____

13. What was the first settlement in Pennsylvania? _____

14. Who founded Pennsylvania? _____

15. Pennsylvania was founded to be a refuge for what type of people? _____

16. What was the main settlement in Pennsylvania, personally designed by William Penn? _____

17. What does *Philadelphia* mean? _____

18. Whose idea was it to begin the colony of Maryland? _____

19. Maryland was intended to be a refuge for the people of what religion?

_____

20. What two ships brought the first settlers to Maryland? _____

21. What was the first settlement in Maryland? _____

22. What were North and South Carolina called when they were both one colony?

_____

23. What was the first settlement in Carolana? _____

24. What was the name of the valuable blue dye produced in South Carolina?

_____

25. What were the large farms in the Southern Colonies called? _____

26. What kind of people settled Georgia? _____

27. Who founded Georgia? _____

28. What was the first settlement in Georgia? _____

29. What famous preacher went to Georgia to start America's first orphanage?

_____

A Picture of Colonial Life

Life in colonial America was quite different from life in America today. Yet the way people lived back then influenced the way we live now.

Homes

The first crude cabins built by the colonists were not very pleasant to live in. The colonists had come to America to stay, and they wanted to build permanent homes. Soon larger, nicer houses began to dot the American countryside, and the one-room cabins began to disappear.

Building a new house was quite a task. Fortunately, the colonist did not have to do it all by himself. When a new house had to be built, all the men in the village would gather for a "house raising." With the help of his neighbors, the colonist would clear his land of trees. Then the men would cut the trees

This sturdy New England home is still standing after three hundred years.

into lumber and build the new home. A colonist would even have to build all of his own furniture unless he had brought a few pieces over from Europe.

Most of the time the settlers built houses that were copies of their homes in Europe. A few of the designs, however, were American.

Inside, the colonial houses were simple. There were one or two large beds, a table (usually with benches, not chairs), and perhaps a few other pieces of furniture. The bowls and plates—even the

This is the governor's palace in Williamsburg, Virginia, a colonial city that has been reconstructed. Visitors to Williamsburg can see what life was like in colonial America.

This instrument is called a froe. It was used to split logs to make lumber. Then the colonists would use the lumber to build such things as tables, benches, and chairs.

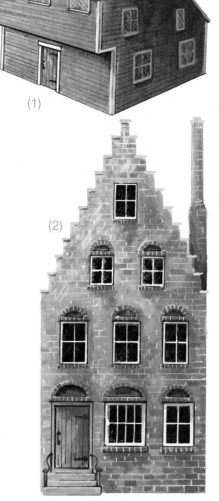

(1)

(2)

(3)

Three colonial homes: (1) A house built by English colonists in Connecticut. (2) A Dutch house in New York. (3) A southern colonist's home in Virginia.

A colonial kitchen. In the background, one woman is churning butter while the other works at a spinning wheel. The fire was for both light and cooking.

99

These were the kinds of clothes that colonial Americans wore: from left to right, a wealthy planter, a Pilgrim, and a farmer.

spoons and forks—were carved out of wood. Candles gave light to the cabin, and a huge fireplace was used for both cooking and heating.

As you can see, colonists did not enjoy the luxuries we have today. *But for almost every colonist, life in America was far better than life in Europe.* And the colonists were willing to work hard to make life in America even better.

During the day, most colonists were busy farming or hunting. Colonial wives also stayed quite busy. One of their most important jobs was making clothes for the family. Using a spinning

New Words

1. **house raising**—a time when all the neighbors got together to help a new settler build his house
2. **homespun**—a coarse, gray material made by colonial housewives
3. **town criers**—men who called out the latest events because most colonial villages had no newspapers
4. **dame school**—where many colonial children started their education
5. **hornbook**—a printed school lesson attached to a wood paddle and protected by a thin sheet of cow's horn
6. **old-field schools**—small schools started by parents in the Southern Colonies

Colonial families made their own candles. Candle wax was made from animal fat. Candles were necessary for daily life. They were the main means of lighting the homes.

wheel, the wife would spin sheep's wool into yarn. Then she would use a loom to make a rough, gray material called *homespun* from the yarn. The homespun was useful for making shirts, dresses, and pants. If the husband were a good hunter, deerskin would also be available for making clothes. The richer colonists avoided wearing homespun clothes; they bought the latest fashions from Europe instead.

The town crier called out the latest news.

New Names

7. *New England Primer*—famous colonial schoolbook which was used by millions of children
8. **Christopher Dock**—a German Mennonite schoolteacher who greatly influenced education in America
9. **Harvard**—the first college started in America

New Dates

10. 1636—Harvard, America's first college, was started
11. 1647—New England passed laws requiring cities to provide schools for children

At night, colonial families usually gathered around the fireplace, for it provided light as well as heat. The family would perhaps work on some project, such as making candles or stitching a quilt together or cooking molasses candy. Since there was no radio or television, they would spend their time talking about the latest news—new settlers in the area, trouble with the Indians, rumors about war with England, the latest happenings in Europe. Some colonial towns had newspapers, but most colonists got the news from *town criers*. Town criers were men who were paid by the city to wander about the streets and call out the latest news as loudly as they could. The colonists also heard the news in their churches on Sundays.

In most homes the Bible was read aloud every night. The Bible could be found in almost every home. Other books, such as *Pilgrim's Progress* and John Foxe's *Book of Martyrs,* were also widely read. But the Bible was the most important book in the lives of most colonists.

Churches

Most settlers came to America so that they could worship God freely. In America, once freedom of religion was allowed, no one had to worship secretly.

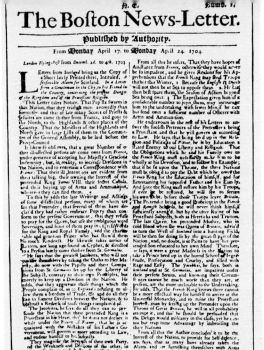

The Boston News-Letter, which began in 1704, was America's first newspaper. Newspapers replaced town criers in America's cities.

Large public houses of worship were built throughout the colonies. The early churches were also used for town meetings, where matters of government were discussed. Thus the ideas of political freedom and religious freedom took root in America's church buildings.

New England was a land filled with churches. At first, most of them were Puritan churches because the founders and early settlers of New England were Puritans from England. The first settlers of New England built churches which, like their homes, were plain and

This simple, sturdy New England church was built about 1740.

simple. They were well built, however, and some of them are still used today.

As more and more people came to New England, changes took place. Larger and more decorative Congregational (Puritan) churches were built, and other religious groups began to build their own churches as well. Baptists, Methodists, Quakers, Jews, and many others built meeting houses in New England. By the end of the Colonial Period (1776), New England had changed from a land dominated by Puritans to a place where people of many faiths could live and worship. For a long time, however, all the people in some New England colonies had to pay taxes for the Congregational church whether they belonged to it or not.

The settlers who built their homes in the Middle Colonies represented many different religions, and the Middle Colonies quickly became known as a land of religious freedom. Many Quakers came to the Middle Colonies to escape the persecution they had faced in England. Other groups who came there included Mennonites, Presbyterians, Baptists, Anglicans, and Dutch Reformed. In the Middle Colonies, these

103

This meeting house in Pennsylvania is an excellent example of churches built in the Middle Colonies.

A typical colonial church service.

groups were free to worship God in the way they thought was right.

There were fewer churches in the Southern Colonies than in the other colonies. The Southern colonists planted large farms that separated Southern families from each other. They would have to travel miles each Sunday just to meet. Rather than churches, traveling preachers brought religion to the Southern colonists. Sometimes an Anglican (Church of England) priest would travel around to the farms and perform an Anglican service for the many Southerners who belonged to the Church of England. Later, men called circuit-riding preachers traveled on horseback throughout the South preaching the Bible, and great revivals broke out.

Going to church was the most important part of the week in colonial America. *Absolutely no work was done on Sunday; the Sabbath was a special time that all the people honored.* Different churches worshiped in different ways, but the services usually included singing, Bible reading, and a long sermon. In fact, most of the services lasted over two hours—some longer than three!

Such long services were bound to cause some people to snooze. But a man strolling through the congregation made sure that everyone stayed awake —he had a pole with which he poked anyone who had closed eyes!

Schools

Almost every colonist believed that children in America needed a good education. The colonists built schools that would give their children what they needed.

Many children began their education in a *dame school*. A lady would agree to teach children in her home. She taught the children reading, writing, and basic arithmetic. The children had no nice classrooms, and there were very few schoolbooks.

Most colonial children got their first schooling in a dame school.

A hornbook.

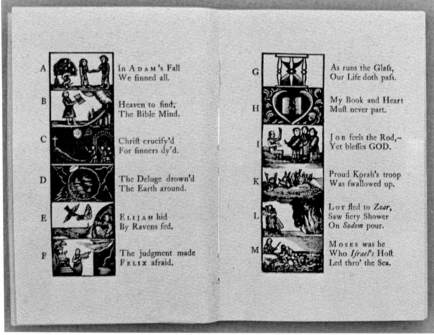

The *New England Primer* was the most widely used textbook in all of colonial America. It offered religious instruction as well as training in reading. The Primer was first printed in 1690 and was used for over 150 years. Millions of copies were printed.

Most children used a hornbook to learn their alphabet. A *hornbook* was a paddle-shaped board to which was attached one sheet containing the alphabet and the Lord's Prayer. The book was called a hornbook because a thin sheet of transparent cow's horn covered the paper to protect it.

After a child had memorized the hornbook, he could begin reading in the *New England Primer.* This book had lists of words, prayers, poems about Bible stories, and short stories about doing right for the children to practice reading. For over 150 years millions of American children learned to read from the *New England Primer.* After that, they would read the Bible, and almost all of them also read *Pilgrim's Progress.*

After staying in dame school for a year or two, the boys might go on to get more education. Girls usually stayed home and learned to bake, cook, and sew, and to make yarn and cloth and candles and soap so they could care for

Harvard University, opened in 1636, was the first college in America. It was created to train ministers.

their families when they were older.

Because American colonists wanted to make sure that their children got a good education, they passed laws ordering cities to build schools and provide education for the public. People knew that learning about God meant reading the Bible, and reading the Bible meant learning to read.

The first public schools in America were built by the Puritans in New England. *As early as 1647 New England had passed a law ordering cities to build schools for children.* Many schools opened their doors to eager children throughout New England. *New England even opened the first college in America—Harvard, which was started in 1636 to train ministers to preach the gospel.* When Harvard College was started, its leaders said:

> Let every student be plainly instructed, and earnestly pressed to consider well, the main end of his life and studies is, to know God and Jesus Christ which is eternal life (John 17:3) and therefore lay Christ in the bottom, as the only foundation of all sound knowledge and learning.

There were fewer schools in the Middle Colonies than there were in New England. Farms were larger here and people lived farther apart than in New England. Schools were so far apart that many children could not walk the distance. Even so, when there was a school, children had to walk as far as two to four miles one way to reach the one-room schoolhouse. Those who lived farther away were taught by their parents or were not taught at all.

Schools in the Middle Colonies usually had just one room with roughly made benches. Almost always, these children were taught by strict men teachers. Sometimes a minister of a church would be the teacher of a school. He would hold his school in the church.

In colonial days, paper was much too expensive for students to use. Pieces of birch bark were stripped from trees and used in place of paper. A piece of lead or coal was used as a pencil. Books were not very plentiful. Usually the school had only one copy of each book it used. Each student waited his turn to use the book.

For a long time, there were not many schools in the South. Wealthy farmers lived in huge homes far apart from each other; they could afford tutors to come to their homes and teach their children privately. And of course the poor people could not afford to build schools.

Eventually, parents in some areas of the South started to get together to hire a teacher for their children. The teacher and students would meet in a shabby building in an old field, in what was called an **old-field school.** This is the kind of school that a boy named George Washington attended. One year, he had to ride on horseback every day to his field school, which was ten miles from home. Another year, he rowed a boat across the river every day, even when it was storming, to get to school.

Industry

America offered Europeans the promise of a better life. Europeans who came to America found that the promise was true. Not only could they worship God freely and give their children a good education, but they could also work and enjoy the fruit of their labors. People who had lived in poverty in Europe came to America and grew wealthy. America was a land of economic freedom.

For the first part of its history, America's chief industry was farming. One of the first things that most colonists did in America was to plant a garden. After the Indians showed them how to plant corn, the colonists planted large farms, and corn became a chief food crop. Colonists ate corn at every meal. They even ate popcorn with milk and sugar as a breakfast food!

New England farmers had to work hard, for the rough New England soil was rocky and hilly. The colonists in the Middle Colonies found farming much easier. But the Southern farmers were the most prosperous of all. The soil was

From *The World Book Encyclopedia*. Painting by H. Charles McBarron. ©1980 World Book–Childcraft International, Inc.

A plantation was like a miniature city. Note the ships on the river—rivers were often the only "road" between plantations.

rich, and the weather was warm. Anything that the farmers planted grew. Cotton proved to be a good crop. Unfortunately, tobacco became popular in Europe, and many farmers in the South planted it.

The large Southern farms were called *plantations*. They resembled a miniature city. Everything the farmer needed was right on his farm. The farms were so large that sometimes there were no roads between them. The people would travel down a river to reach the next plantation!

Gradually, some colonists left farming and began to manufacture goods. The goods were mostly everyday necessities. Such things as cloth, pots and pans, molasses, and other goods were produced and sold in America. People in New England made fishing a major industry.

People in Europe were not interested in most of America's products. For example, no one wanted to buy plain American cloth (homespun). Most of the goods sent to Europe were raw materials. Europeans purchased indigo, a blue dye common in America but precious in Europe. They bought lumber from the vast forests of America. They bought American iron, tobacco, and furs, including beaver furs to make hats and other articles. The trade ships carrying these things to Europe would bring back the goods that the colonists wanted to buy. One of the most popular items was European cloth. Clothes from Europe were much nicer than American clothes and were valued highly in the colonies. America needed Europe's manufactured goods, because there were still not very many factories in America.

Still, there were a few American products that were valued in Europe. The colonists' simple, durable furniture appealed to the Europeans. For example, Benjamin Franklin attached rockers to a slat-back chair to produce the classic American rocking chair, which then became extremely popular throughout Europe.

Paul Revere was one of the greatest colonial silversmiths. He would later win fame as a patriot.

Iron was an important American product. Iron was produced at factories such as the one shown here, which was built at Saugus, Massachusetts, in the 1640's.

The silversmiths of America also manufactured goods that came up to European standards. These fine craftsmen turned lumps of silver into fine pieces of art—tea services and dinnerware that graced the tables of many wealthy people. One of the best silversmiths in America was named Paul Revere. Revere loved his silver, but he also loved freedom as all American colonists did. His love of freedom was to make him famous during the years that ended the colonial age: the years of revolution.

People Worth Knowing More About

Christopher Dock prayed for his students by name every day.

Christopher Dock was a German **Mennonite** schoolteacher in Pennsylvania. Today, he is remembered as a man who made many changes in the way school was taught.

Christopher Dock was the first teacher to use a chalkboard. Today, almost every classroom has a chalkboard in it.

In many colonial schools, a student might be whipped for not knowing the answer to a question. But Christopher Dock said that if the student was working hard and paying attention, there was no reason to spank him if he did not know an answer. Students who misbehaved were a different matter; Dock punished children who lied, cheated, or swore. He felt that a teacher should help "train up a child in the way he should go."

Christopher Dock wrote the first school manual ever published in this country. He hoped that other teachers would read about his methods so that those teachers could improve their own schools.

Christopher Dock had a sincere desire to help young people that lasted through his long life. He cared so much for his students that he prayed for each one of them by name every day. In fact, it was while he was praying for his students that Christopher Dock died in 1771 at his Pennsylvania schoolhouse.

Facts to Remember

1. What is a "house raising"? _____

   _____

2. What did the fireplace in a colonial home provide? _____

3. What did men in the colonies spend their days doing? _____

4. What was one of the most important jobs of a colonial housewife? _____

   _____

5. What was the rough, gray material made by colonial women?_____

6. Since colonial villages often had no newspaper, where did colonists get the

   latest news?_____

7. What was the most important book in colonial homes? _____

8. What were New England churches like? _____

9. What were two religious groups which settled in the Middle Colonies? ___

   _____

10. Why were there so few churches in the Southern Colonies? _____

   _____

   Who preached to Southern families? _____

11. Where did most colonial children begin their education? _____

12. What was a hornbook? _____

   _____

13. What textbook was used by millions of children for over 150 years? _____

   _____

14. What section of the country had more schools than any other, and even passed laws requiring towns to build schools? _____

15. What was America's first college? _____

16. What type of school was common in the South? _____

17. What was the first thing most colonists did when they came to America?

    _____

18. What was the chief food crop in the colonies? _____

    What two crops earned money for Southern farmers? _____

    _____

19. What became a major industry in New England? _____

20. Which American products sold well in Europe?_____

    _____

21. What piece of furniture was invented by Benjamin Franklin and became popular in Europe? _____

22. Who was one of the most famous American silversmiths? _____

23. Who was the Mennonite schoolteacher who greatly influenced American schools? _____

The Great Awakening

One of the most important things that happened in colonial America was the **Great Awakening.** The leaders of the Great Awakening have been called the spiritual Founding Fathers of America, and their teaching did much to shape the spiritual heritage of America.

Revival

The Great Awakening was a spiritual revival that swept through the colonies in the years around 1730 to 1760. It may surprise you that such faithful church-goers as the colonists needed a revival, but the fact is, many of them had never been saved. *They went to church and were good citizens and lived good lives, but many of them had never accepted Christ as their personal Savior.* Many were depending on their good lives to save them.

A Methodist camp meeting

Most of the colonies had laws saying that only church members could vote. Nine of the colonies had official churches, and the people of the colonies had to pay taxes to support those official churches. Often, people joined churches to get in good with the government rather than in obedience to the Bible. This kind of religion was good for the church leaders who wanted many members, but it was not good for the people, because it did not help them to personally accept Christ.

Jonathan Edwards's preaching helped the Great Awakening get started.

Jonathan Edwards— A Great Puritan Preacher

Jonathan Edwards *was one of the first leaders in the Great Awakening.* Jonathan Edwards was born in Connecticut in 1703. He was the only boy in a family of eleven children, and he began to read almost as soon as he could speak. When he was just seven years old he could read books in English and Latin, and he knew some Greek and Hebrew, too. He was also very good at arithmetic and science. When he was twelve he studied spiders by observing their ways. Then he wrote an amazing paper about them, describing their size, kinds, flight, and web-spinning activities. When he was thirteen he went to college, where he was a top student.

Jonathan thought much about God when he was a boy, and he tried very hard to be good. He made up a list of very good resolutions that he tried to follow, and for a while he prayed five times a day. But none of this gave him

115

peace with God. Finally, when he was eighteen years old, he stopped trusting his good works and accepted Christ as his personal Savior. From that time on he was a changed person.

In 1734 Jonathan Edwards preached a sermon about salvation in his Congregational (Puritan) church in Northampton, Massachusetts. A wonderful thing happened. The Spirit of God moved over the congregation convicting them of their sins and their need of Christ. "There was scarcely a single person in the town, old or young," Edwards wrote, "who was left unconcerned about the great things of the eternal world." Good people and bad people, parents and children, wealthy and poor, "from day to day, for many months together," came "by flocks to Jesus Christ."

What a change this brought to the town of Northampton! Jonathan Edwards wrote this about it:

> This work of God, as it was carried on, and the number of true saints multiplied, soon made a glorious alteration [change] in the town; so that in the spring and summer following...the town seemed to be full of the presence of God: it was never so full of love, nor of joy, and yet so full of distress, as it was then.

There was a change in the homes of the town, too:

> There were remarkable tokens [signs] of God's presence in almost every house. It was a time of joy in families on account of salvation being brought unto them; parents rejoicing over their children as new born, and husbands over their wives, and wives over their husbands.

This great move of the Spirit of God upon individuals, households, and whole communities spread throughout New England and eventually to most of the colonies. However, opposition arose.

Jonathan Edwards's church, which

New Words

1. **the Great Awakening**—a revival which swept America in the 1700's
2. **circuit-riding preachers**—men who traveled from town to town, preaching wherever they went

New Names

3. **Jonathan Edwards**—a great Puritan minister whose preaching stirred a great revival in New England
4. **John and Charles Wesley**—English preachers who started the Methodist church
5. **Susanna Wesley**—the mother of John and Charles Wesley
6. **Holy Club**—a Bible club started by the Wesley brothers at Oxford University
7. **Francis Asbury**—a preacher who came to America from England and became a famous circuit-rider
8. **George Whitefield**—the Great Awakening preacher who came to America from England seven times to preach the gospel
9. **David Brainerd**—a Presbyterian missionary to the Indians
10. **Tattamy**—an Indian who helped David Brain-

was supported by the Massachusetts government, would not let him preach any more in Northampton. The wonderful things that were happening were too exciting for the strict Puritan leaders who wanted to be religious without personal salvation.

Edwards moved to the little frontier town of Stockbridge, Massachusetts, where he served as church pastor and missionary to the nearby Indians. He was poorer now, and it was harder for him to provide for his wife and the eight children who were still at home, but he was faithful in the Lord's service. He had more time here, too, and he was able to write some important books about the Bible. His preaching and writing did much to turn the people of America back to the Bible, and it is the Bible, above all else, that has made America a great nation.

Jonathan Edwards was probably the most intelligent man in colonial America as well as one of the best educated. (He became president of Princeton University, a Presbyterian school, before he died.) *But it was his faithful preaching of God's Word that made him great and that blessed America.*

John Wesley— Founder of the Methodist Church

Another man who was very important in the Great Awakening was **John Wesley,** the founder of the Methodist church. Wesley came to America only once, but his influence on our country was very great. You have already read about his missionary work with the Indians in Georgia and how he tried to persuade the colonists not to let rum and slavery into Georgia.

erd preach the gospel
11. **Isaac Backus**—a Baptist pastor who worked to give America religious freedom

New Places
12. **Northampton, Massachusetts**—the city where Jonathan Edwards pastored a church
13. **Princeton**—the college where Jonathan Edwards was president for a brief time
14. **Oxford**—a college in England attended by the Wesleys and George Whitefield
15. **Middleborough, Massachusetts**—the city where Isaac Backus pastored a church

New Dates
16. **1730–1760**—the Great Awakening
17. **1734**—a revival broke out in Jonathan Edwards's church
18. **1736**—the Wesleys traveled to Georgia
19. **1737**—Whitefield first came to America
20. **1739**—Whitefield landed in Philadelphia for the second of his American tours
21. **1744**—David Brainerd began his missionary work among the Indians

Susanna Wesley

John Wesley, the founder of Methodism.

John Wesley was born in 1703 in England, where his father was an Anglican minister. There were nineteen children born into the Wesley family, though, as often happened in those days, some of them died while they were still very young. *The Wesley children owed much of their training to their wonderful mother, Susanna.* Susanna Wesley made sure that her children learned to obey and respect authority at a very early age, and she taught them how to read, too. On John's fifth birthday she taught him the alphabet, and by the end of the day he was able to read from the first chapter of Genesis.

When little John Wesley was six years old, the family home burned down and John was just barely rescued from the flames. He and his mother always believed that God had spared him for a special purpose.

John Wesley was an intelligent, eager learner. After he had learned all he could at home and in school, he went away to Oxford University, where he became known as an excellent student and an outstanding writer. After graduation he stayed at Oxford to teach and to study more.

At Oxford John and his brother Charles started a Holy Club. They studied many books with some friends and tried very hard to live good lives. *In 1736, John and Charles Wesley went to Georgia as missionaries.* Something was wrong, though, and their work was not successful. Charles went back to England after only a few months, and John returned to England after about two years.

Back in England, John studied the Bible with all his heart. Then, with the help of a friend, he discovered what was wrong with him. *He needed to know Christ personally.* The Church of England had taught him to be religious, but it had not taught him that he needed to personally accept Christ. *In 1738 he stopped trusting his good works and turned to Christ for salvation.* Now he was sure that he was right with God, and he found out that his brother Charles had been saved just a few days earlier.

Now John Wesley began to preach in earnest. The ministers in the Church of England, which was supported by the government, did not want him to preach in their churches. So he started preaching in the open air. He would travel by horseback from town to town and preach in the fields, sometimes to thousands of people at once. While he was riding, he would read books.

People were saved wherever Wesley preached, and he organized the new Christians into Methodist societies. The Methodists would meet to pray, study the Bible, and tell others about Christ.

Ministers were sent out from these societies to spread the gospel, and England became a changed country as her people began to turn back to the Bible.

Many great leaders of England have said that John Wesley did more than perhaps anyone else to make England a strong, free country during a difficult time in her history. The Methodists sent many ministers to America as well, and they played a great part in preaching the Word of God throughout our land.

Circuit-Riding Preachers

One Methodist who came to America from England was **Francis Asbury.** He had learned from John Wesley the method of riding from town to town on a horse to preach in as many towns each week as possible. When he became a **Methodist** leader in the American colonies in 1771, he, too, spread the gospel in this way, and he taught many other Methodist preachers to do it.

These men were called circuit-riding preachers, because regularly they would make the same circuit (circle) of towns, preaching wherever they went. They preached every day of the week, and sometimes as many as six sermons a day. You can imagine what a great number of colonists heard the gospel when this method was used! Another famous circuit-riding preacher, who lived a little later in our country's history, was **Peter Cartwright**.

George Whitefield— The Great Evangelist to America

While John Wesley was traveling throughout England, **George Whitefield** was doing the same thing in America. Whitefield first came to America from England in 1738, and he preached in many different kinds of churches. Soon the crowds were too big for buildings, and he started preaching in the fields. He preached to the people, and he also preached to the ministers. *After hearing George Whitefield, many preachers started telling their own people how to get right with God, a thing they had sadly neglected to do.*

George Whitefield was born in England in 1714. When he was eighteen he went to Oxford University, where he studied hard. He was concerned about his salvation, though. Somehow he knew that just being a member of the Church of England was not enough. He started to do good deeds. He visited poor people in jail and read to them to cheer them up. He joined John and Charles Wesley's Holy Club. He ate poor food, dressed in old, patched clothes, and wore soiled shoes. But nothing could bring him peace.

Finally he started studying books about the Bible, and then he turned to the Bible itself. It was in the Bible that he found the answers to his questions. "I got more true knowledge from reading the Book of God in one month than I could ever have acquired from all the writings of men," he said. In 1735 he came to understand that a person is saved by faith in Christ, and he preached this truth for the rest of his life.

Whitefield preached in England for a while, and then he sailed for Georgia in 1738, where he started America's first orphanage and preached the gospel. He returned to England the next year, but the Anglicans would not let him preach in their churches. *Instead, Whitefield started preaching in the fields.* (In fact, John Wesley got the idea of preaching outdoors from George Whitefield.) Sometimes he preached to crowds of 20,000 people at once. He traveled thousands of miles to carry the gospel to the people in England, Scotland, and Wales.

In 1739 Whitefield sailed to Philadelphia to begin the second of his seven tours of America. During his seven tours he preached throughout all the colonies, spreading the gospel and collecting offerings for his orphanage. Many of the churches in America that were supported by the colonial governments were against Whitefield's preaching, and so he preached outdoors.

One good friend of George Whitefield was the great American inventor and statesman, Benjamin Franklin. We do not know whether Ben Franklin ever accepted Christ, but he was moved by the preaching of Mr. Whitefield. When Whitefield preached in Philadelphia, Franklin was impressed by the change that took place in the people. Here is what Franklin wrote:

> It was wonderful to see the change soon made in the manners of our inhabitants. From being thoughtless or indifferent about religion, it seemed as if all the world were growing religious, so that one could not walk through the town in an evening without hearing psalms sung in different families of every street.

George Whitefield believed that the gospel is for all people. That belief made him want to help everyone—children, adults, Indians, black slaves, poor people, rich people, orphans, people with no education, and people with much education.

Whitefield was very concerned about the slaves in America. He got Ben Franklin to print a letter from him urging the colonists to treat the slaves with more kindness. This letter was soon printed in newspapers all over the colonies. Many times Whitefield preached directly to the slaves and told them that they needed to come to Jesus just like everyone else. Here is what he said to them toward the end of one sermon:

> I must not forget the poor Negroes. No, I must not. Jesus Christ has died for them, as well as for others. Nor do I mention you last, because I despise your souls, but because I would have what I shall say make the deeper impression upon your hearts.
>
> Oh that you would seek the Lord to be your righteousness! Who knows but that

Thousands came to hear George Whitefield preach.

He may be found of you. For in Jesus Christ there is neither male nor female, bond nor free; even you may be the children of God, if you believe in Jesus. Did you never read of the eunuch belonging to Queen Candace? A Negro like yourselves. He believed. The Lord was his righteousness. He was baptized. Do you also believe, and you shall be saved. Christ Jesus is the same now as He was yesterday, and will wash you in His own blood. Go home then, turn the words of the text into a prayer, and intreat the Lord to be *your* righteousness. Even so, come Lord Jesus, come quickly into all our souls! *Amen, Lord Jesus, Amen* and *Amen!*

Whitefield was also interested in the Indians, and he wrote a gospel tract for a trader to read to them.

George Whitefield preached over 18,000 sermons in his lifetime to over ten million people. His preaching of the gospel—that each person needs to be saved—affected all areas of American life. Whitefield's care for the orphans was an example to others to help and educate young children. His interest in the slaves and his efforts to preach to them helped others to feel more kindly toward them. His interest in the Indians encouraged many people to become missionaries. Because he saw the importance of education, he influenced the founding of about fifty colleges in America.

Missionary Work in America

Because of the Great Awakening, many Americans became missionaries. The first American missionaries went to settlers in the frontiers of America, and to the Indians. Later, America would become known as a great missionary nation, and Americans would go to all corners of the earth to preach the gospel. Even today, America has more Christian missionaries around the world than any other country. *The missionary spirit of Americans is probably one of the great things that has caused God to bless America.*

One man who gave his life as a missionary to the Indians during the Colonial Period was David Brainerd. David Brainerd was born in Connecticut in 1718. When he was fourteen years old he became an orphan and went to live with his older sister and her family. His parents had taught him the importance of reading the Bible, and he came to know Christ in 1739.

The next fall he went to Yale to prepare to be a preacher. From the start he was an excellent student. In 1740 many students at Yale suffered from smallpox. Brainerd became very ill and was forced to go home for several months. He returned to school as soon as he

David Brainerd was a missionary to the Indians during the Great Awakening.

losis. Tuberculosis was a disease that killed many people in colonial America. David Brainerd would not go home, though, and he kept up with his studies.

While Brainerd had been home with smallpox, the Great Awakening had come to Yale. George Whitefield had preached there often, and many of the students were living changed lives. Brainerd, moved by what was happening, felt that God was calling him to be a missionary to the Indians. The tuberculosis made him very sick, but he was determined to reach the Indians for Christ.

In 1744 the **Presbyterian** church sent David Brainerd out to minister in Indian villages. He traveled regularly on horseback, preaching in villages wherever he could. His travels took him to Indians of New York, New Jersey, and Pennsylvania. He preached in English, and a faithful Indian helper named **Tattamy** interpreted his words into the Indian language. Later he trained six Indians to preach to their people.

When Brainerd went to the Crosswelksung Indians in New Jersey, a wonderful thing happened. Up to seventy Indians at a time came to hear him preach of Christ's salvation. They listened carefully to several sermons in one day. The Indians were having a Great Awakening!

could and studied even harder than before, but soon it was clear that he had a much more serious illness—tubercu-

Brainerd wrote this in his diary about one Indian woman who heard the preaching:

A young Indian woman, who, I believe, never knew before she had a soul, nor ever thought of any such thing, hearing that there was something strange among the Indians, came, it seems, to see what was the matter. In her way to the Indians, she called at my lodgings, and when I told her I designed presently to preach to the Indians, laughed, and seemed to mock; but went however to them. I had not proceeded far in my public discourse, before she felt *effectually* that she had a soul; and before I had concluded my discourse, was so convinced of her sin and misery, and so distressed with concern for her soul's salvation, that she seemed like one pierced through with a dart, and cried out incessantly.

David Brainerd traveled about one hundred miles on his horse each week, even though the pain from his illness grew worse and worse. Finally, he could work no longer, and he had to leave his Indians for the last time. He went to the home of Jonathan Edwards to rest, and there he died in 1747.

David Brainerd was one of the first missionaries to be spurred by the Great Awakening to do great things for God. Other great missionaries followed his example after his death. John Wesley, Francis Asbury, William Carey, and Jim Elliot (who was killed by the Auca Indians of Ecuador in 1956) all said that David Brainerd had greatly influenced their lives. Through the lives of great men who have followed the example of David Brainerd, the effects of the Great Awakening are still being felt around the world.

How the Great Awakening Shaped America

The preaching of George Whitefield, John Wesley, Jonathan Edwards, and the other leaders in the Great Awakening helped the colonists to see more than ever that all men are equal in worth to God. *The preaching of the Great Awakening did more than perhaps anything else to draw the colonists together so that our country would truly become one nation under God.*

The colonists saw that since all men are equal in the eyes of God, then no man is better than any other man. Therefore, all men should be equal in the sight of the law. All deserve equal justice, no matter who they are and no matter what their religious beliefs may be. This truth paved the way for the colonists to write, just a few years later:

We hold these truths to be self-evident,
that all men are created equal;
that they are endowed by their Creator
with certain unalienable rights;

> that among these are
>> life,
>>> liberty, and
>>>> the pursuit of happiness.

Many years later, Calvin Coolidge, who was President of the United States from 1923 to 1929, said this:

America was born in a revival of religion. Back of that revival were John Wesley, George Whitefield, and Francis Asbury.

The Bible truths of the Great Awakening also paved the way to the most wonderful freedom in America—the freedom of religion.

Methodist churches grew up in our land, and Methodist circuit-riding preachers rode on horseback to preach from town to town. Many Presbyterian, Congregational, and Dutch Reformed churches were brought back to preaching the gospel, and Baptist churches sprang up throughout the colonies. The Baptists were especially eager to bring freedom of religion to America, for they had often been persecuted for preaching the gospel in Europe, in England, and even in America.

The great idea of separation of church and state that Roger Williams and his Baptist friends gave to Rhode Island would soon be spread to the whole country, and America would be seen as a vast mission field, open for the free spread of the gospel.

People Worth Knowing More About

Isaac Backus

Isaac Backus—Defender of Liberty

One colonist who came to know Christ during the Great Awakening was **Isaac Backus.** He became a traveling evangelist. In 1756 he became pastor of the First Baptist Church in Middleborough, Massachusetts, and he was pastor there for fifty-eight years.

During those fifty-eight years, he preached to his congregation and helped many Christians in Massachusetts, Connecticut, Rhode Island, and other colonies. He also worked very hard to make our country free from England and to bring religious liberty to America.

He especially spoke out against the religious taxes that all the people of a colony had to pay to support the Congregational churches. He said that people should be free to support their own churches, not a state church that they did

125

not believe in. Finally, partly because of the work of Isaac Backus, America became a land that had freedom of religion through the separation of church and state.

Facts to Remember

1. What was the Great Awakening? _____

2. Why did such good people as the colonists need a revival? _____

   _____

3. What American Puritan preacher helped the Great Awakening get started?

   _____

4. Did New England have separation of church and state in colonial times? ____

5. What problems did this cause? _____

   _____

6. What happened to make Jonathan Edwards a changed person? _____

   _____

7. What was another name for the Puritan churches? _____

8. Why did Jonathan Edwards move to the frontier? _____

   _____

9. Jonathan Edwards became president of what university just before his death?

   _____

10. Who founded the Methodist church? _____

11. Who was the mother of John and Charles Wesley? _____

12. Where did John and Charles Wesley go to college? _____

    What did they start there? _____

13. Why did the Wesley brothers *NOT* have success on their first trip to America?

_____

14. Why did John Wesley start preaching in the open air? _____

_____

15. What did John Wesley do while he was riding his horse from town to town?

_____

16. What were circuit-riding preachers? _____

_____

17. Who learned this method of preaching from John Wesley and then taught it

to other preachers? _____

18. What Great Awakening preacher came to America seven times to preach the

gospel? _____

19. Why did George Whitefield preach outdoors? _____

_____

20. Who was Whitefield's famous American friend? _____

21. Who was a famous American missionary to the Indians?_____

22. What was the name of Brainerd's faithful Indian helper?_____

23. In whose home did David Brainerd die? _____

24. How did the Great Awakening affect America?_____

_____

25. Who pastored a church in Middleborough, Massachusetts, for fifty-eight

years and also worked to make America a free country? _____

_____

The French and Indian War

French soldiers and Indian warriors fought British soldiers during the French and Indian War.

New France and Its Colonies

In the year 1608, when the English were building their first successful settlement at Jamestown, the French were also building their first successful settlement in **New France.** *New France covered most of what is now Canada plus land far down the Mississippi River which is now part of the United States.* The first settlement in New France was **Quebec** [kwe-bek′].

New France was huge, but there were few settlements there. Most Frenchmen who came were interested in becoming fur traders.

Since the French fur traders depended upon the Indians' friendship, the traders were eager to become friendly. They came to New France with glass beads, knives, cloth blankets, and anything else that the Indians desired. These items were traded to the Indians for beaver skins and other furs that were valuable in Europe.

The Differences between New France and the American Colonies

Unlike the English, most French could not become farmers, so they had no desire to take land from the Indians. The king of France did not allow the

New France was a valuable colony for its natural resources, especially its valuable furs.

French colonists the rights the English colonists had. The people who went to New France were expected to work as the king told them. He was not interested in family life or farm life. He was interested in the valuable fur trade. So while the English brought their families, most French colonists were unmarried men. As they moved about trading and trapping furs, they often lived with the Indians instead of building their own homes.

France was a Catholic country, and no one was allowed to go to New France except Catholics. The French sent Catholic missionaries (priests) to the Indians.

The French and English Become Enemies

France's claim that she owned the land along the **Mississippi Valley** and the **Ohio River** caused problems. To strengthen this claim, she built forts along the Ohio River.

Meanwhile, the English colonists of the thirteen colonies were beginning to move west of the Appalachian Mountains onto land that both the French and English claimed as their own.

The English began chopping down trees to clear the land and build homes. The French fur traders became angry. The forests were the homes of fur-bearing animals. If the forests were disturbed, the animals would move and become scarce. This would affect the way of living for the French colonists. As a result, the French strengthened their forts. Then they began talking to the Indians.

"The Frenchmen are your friends. We do not come to take your land. We do not chop down trees and destroy your hunting ground," the French told the Indians. "We think of you as our brothers. The English think of you as enemies."

"The English come as enemies of both of us. When they chop down trees, they destroy the Indians' hunting ground and the Frenchmen's trade. If we do not stop the English from coming, both the French and the Indians will be forced to move off this land. Will you allow this to happen? Will you help the French fight the English?"

The Indians listened and nodded in agreement.

Bands of Indians encouraged by the French began raiding English frontier settlements in the early 1700's. Without warning, in the early morning hours,

Indians attack and burn a British village without warning.

the Indians would attack an English settlement while the settlers were still in their beds. They would burn the cabins and kill most of the men. Even women and children were often killed, but sometimes they were taken captive by the Indians. The Indians would then either sell them as servants to the French colonists or keep them as their slaves. Many times white children taken as captives were adopted into the Indians' tribes. They were then treated as real Indian children.

New Names

1. **French and Indian War**—the war that decided who would be the most powerful in North America— England or France
2. **George Washington**—a young soldier who became a well-known hero during the French and Indian War; later, the first President of the United States
3. **Edward Braddock**—a famous English general who was killed in the French and Indian War

Map Study: America at the Time of the French and Indian War

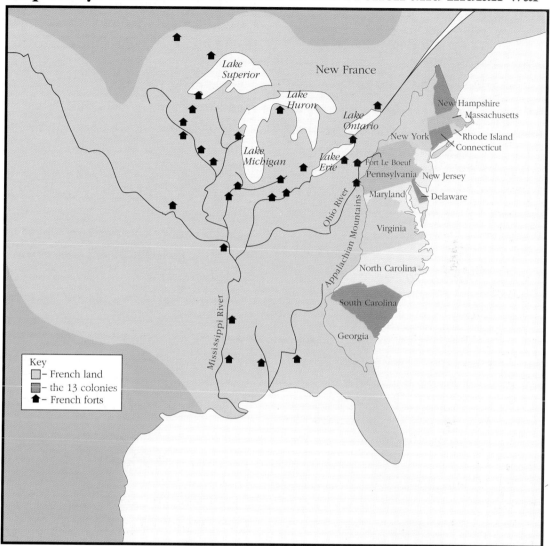

Key
- French land
- the 13 colonies
- French forts

New France

Lake Superior
Lake Huron
Lake Ontario
Lake Michigan
Lake Erie

New Hampshire
Massachusetts
New York
Rhode Island
Connecticut
Fort Le Boeuf
Pennsylvania
New Jersey
Maryland
Delaware
Virginia
North Carolina
South Carolina
Georgia

Ohio River
Appalachian Mountains
Mississippi River

New Places
4. **New France**—France's land in America
5. **Quebec**—the first settlement in New France
6. **Fort Le Boeuf**—French fort in the Ohio Valley

7. **St. Lawrence River**—the river which flows by Quebec

New Dates
8. **1608**—the settlement of New France begins
9. **1754-1763**—the French and Indian War

131

The French and Indian War

Both France and England were powerful countries. Each wanted to control the New World. As a result, between the years 1689 and 1763, France and England fought four wars. The first three wars were unimportant. *The last war had a great effect on the history of our country. It lasted from 1754 to 1763 and was called the* **French and Indian War.**

Events Leading to the French and Indian War

"The Ohio country belongs to England. The French have no right to build forts on our land," insisted the governor of Virginia. "I shall send a messenger to the French officer at **Fort Le Boeuf** (lə buf) and ask them to leave. Fort Le Boeuf is hundreds of miles from Virginia. Whom can I trust to take a letter that far? He certainly should be a brave man, one that is not afraid to spend weeks in the wilderness."

A young man from Virginia by the name of **George Washington** *already had a reputation for being both wise and brave. He was chosen to deliver the message.*

Several men went with him. They left on a chilly October day. Together they crossed the mountains and watched for Indians. After weeks of traveling through the wilderness, they reached Fort Le Boeuf. The French officer took the message that young George Washington handed him from the governor of Virginia and read it. Then the French

Young George Washington was sent by the British to Fort Le Boeuf.

officer politely explained that the French had claimed this land for France. "We do not intend to give up what is ours," he told Washington.

Discouraged, the men from Virginia began their long trip home. It was now winter. The men had to battle heavy snowstorms. Once George Washington nearly drowned when he fell off a log raft into an icy river. After several weeks of hardships, Washington finally reported the bad news to the governor of Virginia.

The governor decided that there was only one thing left to do. He must raise a small army of colonists to drive the French out of the Ohio Valley. By now, George Washington's brave trip through the wilderness to Fort Le Boeuf had made him a hero among the Virginians. The governor made Washington an officer of the Virginia army. He led his men bravely, but the colonists were not trained to fight as soldiers. The French army defeated them. The year was 1754. George Washington had led the first battle of the French and Indian War.

Help Arrives from England

Seeing that the colonists could not defeat the French by themselves, the king of England sent an army of trained soldiers to America. Along with them came **General Edward Braddock,** who would command the English army.

Colonists from the thirteen colonies were asked to volunteer. Among the volunteers was George Washington.

The English army was very fine looking in their red uniforms. They could march together in perfect step. They knew all the rules for war in Europe. The English soldiers would not think of hiding behind a tree or rock to shoot. That, to them, would be cowardly. The rules for war in Europe said that they must fight out in the open. There was only one thing wrong with their plans. This was not Europe. This was America. The Indians had their own rules for fighting a war.

The colonial soldiers had clothes made out of homespun material and buckskin. They could not march in perfect step, nor did they know the rules for fighting in Europe. Yet they knew better than anyone else the rules for fighting in America.

Washington, as well as other colonists, tried to warn General Braddock. "If you are fighting Indians, you have to fight like an Indian. Indians hide behind trees and bushes while they shoot. Your red uniforms will make fine targets."

"My men will not fight like cowards," came the answer.

General Braddock and his men marched through the forest in a narrow line.

With drums beating, General Braddock led his army through the forest. The forest was thick with trees and bushes. The English had to make a narrow road as they moved forward in order that their wagons of food and supplies could move through the forest. A long line of unprotected soldiers and wagons stretched out for miles.

Suddenly shots seemed to ring out from nowhere. The woods were full of French soldiers and Indians hiding behind trees, rocks, and bushes. The English army had not noticed them until it was too late.

The colonists jumped behind bushes and fought back Indian style. But the British soldiers fought where they stood. Because they could not see their enemy, they did not know where to aim their guns. The British soldiers were easy targets for the well-hidden Indians. Many were killed. Suddenly, a bullet hit General Braddock.

With their leader wounded, the British soldiers lost courage and ran. George Washington rode among them, encouraging them to keep fighting. The horse he was riding was shot out from under him. Washington quickly mounted another, and that, too, was shot. He bravely got on a third horse and kept fighting. Pieces of his coat were torn by bullets, but he himself was not hurt.

The British lost this battle. Even the courage of George Washington could not save them. At the time, George Washington was only twenty-three years old. He seemed to be a born soldier. What did he have to say about this battle?

I heard the bullets whistle, and believe me there is something charming in the sound.

134

Victories Come at Last

General Braddock died shortly after the battle, and the British had no great general to lead their army.

The war continued for many years. The British lost many battles. The French army was strong and had the help of many Indians. The frontier covered a large area. While the British army could not be everywhere at once, there were many Indian tribes all along the frontier who did their part in destroying homes and killing and capturing the settlers who were too spread out to fight together.

Finally the king of England sent another army to the colonies. At last, one after another of the French forts in the Ohio Valley was taken away from the French. *At last the day came when the French were driven completely out of the Ohio Valley.*

The French still controlled most of what is now Canada. If they were allowed to stay there, they could rebuild their strength and threaten the English colonies again. Since Quebec was the most important settlement in New France, the British decided that it must be captured. The French army must be driven out of North America. Until then, the war would not be over.

Victory at Quebec—The French and Indian War Ends

Attacking Quebec was not easy. Quebec is built high on a cliff beside the St. Lawrence River. The French thought it would be impossible for the English to climb such a steep rock without being

The British finally began to win victories. This picture shows a battle which occurred in 1755. The British are in red uniforms.

seen, so they guarded another place where they thought the English might try to attack instead.

Late one night, a line of British soldiers worked noiselessly to climb the steep rock. They were not seen or heard by the enemy. Imagine the surprise of the French the next morning when they saw nearly 5,000 British soldiers outside their city, ready to attack. This time, the French were taken by surprise. They fought but had to surrender. The British flag was raised over Quebec. *The English victory at Quebec ended the French and Indian War.*

British soldiers climb a steep cliff to attack the city of Quebec. The English victory at Quebec ended the French and Indian War.

The Importance of the French and Indian War

The French and Indian War was important to the history of our country for many reasons.

1. **It answered the question: Which country would be more important in North America—France or England? The answer, of course, was England.**

2. **Before the war, the colonists had had no experience in fighting wars. Their experience as soldiers in the French and Indian War would be needed when they fought during the American Revolution.**

3. **George Washington became a great hero to the people in all thirteen colonies. Soon they would begin to think of him as their leader.**

4. **More colonists began moving into the Ohio Valley. America now had more room to grow.**

Facts to Remember

1. What was the name given to France's territory in America?_____

2. What was the first settlement in New France? _____

3. What did France build to strengthen her claims in New France? _____

_____

4. The French were aided by whom in their war against the British? _____

_____

5. When was the French and Indian War fought? _____

6. To what fort did British soldiers go to tell the French to leave? _____

_____

7. What man led the first battle of the war and later became a famous hero?

_____

8. Why did England almost lose the French and Indian War? _____

_____

9. What great English general was killed in the French and Indian War? _____

_____

10. What city did the British attack to force the surrender of France? _____

Why was it so difficult to attack this city? _____

_____

11. What were four important results of the French and Indian War?

_____

_____

_____

_____

The American Revolution

With the close of the French and Indian War in 1763, England became the most powerful kingdom in the world. Many American colonists were proud to be a part of their mother country. England allowed her colonists in the New World much more freedom than France had allowed hers. The colonists of New France could not own homes or land. They could not have any part in making their laws. English colonists could own their homes and lands, and they had a part in making their own laws.

Though 3,000 miles of ocean separated England from her American colonies, the colonists were promised the same rights that the people in England had. This promise had made the colonists happy. Would the king of England ever dare to break it?

The American Colonies Demand Their Rights as Englishmen

Money Problems

England may have become the greatest power in the world, but she had also become very poor. She had fought four wars with France. Wars are expensive.

France and Spain still wished for a larger part of the New World. If they fought England, England wanted to be powerful enough to win. England must find a way to make money.

Stamp Act

At that time, **King George III** was king of England. He decided that the colonists themselves must pay for the protection that the English army had given them during the French and Indian War. This sounds fair, but remember, the colonists believed that they were to have a part in making their own laws. This was part of the rights which Englishmen were supposed to have. King George put aside this promise when he told the British government to pass laws for the Americans to obey.

The colonists had no part in making these laws.

One law was known as the **Stamp Act.** Special stamps were to be sold by the British government to the American colonists. These stamps were really seals. The law said that all newspapers, marriage certificates, almanacs, and other documents bought by the colonists had to have a seal or stamp placed on them. The colonists were to buy the stamps when they bought the paper. So each stamp was really a tax that the colonists had to pay. *A* **tax** *is money that people pay to their government to help run the government.*

In England, people could choose men to represent them and make their decisions for them about the tax. But the colonists in America had no such

The Stamp Act aroused the anger of the colonists. A group of colonists is shown here burning a pile of the hated British stamps.

representatives. The colonists had no say in the taxes they had to pay. They believed that the laws of England said that the colonists were supposed to have a say in their taxes, for they believed they were supposed to have the rights of Englishmen. In their minds, King George was breaking the law of England as well as breaking his word.

More Problems

The English government tried to force the colonists to do other things, too. Most colonists were hardworking.

They grew crops such as tobacco, cotton, sugar, and indigo with hopes of selling their products to other countries. But England began telling them, "No, you may not sell your products to any other country, except England." The colonists were forced to accept the low prices that England offered them, because they could not sell their products anywhere else.

Some colonists made cloth. From this cloth, some colonists began to make beautiful clothes. England told the colonists that they could make only

New Words

1. **tax**—money that people pay to their government to help run the government
2. **representative**—a person chosen by a group of people to make decisions for that group
3. **massacre**—the cruel killing of many people at one time
4. **patriots**—those American colonists who wanted to fight for independence from Britain
5. **loyalists or Tories**—those American colonists who remained loyal to England
6. **trench**—a hole or ditch dug in the ground to protect soldiers from gunfire
7. **Hessians**—German soldiers who were hired by the British to fight against the American colonists

New Names

8. **George III**—the king of England during the Revolutionary War period
9. **Stamp Act**—an unfair tax law that angered the colonists
10. **Boston Massacre**—a fight between angry colonists and British soldiers in which five Americans were killed
11. **Boston Tea Party**—an act of protest by American colonists, who threw British tea into the Boston Harbor
12. **Continental Congress**—the group of men who met before and during the Revolutionary War to decide what America should do
13. **Minutemen**—Massachusetts soldiers who got their name from their boast that they could be ready in a minute to fight the British
14. **Patrick Henry**—the patriot who said, "Give me liberty or give me death!"
15. **Paul Revere and William Dawes**—two men who warned American soldiers to get ready for a British attack
16. **Ethan Allen**—a daring American soldier who captured Fort Ticonderoga
17. **Green Mountain Boys**—the nickname for the soldiers who fought with Ethan Allen
18. **Declaration of Independence**—the document which proclaimed that America was fighting to be free of English rule
19. **John Hancock**—president of the Continental Congress
20. **General George Washington**—commander in chief of the colonial army; "the Father of His Country"
21. **Nathan Hale**—a brave patriot who gave his life for his country and said, "I only regret that I

enough clothes for their own families. Clothes made in one colony could not be sold in another colony. Where could a wealthy colonist buy fine clothes? He had to order them from England.

Iron was important to the colonists, for many utensils, pots, and pans of that time were made from iron. England said the colonists could make their own iron, but they were not allowed to make anything with the iron. The colonists must sell their iron to England where it would be made into the things that the colonists needed. Then, the English ships would take the iron products back to the colonies, where they would be sold for high prices.

Who would get wealthy under such laws? Who would become poor? Since the colonists had no voice as to the price of their products, they were the ones to become poors.

Such things would not happen to the people who lived in England. Where had the colonists' rights as Englishmen gone? The king had little concern for the colonists in America except for the money he made from them.

have but one life to lose for my country"

22. **Flag Day**—the day which commemorates the day on which George Washington first presented the stars and stripes to Congress

23. **George Rogers Clark**—the soldier who reclaimed the Northwest Territory for America

24. **John Paul Jones**—a brave sea captain who helped start the American navy and who won the greatest naval victory of the war

25. *Bonhomme Richard*—John Paul Jones's ship

26. *Serapis*—a ship captured by John Paul Jones

27. **Cornwallis**—a general of British troops; he surrendered to Washington

28. **General Greene**—an American general who fought the British in the Southern Colonies

29. *Treaty of Paris*—the agreement which ended the Revolutionary War and which granted America its independence

New Places

30. **Lexington and Concord**—the site of the first battle of the Revolutionary War

31. **Bunker Hill**—the place where Americans proved they would be a tough enemy

32. **Fort Ticonderoga**—a strategic fort captured by Ethan Allen

33. **Trenton**—the site of one of America's first major victories in the war

34. **Saratoga**—the site of the turning point of the American Revolution

35. **Valley Forge**—the place where Washington's army stayed during the cruel winter of 1777–1778

36. **Northwest Territory**—the important frontier land reconquered by George Rogers Clark

37. **Yorktown**—the place where the British surrendered

New Dates

38. **1773**—the Boston Tea Party

39. **1775**—the Second Continental Congress begins meeting; the war begins

40. **1776**—the Declaration of Independence

41. **1777**—the new flag is presented to Congress; the Battle of Saratoga

42. **1778**—the British shift the fighting to the Southern Colonies

43. **1781**—Cornwallis surrenders at Yorktown

44. **1783**—the Treaty of Paris is signed

You can imagine how upset the colonists became when the Stamp Act was passed. The colonists decided not to buy the stamps. "If we buy the stamps, the king will soon tax other things, too," they told each other.

The Colonists Speak Out

Although there were some colonists who agreed with England, many colonists felt that England was treating them wrongly. Men from nine colonies decided to hold a meeting in New York. In this meeting, it was decided that the colonists should complain to the king. At last the British government felt forced to drop the Stamp Act.

New Taxes

But the king of England was not happy at all. He was determined to make the colonists pay taxes without their consent. He now had the British government place a tax on glass, paint, paper, and tea sold in the American colonies. Again, the colonists refused to buy the goods that carried the new tax.

The Boston Massacre

The people of Boston, Massachusetts, grew very angry and restless at the new taxes. England sent soldiers to Boston to help keep the peace and force the colonists to obey. Because the British soldiers wore red coats, some colonists teased them and called them "red coats" or "lobster-backs."

One cold, snowy evening, a small mob began throwing snowballs at a British soldier. Some of the mob began throwing stones as well. British soldiers came running to stop the fight. Suddenly, without orders, and perhaps by accident, a gun was shot. In the confusion, more soldiers fired their guns. Five colonists were killed.

Each side was partly to blame for this terrible mistake. The colonists were teasing, irritating, and threatening the British soldiers. And the British soldiers fired without orders.

Hot tempers on both sides erupted in the Boston Massacre in 1770. This picture of the Boston Massacre was engraved by Paul Revere.

Americans disguised themselves as Indians and threw British tea into Boston Harbor at the Boston Tea Party.

The people of Boston angrily called this incident the **"Boston Massacre."** *A massacre is the cruel killing of many people at one time.* Preachers preached against what the British were doing, and many of their sermons were printed in pamphlet form so that many people could read them. As always, the ministers had a great influence on the people.

England saw that the tax on the glass, paint, paper, and tea was not worth all the trouble it was causing. All the taxes were dropped except one. England wanted to show the colonists that the British government still had the right to tax the colonists. So a small tax was still kept on tea. You can imagine what drink the colonists refused to buy from England—tea!

The Boston Tea Party

Three years had passed since the Boston Massacre. Most colonists still refused to buy tea from England. King George III decided to force the colonists to accept the tea. Three ships loaded with tea sailed into Boston's harbor.

On a chilly December night in 1773, about fifty colonists dressed up to look like Indians. Carrying tomahawks, they boarded the three ships where there were 342 chests of tea. Each chest was smashed open with a tomahawk and then thrown over the sides of the ships into the water. When they destroyed the last chest of tea, they quietly went back to their homes. This event became known as the **Boston Tea Party.**

News of the Boston Tea Party spread quickly to the other colonies. Many colonists cheered the people of Boston for their courage. Others wondered with fear, "What will England do now?"

The English government saw no excuse for the Boston Tea Party. The English government passed harsh laws to punish the thousands of people in Boston, even though only fifty men did the damage.

More English soldiers were sent to Boston. England closed Boston's harbor. Since no ships could sail in or out, the people of Boston had no way of buying supplies or food.

"The port of Boston shall stay closed until its people pay for the tea they destroyed," the British government said. If the harbor remained closed, the people of Boston could starve to death.

The other colonies soon heard of the unfair laws forced upon the people of Boston. South Carolina sent gifts of food. Connecticut and New York sent herds of sheep and cattle. Other colonies also sent gifts. The English were

The building where the Continental Congress met is now called Independence Hall.

able to keep ships from sailing into Boston, but they couldn't keep other colonists from traveling over the New England paths and hills to help the people of Boston.

"How can we protect ourselves from these regulations that the government of England has no right to impose upon us?" each colony asked itself.

One of the patriots suggested that representatives from each colony meet together in Philadelphia to decide what to do.

The War Begins

The First Continental Congress

Fifty men met in Philadelphia in September, 1774. They all agreed that England was unfair to her colonies, but they did not agree about what to do. Most men only wanted England to be fair to the colonists. Only a few men had decided that it was time America became independent from England.

Finally they made a list of complaints against England. They were supposed to have the same rights that all Englishmen had; the king acted as though they had no rights at all. The colonists asked that their rights as Englishmen be respected. Then they agreed that the people of Massachusetts should not obey the laws that England had forced upon her. To show that they meant business, the colonists agreed not to buy goods made in England. This meeting was called the **First Continental Congress**.

"If England does not listen, then we will return in May to hold a second Continental Congress."

How did King George react? He sent warships and more soldiers to the colonies. He was determined to force the colonists to obey.

The Colonists Prepare to Fight

The British warships and soldiers upset the colonists. They began to drill and train as soldiers. Colonists began to hide gunpowder and ammunition.

Many Massachusetts men called themselves "**Minutemen**" because they said they could be ready to fight at a minute's notice.

Fight for what? They were willing to fight for the rights of Englishmen. They thought that once King George realized they meant business, he would give the colonists their rights again.

Meanwhile, in Virginia, a young man named **Patrick Henry** gave a stirring speech which began changing the minds of many colonists. In his argument for fighting for independence, Patrick Henry cried:

Gentlemen may cry, peace, peace—but

"Give me liberty or give me death!" Patrick Henry's stirring speech began to change many colonists' minds.

there is no peace....Why stand we here idle? What is it that gentlemen wish? What would they have? Is life so dear, or peace so sweet, as to be purchased at the price of chains and slavery? Forbid it Almighty God! I know not what course others may take; but as for me, give me liberty or give me death!

Those who, like Patrick Henry, now wanted America to be free from England's rule were called **patriots**. Those who remained loyal to England were called **loyalists** or **Tories**.

How did the British react to the colonists in Massachusetts? The British general heard that the patriots had secretly stored guns and ammunition in the town of Concord. He also knew that two patriot leaders were staying in the town of Lexington. Both Concord and Lexington were close to Boston. The British began making plans to march to Lexington and Concord where they hoped to capture the patriot leaders and capture the patriots' supply of guns and ammunition.

The Midnight Ride of Paul Revere

Fortunately, a patriot had heard of the British plan. If the Minutemen were warned, perhaps they could stop the British.

Paul Revere, a patriot from Boston, and another man named **William Dawes,** jumped on their horses and rode through the countryside. It was night. To wake and warn the colonists, they shouted "The British are coming!"

The Minutemen jumped out of their beds and prepared to fight. The two patriot leaders were warned just in time for them to escape being captured.

When the British soldiers reached Lexington, they met a group of brave Minutemen. Suddenly, the silence at Lexington was shattered by the sound of a gunshot. No one knows who fired the shot, but it started the War for Independence, and it signaled the birth of American freedom. From this shot would come a fight for liberty that the whole world watched with interest. And from this shot would come the creation of a new country which would play a great part in world history. Because that one shot changed history, it has come to be called the "shot heard round the world." Ralph Waldo Emerson, a famous American poet, wrote a poem about the battle at Lexington:

By the rude bridge that arched the flood,
 Their flag to April's breeze unfurled,
Here once the embattled farmers stood,
 And fired the shot heard round the world.

Paul Revere rode through the streets and countryside warning the colonists that the British were coming.

The first shots of the Revolutionary War were fired at Lexington, Massachusetts.

After that first battle at **Lexington,** the British marched to **Concord,** but the Minutemen there were able to push them back. The war had begun, but the purpose of the war still was not clear. Were the colonists going to fight for their rights as Englishmen, or were they fighting for their independence?

The American Colonies Fight for Independence

The Second Continental Congress

Because the king of England refused to listen to the colonists' list of complaints, representatives met in Philadelphia for another meeting—the **Second Continental Congress.** It was May, 1775. Many important decisions were made at this meeting. Two of the most important were (1) America must have an organized Continental Army; and (2) George Washington would command the American army.

The meeting of the Second Continental Congress lasted for over a year.

The Battle of Bunker Hill

At the time, the British soldiers were staying in Boston. They did not feel that the American colonists had the strength or power to chase the powerful British army out of Boston.

In the darkness of night, while the British army was sleeping, more than a thousand colonists climbed Bunker Hill and Breed's Hill, which overlook Boston. All through the night, they dug **trenches** to protect themselves. When the British woke, they were very surprised.

British soldiers marched straight into deadly American gunfire. Although the patriots fought bravely, the British eventually won the Battle of Bunker Hill.

On June 16, 1775, the **Battle of Bunker Hill** *was fought.* Many people who lived in Boston climbed on their roofs to watch the battle. The British began to climb the hill, but the colonists beat them back. Again the British tried, and again they were beaten back. When the British tried the third time, the colonists ran out of gunpowder. This time, the Americans were beaten back.

Though the Americans were beaten back, they did show the British that, although the colonists were not trained soldiers, they could fight with determination.

Ethan Allen and the Green Mountain Boys

The British held **Fort Ticonderoga**, which was located on the main road between Canada and New York. This fort was important to the British because of its location, and it also contained supplies of guns, cannons, and ammunition which the colonists so badly needed.

In the land that is now Vermont lived **Ethan Allen** and a group of patriots who called themselves the "**Green Mountain Boys.**" They decided that they would take Fort Ticonderoga from the British.

In the early morning hours while the unsuspecting British slept, the Green Mountain Boys surrounded Fort Ticonderoga. When this was done, Ethan Allen knocked on the British Commander's door. The sleepy commander opened the door, and Ethan Allen demanded that he surrender the fort. The stunned commander looked outside. When he saw that the fort was already surrounded, he knew he had no choice. He surrendered the fort to the daring Ethan Allen.

The supplies inside the fort were most valuable to the Continental Army, for the colonists had few guns and little gunpowder to fight a war with the British. It was the cannons taken from Fort Ticonderoga that finally drove the British army out of Boston.

Ethan Allen roused the British commander and demanded that he surrender Fort Ticonderoga to the Green Mountain Boys.

More Decisions

Meanwhile the Second Continental Congress continued meeting in Philadelphia. It was now 1776. Many of the representatives still hoped that King George would change his mind. Then the Americans could become peaceful colonists of England once again. These hopes were soon crushed when the colonists received the cruel news that King George had hired German soldiers called **Hessians** to help fight against the Americans.

The king had a hard time finding Englishmen who were willing to fight against the American colonists. Many English believed that the colonists were right and just in their demands. Many people of England themselves did not agree with King George or some of the men in the English government. That is why the king was forced to hire soldiers from another country. This news destroyed most of the colonists' remaining loyalty to England. From now on, the king was their cruel enemy. They realized they must fight for their independence from England.

Although the great evangelist John Wesley was a loyal Englishman, he felt that the English would have real problems if they kept fighting the Americans. He knew that the colonists were fierce lovers of liberty and that they would be united in their fight for it. He wrote to the English leader, Lord North, about the colonists:

> These men will not be frightened, and it seems they will not be conquered as easily as was at first imagined. They will probably dispute every inch of ground, and, if they die, die with sword in hand....They are as strong men as you; they are as valiant as you if not abundantly more valiant, for they are one and all enthusiasts, enthusiasts for liberty.

Someone had told Lord North that the colonists were divided among themselves. Wesley wrote to tell him that this was not true. "My lord," he wrote, "they are terribly united." And united they were, because of their beliefs about human freedom.

The representatives of the Second Continental Congress now asked that a *Declaration of Independence* be written, stating the reasons why the colonists wanted their independence.

The Declaration of Independence Is Written

Five men in the Second Continental Congress were asked to work together to write the **Declaration of Independence.** They were Thomas Jefferson, John Adams, Benjamin Franklin, Roger Sherman, and Robert Living-

The members of the Continental Congress signed the Declaration of Independence on July 4, 1776.

ston. Thomas Jefferson did the actual writing of the great document.

After the writing of the Declaration of Independence was finished, the members of Congress discussed it and changed a few words. On July 2, 1776, the colonies voted to accept it. On July 4 (the day which we know as Independence Day or the Fourth of July), the Declaration was signed by **John Hancock**, the president of the Continental Congress. As Hancock wrote his name in large, clear letters, he said, "There, John Bull [England] can read that without spectacles, and now may double his reward of five hundred pounds for my head." He knew what great danger he had put himself in by signing the Declaration of Independence. The English

would know who he was, and they might want to hunt him down for signing his name to this document.

Hancock turned to the other members of the Continental Congress and said, "Gentlemen, we must all hang together."

"Yes," replied Benjamin Franklin, "or we shall all hang separately."

The People Hear the News

An order was given to make copies of the Declaration. Immediately it was taken to the printing press. Copies were made to take to each colony.

On July 8, the Liberty Bell in Philadelphia was rung to call the people of the town together. On the bell are written these words from the Bible: *"Pro-*

claim liberty throughout all the land, unto all the inhabitants thereof'' (Leviticus 25:10).

This is exactly why the bell rang. When the people of Philadelphia gathered, the Declaration of Independence was read to them. It was the first time they heard these wonderful words:

> We hold these truths to be self-evident:—That all men are created equal; that they are endowed by their Creator with certain unalienable rights; that among these are life, liberty, and the pursuit of happiness.

The Declaration went on to state, clearly and simply, exactly *why* the war was being fought:

> ...To secure these rights, governments are instituted among men, deriving their just powers from the consent of the governed...whenever any form of government becomes destructive of these ends, it is the right of the people to alter or to abolish it, and to institute a new government....

> The history of the present King of Great Britain is a history of repeated injuries and usurpations, all having, in direct object, the establishment of an absolute tyranny over these States.

> *We, therefore,* the *Representatives* of the *United States of America*...do, in the name and by the authority of the good people of these colonies, solemnly publish and declare, That these united Colonies are, and of right ought to be, *Free and Independent States;* that they are absolved from all allegiance to the British crown, and that all political connection between them and the state of Great Britain is, and ought to be, totally dissolved....

> And, for the support of this declaration, with a firm reliance on the protection of Divine Providence, we mutually pledge to each other our lives, our fortunes, and our sacred honor.

The Liberty Bell can still be seen in Philadelphia. Because of the crack, the bell has not been rung since 1835.

Of course, there were no telephones, televisions, or airplanes to speed the news to the other colonies. Riders packed copies of the Declaration in their saddle bags and jumped on their horses. Over dusty roads, through shallow streams, and over creaking bridges they rode as fast as possible to carry the good news. Even so, it took as long as two months for the people in some settlements to hear the news. So our country's first Fourth of July was celebrated

151

on many different days, as each town or settlement heard the news.

The people cheered! They rang church bells. They fired guns and cannons to salute the new United States.

Why were the people so excited? Because they were hearing all that they believed about government, written in an almost perfect form. This Declaration was what almost all Americans believed. This was what they were fighting for!

Almost all the people in the churches throughout the land supported American independence. Most of the Anglican (Church of England) ministers did not, because of their ties with the Church of England, but many of the Anglican church members did. Pastors and people in the other churches—Congregational, Presbyterian, Baptist, Dutch Reformed, and many Catholics—supported the patriot cause, and many ministers served as chaplains in the army. Many Quakers, Mennonites, and Moravians did not believe in fighting, but they helped the patriot cause in other ways, such as caring for the wounded and providing food and clothing for those who needed help.

One Presbyterian preacher, James Caldwell, helped in an unusual way. His wife had been shot by the Hessians, and his house was burned to the

News of the Declaration of Independence was spread through the colonies by men on horseback. Here the Declaration is being read to a group of soldiers.

ground. The people of the town rose up to defend themselves and were fighting the Hessians and British in a lot next to Caldwell's church. They were using long guns called muskets as weapons, and they ran out of the paper that they had to stuff into the muskets to keep the powder and ball from falling out. Caldwell ran into the church and gathered all the hymn books he could carry. The books were written by Isaac Watts. He tore pages out of the hymn books and shouted, "Put Watts into 'em, boys! Give 'em Watts!" The soldiers were able to keep on with their defense.

The Americans knew that they would have to set up a whole new government to protect their freedoms. No longer were they fighting for the rights of Englishmen. They were fighting to become free and independent from England. All the world was watching to see what would happen.

The War Continues

The Declaration of Independence did not end the war. Neither did it give the colonists their freedom. It was up to the Americans to prove to the world that they meant what they said. They must win the war.

General George Washington

Congress made **George Washington,** who had been fighting so bravely for the colonists, commander in chief of the colonial army. Washington worked without pay to lead the Americans, and he even gave some of his own money to

General Washington and his army retreated sadly from New York City after losing an important battle there.

buy supplies for the army. George Washington did perhaps more than any other man to help the United States gain independence. That is why he is called "the Father of His Country."

The Colonial Army at New York City

You will remember that the first fighting began around Boston. Now the British made plans to capture New York City. New York City had an excellent harbor. If the British controlled this harbor, British ships could easily bring the British army fresh food and supplies.

General Washington moved his army to New York and prepared for a battle against the British. Just before the battle, Washington made an inspiring speech to his soldiers. He challenged them by saying that if they failed, America would lose its freedom. He made it clear to the men that if they did not conquer, they would die:

> The time is now near at hand which must probably determine whether Americans are to be freemen or slaves; whether they are to have any property they can call their own; whether their houses and farms are to be pillaged [robbed] and destroyed, and themselves consigned [given over] to a state of wretchedness from which no human efforts will deliver them. The fate of unborn millions will now depend, under

God, on the courage and conduct of this army. Our cruel and unrelenting enemy leaves us only the choice of a brave resistance, or the most abject [shameful] submission. We have, therefore, to resolve to conquer or to die.

Washington and his men fought bravely, but they could not win. Now the British army controlled New York City. General Washington moved his army to New Jersey.

Nathan Hale

The defeat of the Americans at New York City made everyone sad and discouraged. But the Americans kept right on fighting. People saw that they would have to fight hard for their freedom. One such person was **Nathan Hale**, a handsome young schoolteacher from Connecticut. Hale decided that he would serve America no matter what the cost. Hale volunteered for a very dangerous mission: he was to sneak behind enemy lines and find out what the British army was planning. The risk was great, for he would be executed as a spy if he were caught. But Nathan Hale was not worried about his own life; he wanted to serve his country. He bravely started out on his mission.

Unfortunately, Nathan Hale was captured by the British and condemned to death. But he was not a coward. He did not beg for mercy, and he did not betray his country. The last words he spoke before he was executed were these: *"I only regret that I have but one life to lose for my country."*

Nathan Hale died, but his words lived on. Even the British were impressed with his bravery and patriotism. And American soldiers everywhere were stirred by Nathan Hale's brave words. His death reminded the soldiers that they, too, should be willing to give up their lives to make America a free land.

The Colonial Army at Trenton, New Jersey

It was almost Christmas. General Washington's army was very discouraged. Their food and supplies were almost gone. Their clothes were ragged. Few battles had been won. Some soldiers gave up and went back to their homes.

Washington was discouraged, too, but he would not give up hope. He knew that over a thousand Hessians were staying at **Trenton,** a town in New Jersey.

"If only my army could capture Trenton," he said to himself, "we could take and use the British supply of guns, ammunition, and supplies." Then he made a plan.

Christmas night was very cold. Large chunks of ice floated down the Delaware River. From dark until dawn Washington's men worked. He had over 2,000 soldiers. By dawn, every one of his soldiers had safely crossed the dangerous, icy Delaware River in small boats. In the early morning hours, his soldiers surrounded Trenton and took the Germans by surprise.

What were the German soldiers doing while Washington's men were crossing the Delaware? They had been celebrating Christmas. Now they were fast asleep. Imagine their surprise when they woke up to find themselves surrounded by the American army. There was nothing for the Hessians to do but give up. They became Washington's prisoners. And their supplies of guns and food were taken by the American army. Hope began to return to the American army.

In a brilliant move, Washington crossed the Delaware River on Christmas night and easily defeated the Hessians the next morning.

A Flag for Our Country

The Second Continental Congress was still making important decisions. Americans had wanted their own flag for a long time. Many people had made their own flags with their own designs. Now congress made this decision:

> Resolved, that the Flag of the United States be thirteen stripes, alternate red and white, that the "Union" be thirteen stars, white in a blue field....

The thirteen stripes and thirteen stars stood for the thirteen colonies. Later, a new star would be added for each new state that became a part of the United States of America. According to an old story, Betsy Ross stitched together the first American flag with stars and stripes. On June 14, 1777, George Washington gave our new flag to Congress. June 14 has become known as **Flag Day.**

America Wins Its Freedom

The Colonial Army at Saratoga, New York

The British had already captured New York City. Now they made plans to capture all of New York state. Why? Because New York separated the New England colonies from the other colonies. If the British controlled New York, the northern colonies would have no way of communicating with those to the South.

Fortunately, the American army was

According to tradition, Betsy Ross stitched together the first American flag with stars and stripes.

This picture shows the British general surrendering to George Washington at Saratoga.

156

George Washington and his troops spent the harsh winter of 1777–1778 at Valley Forge, Pennsylvania.

able to stop the British from capturing New York in the **Battle of Saratoga.** The Battle of Saratoga is often called the turning point of the War for Independence. This battle did not end the war, but it did prove to the world that America had a chance of winning the war. France had been watching. The Battle of Saratoga persuaded the king of France to help the Americans. Remember that news traveled slowly in those days. It would be a while before the French arrived to help.

The Colonial Army at Valley Forge, Pennsylvania—Winter of 1777–1778

More trouble and hard times lay ahead for the colonists. The British had captured the city of Philadelphia. Winter was coming, and the British planned on spending the winter in the warm homes of the colonists in Philadelphia.

Washington's men were not so fortunate. Even the victory of Saratoga did little to cheer them. They had no warm place to spend the winter. Washington's army had tried to win back Philadelphia but failed. Afterwards, Washington marched his men to **Valley Forge,** which is near Philadelphia.

Here, Washington's men would spend the worst winter of the war. It was not the British that bothered them at Valley Forge. Hunger and cold were the worst enemies there.

There were no warm buildings. Log huts were built that would give some protection against the cruel winter storms, but they certainly would not be warm. Neither was there any money to buy badly needed food, clothes, blankets, or supplies for the men.

Soldiers had only thin, ragged clothing. Many men did not even have shoes for their feet. As they walked, they left blood in the snow from their cold, sore feet. For the sick, there was very little medicine.

Cold, hungry, weak, sick, and discouraged—these are the words that described General Washington's army at Valley Forge.

What would you have done under such hardships? Some of Washington's men gave up and went home. Some complained about their leader, but enough men stayed on to wait for springtime when they would begin fighting again. If these men hadn't been brave enough to stay, there would never have been a United States of America. The thought of a free country—their own country—gave them the strength to continue.

The thought of their brave leader gave them courage, too. Someone has painted a picture of George Washington praying in the snow at Valley Forge. From what we know about Washington's character, this is probably exactly what he did, and he probably did it more than once.

The War on the Frontier

There were colonists who moved out of the colonies into the western frontier. The frontier had only a few small settlements, but the British decided to stir up trouble there, too.

Just as the French had gone to the Indians during the French and Indian War, so the British talked to the Indians during this war: "If the colonists win this war, they will keep moving west," they told them. "They will build houses on your land. They will take away your hunting grounds. You must help us stop them."

Although there were Indian tribes that decided to help the Americans, other tribes made war on the frontier settlements, killing and burning as they went.

A bold young man named **George Rogers Clark** decided to help. He led a group of men from Virginia down the Ohio River. Then they marched through swamps and forests. One by one, they captured three British forts on the frontier—two in the land that is now Illinois and one fort in what is now Indiana. The British had lost control of the northwest frontier.

And because of the courage of George Rogers Clark, the Indians became less of a problem to the frontier settlements in the Northwest Territory.

A New Navy

Before the American Revolution, the American colonists did not have a navy. There was no need of one, for the British navy had protected her colonies. Now the Americans needed a navy to protect themselves against the British navy. Of course, with little money, our new country could not build a large, powerful navy. It would have to be a small navy run by determined men.

Before the war, **John Paul Jones,** a Scottish seaman, had come to America. He became one of the first officers of our navy. His courage and determination helped our first navy to be successful.

Of his sea battles, the most famous is the one between the American ship named the *Bonhomme Richard* (named

John Paul Jones's bravery and determination helped build the U.S. Navy.

after Benjamin Franklin's "Poor Richard's Almanack") and the British ship named the *Serapis.* John Paul Jones brought his ship so close to the *Serapis,* that the cannons of the two ships almost touched.

The British officer on board the *Serapis* shouted, "Are you going to surrender?"

With a clear, determined voice, John Paul Jones answered back, "I have not yet begun to fight!"

When called upon to surrender, John Paul Jones said, "I have not yet begun to fight." Jones kept fighting and eventually defeated the British ship *Serapis.*

With that, guns of both ships boomed. Many on both sides were killed. Finally, the Americans were able to board the British ship and fight hand to hand. At last, the British officer surrendered his ship.

The War in the South

In 1778, the British decided to move their fighting to the Southern colonies. From this time until the end of the war, most of the fighting took place in the southern part of America.

First the British captured Georgia and then almost all of South Carolina. The British leader at this time was General Lord Cornwallis.

General Washington sent one of his trusted generals, **Nathanael Greene,** to fight in the South. With Greene's help, South Carolina and Georgia were won back from the British.

English General **Cornwallis** then moved up to Yorktown, Virginia. It was here that General Washington saw the chance he had been waiting for for a long time.

Victory at Yorktown— October, 1781

The French had sent their navy to help the Americans. When English General Cornwallis moved into **Yorktown,** he expected help from the British navy. But before the British navy could help, the French navy sailed into the Chesapeake Bay and blocked the Bay. Now, no help could get to the British without attacking the powerful French navy. Cornwallis was in a trap. He could not sail out to escape, and no British ship could sail in to help him.

Meanwhile, General Washington began marching his army to Yorktown. Thousands of French soldiers joined him, until General Cornwallis's army was surrounded by both sea and land. Although it was hopeless, Cornwallis fought bravely.

At last, the entire British army surrendered. The date was October 19, 1781. *The Americans had fought for six long, hard years. At last they had won their independence.*

Americans realized that God had been with them in their struggle for freedom. Now, as General Washington himself recommended, prayers of thanksgiving could be heard in the American army, in the churches across this new nation, and in the homes and hearts of thankful Americans.

The Treaty of Paris

A **treaty** *is an agreement or understanding between two or more countries.* The fighting had stopped in 1781, but almost two more years passed before England signed the agreement known as the **Treaty of Paris** in **1783.** In this treaty, England gave up her thirteen American colonies. These colonies were now free and independent states.

How big was our country at that time? The Treaty of Paris gave the Americans the land from Florida to Canada, and from the Atlantic Ocean to the Mississippi River. This new land that was not a part of the thirteen colonies became known as the **Northwest Territory.** You will remember that George Rogers Clark battled his way through this wilderness to win three forts from the British. His triumph in winning these forts was of great importance to our country. If Clark had not won, it is possible that our land would have gone only as far as the Ohio River.

Facts to Remember

1. Who was king of England during the Revolutionary War period? _____

_____

2. What tax angered the colonists because it added to the cost of newspapers,

documents, etc.? _____

3. What is a tax?_____

_____

4. What is a representative? _____

_____

5. What is a massacre? _____

_____

6. What was the Boston Massacre? _____

_____

_____

7. What was the Boston Tea Party? _____

_____

_____

8. What was the group of representatives who met before and during the Revolution to decide what America should do?_____

9. Who said, "Give me liberty or give me death"?_____

10. Who were the patriots? _____

_____

11. Who were the loyalists or Tories?_____

_____

12. Who were the Minutemen?_____

_____

_____

13. Who rode across the countryside, warning of a British attack?_____

_____

14. Where did the first battle of the War for Independence take place?_____

_____

15. What is a trench?_____

_____

16. Who commanded the American army during the War for Independence?_____

_____

17. During which battle did the Americans show the British that the Americans would not be easy to defeat? _____

18. Who captured Fort Ticonderoga? _____

19. What were the Germans called who fought for England? _____

20. What important document was signed on July 4, 1776? _____

_____

21. In what city did the Americans win an important victory at Christmas, 1776?

_____

22. What happened on June 14, 1777, the day which we now know as Flag Day?

_____

23. What is considered to be the turning point of the War for Independence?

_____

24. Where did General Washington and his troops spend the harsh winter of

1777–1778? _____

25. Whose bold adventures secured the Northwest Territory for America?

_____

26. What Scotsman helped build the American navy? _____

What was the name of his ship? _____

In his most famous victory, what ship did Jones capture? _____

27. Which general led the British army near the end of the war and eventually sur-

rendered to Washington? _____

28. When the war shifted to the Southern Colonies, who was sent to lead the

American forces? _____

29. What treaty ended the War for Independence? _____

Building a New Nation

The thirteen colonies had gone through a hard struggle to become thirteen free and independent states. They had faced the problems of fighting the British. Now that they had won, they would face problems of a different kind—that of building a new nation.

The thirteen states did not feel united as one country. The people from Georgia thought of themselves as Georgians. Those from Virginia thought of themselves as Virginians, those from Pennsylvania as Pennsylvanians. Hardly anyone thought of himself first as an American. Instead of one big country, the thirteen states were acting as if they were thirteen small countries, each ruling itself.

Many people were afraid of one strong government. That reminded them too much of the powerful British government from which they had just won their freedom!

The Articles of Confederation

The first plan of government that the states agreed upon was called the **Articles of Confederation.** Under this plan, the government could not be strong.

The government had no power to tax the people of the United States. Requests went out to the states for money, but very little came in, because the states knew that the government could not force them to give. There was little money for anything.

This government had no power to settle quarrels that might arise between two states. The states could refuse to do anything that the government asked them to do. In order for this government to work, each state would have to agree with all the others all the time. Do you think this was possible?

Already you can see problems that would arise. This government was too weak to work.

The Constitution of the United States

A meeting was held in **Philadelphia** to discuss what could be done to make our government stronger. This meeting was called the **Constitutional Convention.** The meeting lasted all through the summer of 1787. It was held in Independence Hall, where the Declaration of Independence had been signed eleven years earlier. Many wise and important men gathered for this meeting. George Washington was chosen as the president of this meeting. Ben Franklin, now 81 years old, was there to help. *The man who did the most important work at this Convention was* **James Madison,** *who would later become fourth President of the United States.*

The men quickly decided that just a few changes in the Articles of Confederation would not do. A brand new government was needed. The plan for that new government, which our government still follows, is the **Constitution of the United States.**

Many discussions were held. Many committees met. Many ideas were talked about. In debate after debate the men challenged one another to find what was best for America. In the history of the world there has probably never been such an assembly of geniuses. The wisdom about politics that our Founding Fathers at the Convention showed has never been equaled. *The writing of the* **Constitution of the United States** *and the writing of the* **Declaration of Independence** *are two of the most important events that have contributed to the happiness and progress of all mankind.* They were written for America, but the whole world has learned a lesson from them—what it means to be free men. Everybody was convinced that the hand of God was in the work that was being done at this Convention. They also knew that no country can be strong without God's continuing help. At one point during the Convention, Benjamin Franklin stood and said:

> I have lived a long time, and the longer I live the more convincing proofs I see of this truth: that God governs in the affairs of men. And if a sparrow cannot fall to the ground without His notice, is it probable that an empire [great country] can rise without His aid?

Everyone agreed on the purpose of the new government. The government would protect the freedoms that the Declaration of Independence talks about and that the War for Independence was fought over. Everyone wanted this. They disagreed, though, over just what kind of government could best protect our freedoms. *The government would have to be powerful, but not too powerful. It would have to be strong enough to protect people from criminals and yet not so strong that it could take away the freedoms of people who obey the laws.*

Here are some of the questions that were discussed:

- What powers should the government for the whole country have? How much power should be left with the states?
- How should the government for the whole country be set up so that it could protect the country from foreign enemies but not become the enemy of the country it was supposed to protect?
- Should there be limits on what the state governments could do?
- What could be done to keep bad men from using government for selfish purposes?

The men realized that no one person or one state could have its own way completely. Each side had to give a little. In this way, they began to work together through the long, hot summer months to answer these questions:

Who would carry out the laws of our new nation?

It was decided that the head of our new government would be a **President.** The President would have the power to see that the laws were obeyed.

New Words

1. **President**—the head of government; he sees that the nation's laws are obeyed
2. **Congress**—the part of government that makes our country's laws
3. **houses**—the two groups which make up the Congress
4. **Senate**—the house of Congress which contains 100 members, two from each state
5. **House of Representatives**—the house of Congress whose size depends on the population of the states
6. **Supreme Court**—the highest court in the land; it judges whether or not the Constitution has been obeyed
7. **republic**—a government controlled by the citizens, not by any one particular person or group
8. **Inauguration Day**—the day on which the new President is sworn into office

New Names

9. **Articles of Confederation**—the first plan of government agreed upon by the states; it made the government very weak
10. **Constitutional Convention**—the meeting of representatives which produced a new gov-

Who would make our country's laws?

Congress would have the power to make our country's most important laws. *Congress was to be made up of two groups called* **houses.**

One house was to be the **Senate.** Every state was to send two senators to represent their state in the Senate.

The other house was the **House of Representatives.** Each state would send representatives to the House of Representatives. How many representatives? This depended upon how many people lived in a state. A large state like Virginia could send more representatives than the small state of New Jersey.

The idea of a Senate pleased the small states, for there every state, no matter what size, had the same power. The House of Representatives pleased the larger states, for there they had more power. Yet neither house was more important than the other. The Senate and the House of Representatives both have to agree on a law before it becomes a law. *Who would settle our country's arguments? Who would decide between right and wrong?*

There would be many new laws made and enforced by the new government. A new set of courts and judges was needed. *The highest court in the land is known as the* **Supreme Court.**

A Brand New Government

The Constitution was now complete. Each state thought carefully before signing the Constitution. It was a big step. *By signing the Constitution, each state gave up its power to completely govern itself. They were putting their trust in a brand new government, a government of the people, by the people, and for the people.*

ernment for America

11. **James Madison**—the man who did the most important work at the Constitutional Convention

12. **Constitution**—the document which outlines our system of government

13. **Bill of Rights**—a section added to the Constitution which states the rights and freedoms of the American people

14. **George Washington**—the first President of the United States under the new Constitution

15. **John Adams**—the first Vice President; he became the second President when Washington left office

New Places

16. **Philadelphia**—the city where the Constitutional Convention was held

17. **New York**—the first capital of the United States

18. **Washington, D.C.**—the capital of the United States

19. **Mount Vernon**—George Washington's home

New Dates

20. **1787**—the Constitutional Convention is held

21. **1833**—Massachusetts gains complete religious freedom, the last state to do so

The Constitution began with these words:

> We the people of the United States, in order to form a more perfect Union, establish justice, insure domestic tranquillity, provide for the common defense, promote the general welfare, and secure the blessings of liberty to ourselves and our posterity, do ordain and establish this Constitution for the United States of America.

The Bill of Rights

The people of the United States knew from the very beginning that it was important to make sure that no government—even our own government—could take away freedoms that God has given us. To protect the freedom of individuals and groups, they added a **Bill of Rights** to the Constitution. The Bill of Rights is a list of people's rights or freedoms. The Bill of Rights forbids the federal government from taking these freedoms from us.

The Bill of Rights includes the right to print and read what we want, within certain limits. It also includes the right for someone accused of a crime to be tried by a jury in a court of law.

The new government could not interfere in these areas. The Bill of Rights also protected the states and their powers from being taken over by the new government. They believed it was wise

The Bill of Rights guarantees the rights and freedoms of all Americans.

This painting includes a portrait of every man who signed the Constitution. It hangs in the United States Capitol in Washington, D.C.

168

not to give too much power to any one person or group, or even to the government.

The Bill of Rights is written in the form of ten amendments, or changes, to the constitution. The First Amendment is especially important. It gives us freedom of religion, freedom of speech, freedom of the press, and freedom of assembly. It says:

> Congress shall make no law respecting an establishment of religion, or prohibiting the free exercise thereof; or abridging the freedom of speech, or of the press; or the right of the people peaceably to assemble, and to petition the government for a redress of grievances.

The New Republic

It has been said that as Benjamin Franklin left the Constitutional Convention, a woman walked over to him and asked, "What kind of government has been formed?" His thoughtful answer was, "A republic, if you can keep it!"

"A republic, if you can keep it!" What did Benjamin Franklin mean by this statement?

A **republic** *is a government which is controlled by the citizens, not by a king.* Franklin knew that it was dangerous for only one man to rule a country. Yet never before in history had any country as large as ours tried to have self-government. The Constitutional Convention had worked hard to plan a government in which our President could not rule like a king.

A republic is also a government in which no particular group has all the power. Franklin also knew that it is dangerous for the people to have too much power. He knew that in self-government the people can sometimes act like a harsh king. We are fortunate that the Constitution guards against this.

America has so far kept the republican government set up by the Constitution. May we as Americans never let our government take away the freedoms that were guaranteed to us by our Constitution and Bill of Rights.

An Election

Now there was another decision to make. Who would be the first President of the United States? This was not a hard decision. The man who had led our country through the American Revolution was already loved and trusted. **George Washington** *was elected our first President;* **John Adams** *was our first Vice President.*

After being elected, Washington traveled in a horse-drawn coach to our nation's first capital—**New York.** There was no Washington, D.C., yet.

People crowded the roads that George Washington's coach traveled. All along the way, he was met by cheering crowds. Little girls threw flowers in his path. Guns were fired to salute the first President of the United States. On the first **Inauguration Day,** Washington asked that a Bible be brought to him. With his hand resting on the Word of God, Washington took the oath of office. Washington set a good example that day; all the Presidents since then have been sworn in on a Bible.

George Washington was a good President. He was well aware that as the first President, he would be setting an example for all the Presidents who would come after him. Therefore, all his official actions were done carefully, cautiously, and thoughtfully. *Because*

he set such a good example, Washington is regarded by historians as one of the greatest of all Presidents. He served his first term of four years so well that the people elected him for a second term. When it came time for the third election, the people wanted to elect him again—but this time he refused. He and his wife, Martha, returned to their beautiful plantation farm, **Mount Vernon,** in Virginia.

Before he left office, Washington wrote a long farewell address. In the address he thanked the people of America for voting for him and for allowing him to serve his country as President for eight years. Then he warned the people that unless they acted like responsible citizens, the freedom for which they had fought so hard might disappear. He told them that respect for and obedience to the nation's

Washington became the first President on April 30, 1789. He took the oath of office with his hand placed on the Bible.

John Adams became the second President of the United States.

On the bottom is the original plan for the city of Washington, D.C., drawn in 1791. Above the drawing is a photograph of modern-day Washington taken high in the air. How closely has the original plan been followed?

laws are vitally important. He warned people that loyalty to their country should never be replaced by loyalty to a political party. He urged people from the North, South, East, and West not to think about what would be good for their part of the country, but what would be good for the country as a whole. Above all, he stressed that a democratic government could work only in an atmosphere of strong morality (doing right according to God's laws). He said that morality would result only when religion held its proper place in the lives of its citizens.

A short time after writing this address, Washington retired to Mount Vernon. *Honest, hard-working John Adams took his place and became the second President of the United States.*

A New Capital

You will remember that our nation's first capital was New York. Soon plans were made to build a new capital. Both Virginia and Maryland gave land to build the city on the banks of the Potomac River. Although George Washington never lived there, the city was named Washington, in his honor. The land that the city was built on was called the District of Columbia. Thus, we get the name **Washington, D.C.**

Facts to Remember

1. What did most Americans feel about having one strong government over them? _____

2. What was the first plan of government that the states agreed upon? _____
_____

3. Was the government under the Articles of Confederation weak or strong? __
_____

   What important power did the government lack? _____

4. What meeting decided to create a brand new government? _____
_____

5. Where was the Constitutional Convention held? _____

6. Who was the president of the Convention?_____

7. Who did the most important work at the Convention? _____

8. What plan of government did the Convention draw up? _____
_____

9. Who has the power to see that our nation's laws are obeyed? _____
_____

10. Who has the power to make our country's most important laws? _____

11. Congress is divided into two groups called what? _____

12. Which house gives equal representation to all states, no matter what size?
_____

13. In which house do the larger states have more power? _____

14. What is the highest court in the land? _____

15. By signing the Constitution, what did each state agree to give up?

_____

16. What was added to the Constitution to insure that certain rights and freedoms

could never be taken away from the people? _____

17. What is a republic? _____

_____

18. Who was elected the first President of this country? _____

Who was the first Vice President? _____

19. What was the first capital of this country? _____

20. On what day does the new President take the oath of office? _____

_____

21. How many terms did Washington serve? _____

22. Who became the second President of our country? _____

23. Where was the country's new capital located? _____

_____

Who gave land for the city? _____

24. What was the name of the new capital? _____

What was the land that the city was built on called? _____

_____

Our Nation Grows

The United States Doubles Its Size

Thomas Jefferson, the author of the Declaration of Independence, became our third President. He made many good decisions for our country. One decision had to do with the city of New Orleans at the mouth of the Mississippi River. Jefferson knew how important this city could be to the United States. American ships could load and trade here freely if the city belonged to them.

The land surrounding New Orleans was called the Louisiana Territory. It had belonged to Spain, but Spain gave the land to France. Jefferson quickly asked the French ruler if he could buy New Orleans for two million dollars. The French decided to sell not only New Orleans, but also all of the Louisiana Territory. The price for all this land

Brave pioneers traveled west to settle the wilderness. This painting shows a group of pioneers traveling west to the Oregon Territory.

would be fifteen million dollars. This may seem like a large amount of money, but it was a small price to pay for so much land. Thomas Jefferson gladly accepted France's offer, and bought the Louisiana Territory in 1803.

The **Louisiana Purchase** more than doubled the size of the United States. *In*

the years to come, the Louisiana Purchase was to provide all or part of the land for fifteen new states.

Exploring the Louisiana Territory

Hardly anything was known about the land that made up the Louisiana Territory. President Jefferson chose to have this land explored. For this job, he chose two young men, **Captain Meriwether Lewis** and **Captain William Clark.**

Along the way, Lewis and Clark met Indians, but the explorers had a hard time understanding the Indians' language. Fortunately, they met a French trapper whose wife was an Indian. Her name was **Sacagawea.** Both agreed to go with Lewis and Clark to translate the Indian language for them.

Together they climbed over mountains. When they came to rivers, they built boats. At last they saw the Pacific Ocean. When they finally returned to Washington, D.C., they had important reports to make to President Jefferson.

Americans heard about Lewis and Clark's exciting trip to see the West. Many people from the original thirteen states in the East became eager to move West. As a result, pioneers began pushing their way West to make new homes.

This painting shows the Indian guide Sacagawea showing the way for explorers Lewis and Clark.

Map Study: The Louisiana Purchase

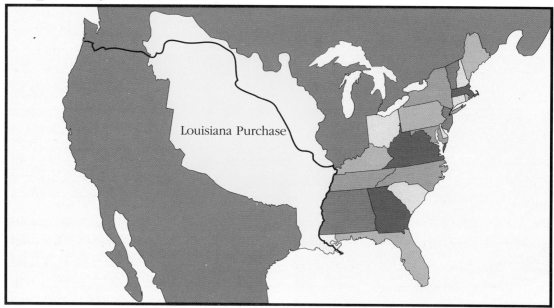

Louisiana Purchase

The Louisiana Purchase doubled the size of the United States, and it eventually provided all or part of the land for fifteen new states. Lewis and Clark were sent out to explore the country's new territory.

New Words

1. **blaze**—to mark a trail
2. **flatboat**—a long boat with a flat bottom
3. **dictator**—a ruler who allows his people no freedom
4. **ghost towns**—towns with empty buildings where no one lived

New Names

5. **Louisiana Purchase**—a section of land bought by President Jefferson which doubled the size of America
6. **War of 1812**—a war fought with England; neither country won this war
7. **Lewis and Clark**—led an expedition which explored America's new territories
8. **Sacagawea**—an Indian woman who acted as a guide for the Lewis and Clark expedition
9. **Napoleon Bonaparte**—the French ruler who sold the Louisiana Territory to the United States
10. **Francis Scott Key**—the man who wrote "The Star-Spangled Banner"
11. **James Monroe**—the President who purchased Florida from Spain
12. **Daniel Boone**—an explorer who began the settlement of Kentucky
13. **Wilderness Road**—the trail blazed by Daniel Boone in Kentucky
14. **Peter Cartwright**—a famous circuit-riding preacher
15. **Santa Anna**—Mexican dictator who tried to crush the Texas rebellion
16. **Davy Crockett**—a famous frontiersman who died fighting at the Alamo
17. **Sam Houston**—the leader of the Texans
18. **James K. Polk**—President during the Mexican War
19. **Gadsden Purchase**—a section of land in the Southwest purchased from Mexico
20. **John Sutter**—the man on whose land gold was discovered in California
21. **Forty-niners**—the nickname for the people who flocked to California to find gold

The War of 1812

The French Purpose in Selling Louisiana

At the time the French were being governed by a very powerful soldier, **Napoleon Bonaparte.** Napoleon sold the Louisiana Territory to the United States, but he was not selling it to be generous to us. At the time, he was trying to become the ruler of all Europe. He needed money to carry on his wars in Europe. Selling Louisiana was a good way to get the money he needed. Although America was certainly far away from Europe, she became a part of the war between France and England.

Problems Arise for American Ships

France and England both had powerful navies, and both were fighting each other. If an American ship tried to sail with goods to England, France tried to prevent the American ship from reaching England. On the other hand, if an American ship tried to take goods to France, England did her best to prevent the ship from reaching France.

Then English warships began stopping American ships. The British would go on board the American ships and force some of the American sailors to board the English ships. These Americans were then forced to fight in the British navy. This happened so often

22. **Marcus and Narcissa Whitman**—a husband and wife who were missionaries to the Indians in Oregon
23. **Noah Webster**—the writer of the *Blue-backed Speller,* history and reading textbooks, and the first American dictionary.
24. **William H. McGuffey**—the author of a series of readers that were used in American schools for over one hundred years.

New Places
25. **Fort McHenry**—the place where "The Star-Spangled Banner" came to be written
26. **Boonesborough**—a pioneer settlement in Kentucky, named after Daniel Boone
27. **the Alamo**—a Spanish mission where 187 men fighting for Texas were killed by the Mexicans
28. **San Jacinto**—the battle where the Texans defeated the Mexican army
29. **Rio Grande**—the river that forms the border between Texas and Mexico

30. **Oregon Territory**—the land which eventually included the states of Oregon, Washington, and Idaho, as well as part of Montana and Wyoming

New Dates
31. **1803**—the Louisiana Purchase; Ohio became a state
32. **1812-1815**—the War of 1812
33. **1819**—Florida was purchased from Spain
34. **1821**—Mexico became independent from Spain
35. **1833**—General Santa Anna became dictator of Mexico
36. **1845**—Texas became a state
37. **1846-1848**—the Mexican War
38. **1846**—the United States and Britain agreed upon a boundary between America and Canada
39. **1848**—gold was discovered in California
40. **1850**—California became a state
41. **1853**—the Gadsden Purchase
42. **1859**—Oregon became a state

During the War of 1812, British soldiers set fire to Washington, D.C. Many important government buildings were destroyed in the fire. Here, the White House is seen going up in flames.

that hundreds of American sailors were kidnapped and forced to serve in the British navy.

There was no respect for American ships on the seas. Since England was causing most of the problems, *the United States declared war on England in 1812*. This is known as the **War of 1812.**

The British and the Americans fought for over two years. The American army and navy were still new and weak. In 1812, the British marched into Washington, D.C., where they burned the Capitol building and the President's house.

Our National Anthem

The British next planned to capture Baltimore, Maryland. During this battle, **Francis Scott Key** of Baltimore was visiting an American prisoner on board one of the English warships. The battle of **Fort McHenry** in Baltimore continued during the night.

As the bombs burst and the rockets gave off a red glare of light, Key had enough light to see that our flag was still flying over the fort. When the dawn finally came, he saw plainly that our flag was still there. The British had failed to capture Baltimore. The sight of our battle-torn flag inspired Francis Scott Key to write our national anthem, ''The Star-Spangled Banner.''

During the battle at Ft. McHenry, Francis Scott Key was inspired to write ''The Star-Spangled Banner.'' His poem became our national anthem.

The Results of the War of 1812

The last battle of the War of 1812 was fought in 1815. The Americans soundly defeated the British at this battle, but neither side won the war. After three years of war, each side gladly made peace. England finally respected our ships on the seas. We also gained the respect of other countries who were watching to see what the outcome would be. The United States proved to herself and others that she was strong enough to protect herself. The people of the United States became prouder than ever of being Americans.

The Purchase of Florida

You will remember that Florida belonged to Spain. However, Spain did not rule Florida well. Men who had broken the law often ran to Florida to hide, and Spain did little to stop them. Many Indians of Florida were warlike.

Map Study: The United States and Its Territories 1819

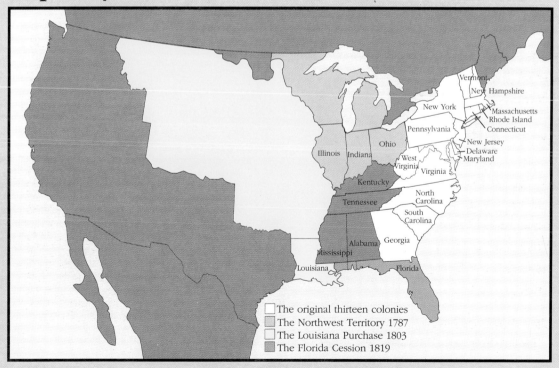

The original thirteen colonies
The Northwest Territory 1787
The Louisiana Purchase 1803
The Florida Cession 1819

Can you name some of the states that had not become a part of the sections that made up the United States in 1819?

Spain did nothing to control these Indians from crossing over Florida's border into Georgia, where they terrorized the settlers. After burning and killing, these Indians would run back to Florida. Florida was not a safe place to live in the early 1800's.

The United States had enough of Spain's poor control. The United States President at that time was **James Monroe.** He offered to buy Florida from Spain for five million dollars. However, this money would not be paid to Spain. Instead, the United States planned to use it to pay back the people of Georgia and other United States citizens who had property damaged by Florida's Indians.

Spain accepted our offer and sold Florida in 1819. The United States as we know it today was beginning to come together like pieces of a puzzle.

America Pushes Further West

Where would you think of if you heard someone say that he was moving West? Perhaps you would say "California" or "Oregon." You would be correct, but if you lived back in the early 1800's, your idea of "West" would be completely different. In those days, the "West" meant any land that was still frontier land. The "West" kept moving further west as America continued to grow.

Daniel Boone and the Wilderness Road

Even before the American Revolution, there were pioneers who were eager to see the West. Most of these early pioneers were unmarried men who wanted to hunt and trap animals for furs. Few had horses. Most walked

Daniel Boone is shown here leading a group of settlers to the Kentucky territory.

through the wilderness. There was not even a path to guide them. There were so many trees and rocks that it was impossible to take wagons. For these reasons, few women and children were among the early pioneers.

Daniel Boone yearned to see the wilderness of Kentucky. When some friends offered to go along with him, Daniel decided to leave his family for a while and see Kentucky. The trip was filled with adventure. They were even captured by Indians.

When he returned home, Daniel certainly had exciting stories to tell his wife and children. He hoped for the day when he could move his family to Kentucky.

The next year, Daniel Boone was asked to return to Kentucky to **blaze** a trail so that other pioneers could follow. Daniel chose thirty strong men to work with him. The trail that they made was barely more than a path through the thick forests and over the mountains. At first, the path was so narrow that it was still impossible for a wagon to travel over it. Yet this path was called the **Wilderness Road.** The first pioneers who traveled this road would have to walk or ride a horse.

Almost the same time that the American Revolution started, a settlement was built in Kentucky. It was named **Boonesborough** in honor of Daniel Boone. Then Daniel returned to his home and brought his family back to live in Kentucky.

Although the Wilderness Road was at first only a rough path, it led many of the first pioneers West. For this reason, *Daniel Boone has been called "the pioneer of pioneers."* With the passing years, the Wilderness Road was made wider. Thousands of wagons and families traveled over it.

Settling the Northwest Territory

The Northwest Territory was given to us after we won the American Revolution. Some day this large piece of land would make up the states of Ohio, Indiana, Illinois, Michigan, and Wisconsin.

Our government knew that many settlers would flock to the Northwest Territory, and Congress passed a law that would bring order and government to the territory. This law was called the **Northwest Ordinance of 1787.**

The Northwest Ordinance made sure that the freedom and democracy which the states enjoyed would also be present in the territories. It guaranteed freedom of religion in the territories. It outlawed slavery in the territories. It set up territorial legislatures and allowed the settlers to send representatives to Congress. In this way the settlers could still take part in the government of the United States.

The Ordinance divided land into squares measuring one mile on each side. These one-square-mile sections would be sold to settlers at $1.00 an acre.

Perhaps the most important part of the Northwest Ordinance was the promise that "education shall forever be encouraged." In order to encourage education, the Ordinance demanded that sections of land be set aside for public schools. Thus, settlers who wanted to move to the Northwest Territory were sure that schools would be there for the children to attend.

Finally, the Northwest Ordinance said that when the population of an area reached 60,000, that area could become a state and enter the Union.

There were men who desired to move their families into the Northwest Territory. Some felt too crowded where they were and wanted to move on. Others just wanted a new way of living and adventure. Together, they formed one courageous group of pioneers, helping our country to grow.

There were no highways to lead these pioneers. Since Ohio was first to become settled in the Northwest Territory, let's see how a pioneer family traveled there from Pennsylvania.

First they bought a covered wagon and loaded it with the supplies they knew they could not get in Ohio—seeds for gardens, a plow, tools, nails, guns, an iron kettle, cooking utensils, a spinning wheel, and blankets. They had to pack enough flour, salt, bacon, and other food to last them until they reached Pittsburgh.

To one side of the wagon, they tied a crate of chickens. To the other side they

These settlers on their way west have stopped to make camp for the night. The pioneers have gathered together and are enjoying some music.

Pioneer families packed all their possessions—including livestock and horses—on a flatboat so that they could travel down river to get to the frontier.

might tie a crate of piglets. Behind the wagon walked a cow. As you can see, there was not much room left to take furniture or fancy dishes. They would have to make their own homemade furniture when they reached Ohio. With chickens cackling and piglets squealing, the wagon began creaking down the rough road.

In a few days, the covered wagon reached the city of Pittsburgh in Pennsylvania. Here, the father sold the wagon and bought a **flatboat,** which was a long boat with a flat bottom. Then the family unloaded their supplies in the wagon and placed them on the boat. Even the chickens, piglets, horses, and cow were placed on the boat. More food and supplies were bought.

Men gave advice to the family before they began their trip down the Ohio River to their new home:

"Beware of Indian traps! To avoid them, keep your distance from the shore."

"Keep your eyes open for fallen trees and sharp rocks in the river. They can tear the bottom of your boat open!"

The trip by flatboat could be even more dangerous than traveling in the bumpy covered wagon. Once the pioneers traveled west of Pittsburgh, they left the protection of forts and soldiers.

When the family reached their new home in Ohio, their flatboat was carefully taken apart to save the lumber and nails. Then their home was built and a garden was planted. There was plenty of work to do.

As more and more pioneers moved into Ohio, it was no longer considered the frontier. Schools were built as well as stores and churches. Then new pioneers who wished to settle in the frontier of the Northwest Territory no longer stopped in Ohio. They kept moving westward into Indiana, Illinois, Michigan, and Wisconsin.

As the population grew in each new section of the country, new states were added to the original thirteen states. Vermont, which at the time of the American Revolution was considered the frontier, too, became the fourteenth state. Kentucky and Tennessee followed.

The population of Ohio grew so quickly that in 1803, she became our seventeenth state. *As the years passed, more of our frontier became settled and more states were formed.*

The Second Great Awakening

As more and more people poured into the western regions and settled there, the need for churches and preachers was great. But the people of the territories were spread out over a large area, and many of them were too poor to build churches and hire full-time pastors. So instead of staying in one place to pastor a church, preachers began to ride around the territories, stopping at a settlement and preaching to all who would listen. These traveling preachers became known as circuit riders, because they followed the same circuit every year. You have already read about Francis Asbury, who trained the first circuit-riders during the Great Awakening. The preaching of these men started what some people call the Second Great Awakening. This great revival began in Kentucky (the territory which Daniel Boone opened up to settlers) and spread to neighboring areas and up into the Northwest Territory. Soon many people were being converted under the preaching of Baptist, Methodist, and Presbyterian evangelists in Indiana, Ohio, Kentucky, and Tennessee.

One of the best-known of the circuit-riders was **Peter Cartwright,** who preached the gospel for over fifty years. Cartwright was a strong and rugged man who seemed to enjoy the life of a circuit rider. Here is his description of what it was like to be a traveling preacher on the frontier:

> A Methodist preacher in those days, when he felt that God had called him to preach,...hunted up a hardy pony of a horse.... He started, and with a text that never wore out or grew stale, he cried, "Behold the Lamb of God, that taketh away the sins of the world." In this way he went through storms of wind, hail, snow, and rain; climbed hills and mountains, traversed [crossed] valleys, plunged through swamps, swam swollen streams, lay out all night, wet, weary, and hungry, held his horse by the bridle all night, or tied him to a limb, slept with his saddle blanket for a bed, his saddle or saddle-bags for his pillow, and his old big coat or blanket, if he had any, for a covering.

Clearly, a circuit-rider had to be a strong man to face up to the many difficulties of his job. The west was not a place for weaklings. And it was not a place for a preacher who wanted to make a lot of money, either; Peter Cartwright says that in his day the average salary paid to preachers in the west was thirty to forty dollars *per year.* So why did these men spend their lives doing such hard work? They preached because they loved God, and they wanted to see the frontier people come to Christ.

Eventually the Second Great Awakening made its way east. New England, where the first Great Awakening had taken place, experienced another great revival.

For many years the spirit of revival was kept alive in America by camp meetings. Each year a camp meeting was held in virtually every county of every state. People from all around gathered together for a solid week to hear gospel preaching. Because people lived so far apart, many of them traveled several miles to the campsite. There they would set up a tent and live and cook camp-style throughout the week.

The United States Gains the Southwest

In 1821, the country of Mexico fought for and won her independence from Spain. At that time Texas, New Mexico, Arizona, and California were all part of Mexico.

Mexico Invites Americans to Texas

The Mexican government was eager to have more settlers come to Texas. Mexico offered to sell land cheaply to Americans if they agreed to become Mexican citizens and obey Mexico's laws.

Thousands of Americans accepted Mexico's offer. By 1834 there were more Americans in Texas than there were Mexicans. The Mexican government began to worry, "What if the Americans try to take over Texas?"

Then Mexico decided to stop any more Americans from coming to Texas. Mexican soldiers were sent to guard the border of Texas. Then the Mexican government tried to take away the freedoms of the Americans already in Texas. You can imagine how freedom-loving Americans felt about that!

Texas Decides to Fight for Independence—The Alamo

In 1833, a Mexican named **General Santa Anna** took complete control of Mexico. He allowed the people no freedom. Such a leader is called a **dictator.**

The Americans in Texas could take no more. They declared Texas an independent country, free from Mexico's rule. General Santa Anna replied by sending an army to beat the Americans.

A group of 187 men gathered inside an old Spanish mission called the **Alamo.** There they prepared to fight. Not all the men in the Alamo were Texans; some of them had come down from the United States to help the Texans fight. One group of men from Tennessee was led by the famous frontiersman **Davy Crockett.** Why did Crockett go to Texas to fight even though Texas was not yet part of the United States? Because the people of Texas wanted to be free, and Davy Crockett was willing to fight anywhere for any people that wanted to be free.

When Davy Crockett had left his home state of Tennessee to head for Texas, he had an idea that he might not ever return. So he wrote a beautiful poem of farewell to his home and his family:

> The home I forsake where my offspring arose;
> The graves I forsake where my children repose;
> The home I redeemed from the savage and wild;
> The home I have loved as a father his child;
> The corn that I planted, the fields that I cleared,
> The flocks that I raised, and the cabin I reared;
> The wife of my bosom—Farewell to ye all!
> In the land of the stranger I rise or I fall.

But Davy was not afraid. He always said that his life's motto was, "Be always sure you're right—then go ahead!" That was his motto when he fought bravely in the War of 1812. And now he felt it was right to fight for Texas's freedom—so he went ahead!

Crockett and the other men in the Alamo fought bravely, but they were no match for the 3,000 Mexican soldiers. But the Texans did make the Mexicans pay dearly for a victory. For *eleven days* the Mexicans could not get near the Alamo. But finally the Texans ran low on ammunition, and the Mexicans poured into the old mission. The men fought on until all 187 of them were killed. Not a man would give up. Even Davy Crockett died in the battle. The night before his death, Crockett made this last entry in his diary:

> March 5. Pop, pop, pop! Bom, bom, bom!—throughout the day. No time for memorandums now. Go ahead! Liberty and independence forever!

The Alamo can still be seen in San Antonio, Texas.

Davy Crockett and many other brave Americans met their death at the Alamo.

It was for liberty and independence that Davy Crockett and the other men in the Alamo gave their lives.

The cry "Remember the Alamo!" swept through Texas as men prepared to fight Santa Anna. Texans led by **General Sam Houston** took the Mexican army by surprise. This was the battle of **San Jacinto.** Santa Anna himself was captured along with the Mexican army. Texas now considered herself a free nation. Sam Houston was elected to be her president.

Texas remained independent until 1845, when she became the twenty-eighth state to join the Union (the United States).

War with Mexico

Mexico remained bitter about the war. She never recognized Texas as being independent. When Texas became a state, Mexico became bitter toward the United States.

Then there was an angry quarrel over the boundary line that separated Texas from Mexico. Texas claimed that the **Rio Grande** River was her western boundary, while Mexico claimed another boundary that gave Texas less land.

James K. Polk, President of the United States, sent a general with an army to guard the Rio Grande boundary line that Texas claimed was hers. Of course, the Mexicans claimed this land was theirs and attacked the American army for being on their land. At the same time, the Americans said they were on land that belonged to the United States. In the fight, some Americans were killed. The United States then declared war on Mexico.

The war with Mexico began in 1846. It lasted for two years. The United States easily won. By the treaty of peace, the Rio Grande was accepted as the border between Texas and Mexico. A large area of land which makes up the present states of California, Nevada, Utah, and parts of Arizona, New Mexico, Wyoming, and Colorado was given to the United States. The United States agreed to pay Mexico fifteen million dollars for this piece of land.

Map Study: Territory Obtained from Mexico

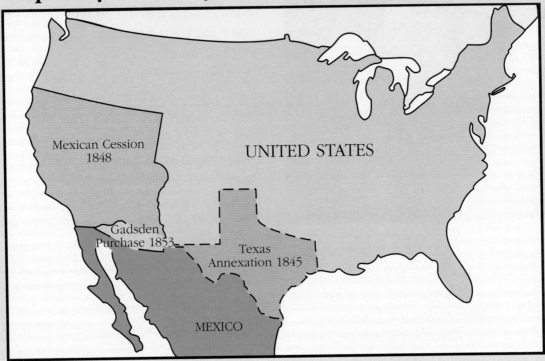

The Gadsden Purchase

Only five years later, in 1853, the United States bought a strip of land from Mexico. This land, known as the **Gadsden Purchase,** made up the southern parts of what are now New Mexico and Arizona. The purpose of this purchase was to build a railroad through the Southwest.

The Great Rush to California

In 1848, gold was discovered in California on **John Sutter's** *ranch. One day* one of his hired workers saw what he thought might be flakes of gold. Gathering some, he took them to John Sutter.

John Sutter studied the flakes for a long time as his worker, John Marshall, watched. Finally, Sutter whispered, "You have found pure gold! But don't tell anyone, for if you do, my land will be destroyed as people search for gold."

The news did spread. "Gold has been found in California! Go to California and become rich."

Before long the whole United States

had heard the exciting news. Many people from the North, South, and East left their jobs and homes to go to California. In those days, such a trip was long and dangerous, for there were mountains and deserts to cross and warlike Indians to deal with.

Gold! Gold! Gold was the only thing these people thought about! So great was their desire for gold that it became known as "gold fever"!

Although gold was discovered in 1848, it was 1849 before the great crowd of gold seekers began arriving in California. For this reason, the gold miners were often called **"forty-niners."** This movement was called the **Gold Rush.**

Most miners did not find enough gold to pay for all their troubles in reaching California. True to John Sutter's words, thousands of greedy, uninvited gold miners swarmed over his land. These men cared nothing about the crops that John Sutter had planted or the animals he was raising. Although gold was discovered on his land, John Sutter's farm was ruined.

Life in a California Gold-mining Town

Towns grew rapidly as thousands of gold miners made their way into California. They found that life was not easy in a gold-mining town.

Storekeepers demanded that their goods be paid for in gold dust rather than money. Perhaps you have heard your parents talk about the high cost of food today, but can you imagine paying these prices? One egg by itself cost as much as fifty cents to a dollar, and one pound of flour often cost more than a dollar's worth of gold! With prices like these, the storekeepers often became richer than those who found the gold.

Along with the honest gold miners came the dishonest who would steal or kill to gain more gold. Why didn't the law stop them? You must remember that at the time, California was not a state. There was little or no law. It was up to the people to protect themselves.

Lumber was so expensive that many men chose to live in tents rather than to build buildings. Some cities were made up almost entirely of tents. As long as gold was found, that town remained prosperous.

What happened to those towns whose miners could no longer find gold? Some of these became **ghost towns**—towns with empty buildings where no one lived. In other towns, some miners finally decided to settle down and build farms or businesses.

California Becomes a State

By 1850, only two years after gold

A "forty-niner" searches for gold. Very few people who came to California actually found gold.

was discovered, the population of California had grown so much that the people who lived there asked if it could become a state. In that same year, *California became the thirty-first state to join the Union.*

The Oregon Territory

The next piece of land to be added to the United States was called the **Oregon Territory.** *This land would include the present states of Oregon, Washington, and Idaho as well as part of Montana and Wyoming.* At the time, the Oregon Territory was owned by both England and the United States. They both agreed to be joint owners of the land, which at the time even included part of Canada.

If you have ever traveled in these states, you know what beautiful country there is to see. You might then ask, why did it take so long for the Oregon

Territory to be added to the United States? Perhaps it was because it involved a long, dangerous trip to get there. The Oregon Trail was almost 2,000 miles long, stretching over wild country and hazardous mountains. Before Oregon could be settled, someone had to see it to know how rich and beautiful it was. Then someone had to travel all the way back East to tell the people how wonderful the Oregon Territory was so that pioneers would be persuaded to come.

Missionaries were among the first to travel to Oregon. They were interested in teaching the Indians. *The most famous missionaries to Oregon were* **Dr. Marcus Whitman** *and his wife* **Narcissa.** They worked hard to teach the Indians, and they worked hard to bring pioneers to Oregon. During one winter, Marcus Whitman traveled back East to tell the people about Oregon.

Dr. Marcus Whitman traveled all the way to Oregon. He established a mission there and encouraged other pioneers to settle the territory.

about Oregon. To make this journey, Oregon-bound pioneers traveled to Independence, Missouri, where the Oregon Trail began. Here they waited until enough pioneer families came to form a wagon train.

All of the families had to work together to make the 2,000-mile journey a success. Each man would be needed to keep the wagons repaired and rolling on their way. Each man would be expected to defend the wagon train in an Indian attack. Many of these pioneers would die of sickness or be killed before they reached Oregon.

When he returned he brought several pioneers with him.

Slowly, the people back East heard

Map Study: The Last Piece of the Puzzle—The Oregon Country

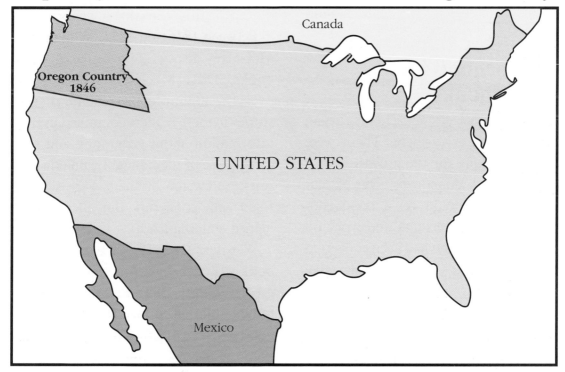

Canada

Oregon Country
1846

UNITED STATES

Mexico

By 1845, thousands of pioneers had been successful in reaching Oregon. It became clear to both England and the United States that there would have to be a boundary line dividing Oregon into British-owned land and American-owned land. In 1846, an agreement was reached giving us the border between Canada and the United States that we have today.

This would be the last piece of land added to the United States for a long time. In 1859, the state of Oregon joined the United States. The state of Oregon did not include all of the Oregon Territory. Later on, Washington and Idaho also became states. Now our country stretches from "sea to shining sea."

New Schools and Schoolbooks

As America grew, schools began springing up everywhere. There were several reasons for the growth of our schools. First, Americans believed that each person should get a good education so he could think and work on his own. Those who had been converted during America's great revivals especially wanted to see schools built so that their children could learn to read the Bible. Second, you will remember that the Northwest Ordinance provided free land for schools. And finally, many states began to pass laws requiring that schools be built in each city. Before long children throughout the country were going to school.

Noah Webster was concerned because there were no American textbooks to be used in American schools. Webster then decided to write textbooks himself. These books taught children to read, but they also taught children to do right, to be loyal Americans and to love God and His Word. Webster's most famous book was The American Spelling Book, nicknamed the "Blue-backed Speller." Some sixty million copies of this book were sold during the fifty years that it was printed.

Between 1836 and 1857, **William H. McGuffey** also wrote a series of textbooks. These McGuffey readers sold over 122 million copies. Some of the stories in these readers contained useful information about geography and science; some of them taught valuable lessons; and some of them were simply filled with good fun. But all of them helped children learn.

Webster, McGuffey, and other textbook writers helped America become a great country because their books taught children to love freedom, to be good citizens, to fear God, and to serve Him by obeying His Word.

What Schools Were Like

This painting shows a typical school in the nineteenth century. Millions of American children went to one-room schoolhouses just like this one. There were not separate classes: all the boys sat together on one side of the classroom, all the girls on the other side of the classroom. The teacher would call the students by groups to the front of the classroom to recite their lessons. First she might help the fourth graders with their history; then she might quiz a sixth grader on his spelling words; then she might help the first graders with their phonics. The teacher always stayed busy teaching the students and making sure they behaved themselves.

The schoolhouse was small and simple, but the children took pride in it and kept it clean. There were few maps or globes, and of course there were no record players or filmstrip projectors or other fancy machines. But still the children learned! They learned because they had the right tools for learning—good textbooks and a teacher who loved them and wanted to help them learn.

Facts to Remember

1. Which purchase doubled the size of the United States? _____

2. Which President made the Louisiana Purchase? _____

3. What two young men explored the Louisiana Territory? _____

_____

4. What Indian woman acted as a guide for the Lewis and Clark Expedition?

_____

5. Why did America declare war on England in 1812? _____

_____

6. What city was burned during the War of 1812? _____

7. Who wrote "The Star-Spangled Banner"? _____

8. At what battle was our national anthem written? _____

_____

9. Which side won the war of 1812? _____

10. Which territory did President Monroe buy from Spain? _____

11. What famous pioneer opened up Kentucky to settlers? _____

_____

12. What trail in Kentucky did Daniel Boone blaze? _____

_____

13. What early settlement in Kentucky was named in honor of Daniel Boone?

_____

14. What states were formed from the Northwest Territory? _____

_____

15. What law established the rules for settling the Northwest Territory? _____

_____

16. Who was one of the most famous circuit-riding preachers during the Second

Great Awakening? _____

17. What did pioneer families travel in after they sold their wagons? _____

18. What dictator tried to take away the liberties of Texans? _____

19. How many men were killed defending the Alamo? _____

20. Whom did the Texans choose to be their leader? _____

21. At what battle was Santa Anna captured and defeated? _____

_____

22. Who was President during the Mexican-American War? _____

23. What was the Mexican-American War fought over? _____

_____

24. How long did the Mexican-American War last? _____

25. What purchase was made so that a railroad could be built in the Southwest?

_____

26. On whose ranch was gold found in California in 1848? _____

_____

27. Why were the men who went to California looking for gold called "forty-niners"? _____

28. Why did many people in gold-mining towns decide to live in tents? _____

_____

29. What were deserted, empty towns in the West called? _____

30. From what territory were the states of Oregon, Washington, and Idaho formed? _____

31. What missionary couple helped Indians and pioneers in Oregon? _____

_____

32. Who wrote the first schoolbooks especially for American schoolchildren? __

_____

What was the name of his first schoolbook? _____

33. What man wrote a series of famous readers in the middle of the Nineteenth Century? _____

The Civil War

Before the War

While our country was growing in size, its problems were also growing. For many years, the North and the South had misunderstood each other. This misunderstanding slowly turned into anger in the minds of some people. The states from the South began talking about withdrawing from the United States and forming their own country. Those from the North said that no state could leave the **Union.**

States quarreled with each other. Neighbors argued. Even many families were split with quarrels. *These quarrels led to the* **Civil War.** To better understand the problems that arose, we will first study the differences in the way the people of the North and the South lived.

The North and Slavery

You will remember from our study of colonial life, that life in the North was very different from life in the South. Until the late part of the 1700's, some negro slavery existed in all American colonies. Then slavery began to disappear from the North. Most Northern farms were small. The Northern farmer could not afford to buy many slaves.

Because the Northerners could not depend on slaves to do their work, they knew they would have to work hard themselves. They knew they would have to think of other ways to get a great deal of work done. Factories began growing in importance in the North.

196

The South and Slavery

Many Southern farms were very large. These large plantations usually grew only one or two crops—cotton and tobacco.

Eli Whitney's cotton gin removed the seeds from the cotton plant much faster than workers could do it by hand.

When **Eli Whitney,** a young schoolteacher from Massachusetts, moved to Georgia, cotton was not a very important crop. It took so long to separate the seeds from the cotton fibers (lint) by hand that the cost of preparing cotton was very high. In 1793, Whitney invented the **cotton gin,** a machine which removed the seeds quickly and greatly increased the speed of turning cotton into cloth. The cotton gin made cotton cloth cheaper to make, and cotton became a valuable crop in the South. Not only the Northern states, but England and France as well bought cotton from the South. Smoking tobacco became a more and more popular habit. *The climate of the North is too cold to grow either cotton or tobacco. Because the world wanted these two crops, the Southern planters happily grew them.*

The Southern planters bought more land as their crops sold more. The purpose of buying more land was to plant more cotton and tobacco. But who could take care of such large fields? The Southern planter could never hire enough people to get his work done, and so he turned to buying slaves.

Slaves easily learned how to pick cotton and tobacco. The Southern weather was warm and the slaves stayed

197

healthy. There was no need of factories in the South, for cotton and tobacco made the South rich.

The South needed many workers. To the South, slaves were the answer. However, only one out of every ten Southerners owned slaves.

The North, which depended largely on its factories for a living, began to dislike slavery. If slaves ran away from their owners in the South, there were some Northerners who were willing to help them get to freedom.

"How can we call this a free country when we allow one man to own another?" the North asked the South. But by this time, the South depended on its slaves. If they freed their slaves, how would they be able to make a living? There was no easy answer to this question.

If slaves were men, then why could they not enjoy the rights of life, liberty and the pursuit of happiness which the Declaration of Independence said belonged to all men?

"...A Firebell in the Night"

As new states were added from the territories, a new argument arose.

New Words

1. **cotton gin**—a machine invented to remove seeds from cotton
2. **compromise**—a decision that tries to satisfy both sides of an argument
3. **blockade**—to close off or prevent communication or trade between nations or cities
4. **ironclad**—covered with iron
5. **emancipate**—to set free
6. **proclamation**—an important statement

New Names

7. **the Union**—another name for the United States, especially during the period of the Civil War
8. **the Civil War**—the war fought between the North and the South between 1861 and 1865

9. **Eli Whitney**—the man who invented the cotton gin
10. **Missouri Compromise**—an effort to make the slave states and the free states live in peace with each other
11. **Abraham Lincoln**—the President during the Civil War
12. **Confederate States of America**—the name which the Southern states gave themselves after they withdrew from the Union
13. **Jefferson Davis**—the president of the Confederacy during the Civil War
14. **the *Merrimac***—a Confederate ironclad
15. **the *Monitor***—a Union ironclad
16. **the Emancipation Proclamation**—Lincoln's

Should the states be admitted as *free states* (states not allowing people to own slaves) or should they be added as *slave states* (states that allowed people to own slaves)?

Why did this turn into an argument? Remember that each state is represented by two senators in the Senate. If there were more slave states, the Senate would be more careful to look out for the slave states. However, if the Senate was controlled by the free states, the Senate would be more interested in the free states. *To keep both the free and slave states happy, there had to be an equal number of both free and slave states.*

In 1819, both Maine and Missouri were asking to become states. In order to keep the Senate equal, since Maine was free, Missouri would have to be admitted as a slave state. But the people who lived in Missouri did not agree. Some wanted to own slaves while some were against it.

Finally, in 1821, Congress admitted Missouri as a slave state, but only after a **compromise** was made. A compromise is a decision that tries to satisfy both sides of an argument. Since Missouri was to become a slave state, no other slave states north of an established boundary line could enter the Union as slave states. This decision was called the **Missouri Compromise**.

When Thomas Jefferson, the author of the Declaration of Independence, heard the news of the Missouri Compromise, he was very saddened. He described the news as "a firebell in the night." He meant that it was a warning that trouble was coming.

announcement that the slaves had been freed

17. **Ulysses S. Grant**—the general who led the Union army
18. **Robert E. Lee**—the general who led the Confederate army
19. **William T. Sherman**—the Union general who captured Atlanta and then marched through Georgia to the sea
20. **John Wilkes Booth**—the man who murdered Abraham Lincoln
21. **Andrew Johnson**—the man who became President after Lincoln's death

New Places

22. **Fort Sumter**—the place where the Civil War began

23. **Gettysburg**—the turning point of the war
24. **Vicksburg**—the city which was captured by the Union army so that the North could control the Mississippi River
25. **Richmond**—the capital of the Confederacy during the Civil War
26. **Appomattox**—the place where Lee surrendered to Grant, bringing the Civil War to an end

New Dates

27. **1821**—the Missouri Compromise
28. **1860**—Lincoln was elected President
29. **1861**—the Civil War began
30. **1863**—the Emancipation Proclamation was issued
31. **1865**—the Civil War ended; Lincoln was shot

Many Southern states felt that the right of each state to do as it wanted was more important than the country as a whole, and they began to talk about separation from the United States. They wanted to form their own nation.

"After the American Revolution, we agreed to join the United States. Now, we can see no reason why we cannot agree to leave the Union," said the South.

"No state can leave the Union!" replied the North.

Indeed, a firebell had sounded in our nation. *A very sad and horrible war was about to begin within our own country.*

Abraham Lincoln Becomes President

A new President of the United States was to be elected in 1860. Throughout the North and West, a tall man from Illinois by the name of **Abraham Lincoln** had become popular. Above all he wanted our country to remain one strong Union. He did not want to see our country divided.

Abraham Lincoln cared about the South's problems, but the South said they would not trust him as their President, for they knew he disliked slavery.

"If Abraham Lincoln becomes President, the South will leave the Union," the South said.

Nevertheless, Abraham Lincoln was elected our President. And true to their word, the South began to carry out their threat of leaving the Union.

The South Leaves the Union

South Carolina was the first state to leave the Union. Within a short time, six other Southern states made the same decision: Mississippi, Florida, Alabama, Georgia, Louisiana, and Texas. These states formed their own nation called the **Confederate States of America.** They elected **Jefferson Davis** as their president.

The people of the United States listened as Abraham Lincoln begged the North and the South not to become enemies. But they had already become enemies.

Abraham Lincoln

This picture shows a group of Union soldiers. Being a soldier was not pleasant: food, uniforms, and supplies were scarce; sickness and disease were common.

The Civil War

A Divided Country—
Its Soldiers

The Union Troops

When Abraham Lincoln asked for soldiers, thousands volunteered. The Northern soldiers wore blue uniforms. Besides being called the Union troops, they were sometimes called the "Yankees," "the Yanks," or "the Billy Yanks."

The Confederate Troops

Answering the South's call for soldiers, thousands volunteered to join the Confederate Army. They wore a gray uniform. Their own Confederate flag waved in the breeze. The Southern Confederate soldiers were sometimes called "Rebels" or "Johnny Rebs."

The First Battle

The United States Army owned several forts located in the Confederate states. The Confederate government demanded that these forts and their guns be given to the Confederate states. Of course, the United States would not give up her forts.

One of these forts was **Fort Sumter** in Charleston, South Carolina. This fort stands on a man-made island of rock in Charleston's harbor. The Confederates wanted to remove the Union soldiers from Fort Sumter.

"Fort Sumter belongs to us," the Confederates claimed.

Early on an April morning in 1861,

The first shot of the Civil War was fired at Fort Sumter, in South Carolina.

Confederate troops aimed their guns at Fort Sumter. The people of Charleston grew excited. Although it was still dark, they came out of their houses to watch. At 4:30 in the morning, the Confederates fired the first shot. *This shot began the Civil War.*

The Union troops inside Fort Sumter had few supplies. They fought bravely for two days, but at last they had to surrender the fort. The United States flag was taken down from the fort and the Confederate flag was raised in its place.

The Confederates cheered, for they had won the first battle of the war. Little did they realize what a long, horrible war lay before them. They mistakenly thought the North would not want to keep fighting. And they mistakenly thought that England and France would come to help them. But the Confederates were wrong.

The Union Must Be Saved

President Lincoln was saddened by Fort Sumter. He knew that the Union must be saved, even if it meant war. He asked for 75,000 Union men to volunteer as soldiers. Within days, thousands of men volunteered to join the Union army.

The Confederacy Grows

There were some states from the South that had not joined the Confederacy yet. When President Lincoln's call for soldiers came, they could not bear the thought of fighting against their own Southern neighbors. Instead, they left the Union and joined the Confederate states. These states were Virginia, North Carolina, Tennessee, and Arkansas.

The Confederate government was now made up of eleven states. Yet twenty-two states stayed with the Union.

A Blockade against the South

The North had many small farms which grew large supplies of food. It also had many factories. During the war, the North could thus supply itself with food and supplies.

The South did not have many factories, and it had depended mainly on cotton and tobacco for its way of making a living. They could not eat tobacco, and they could not wear cotton unless it was turned into cloth by the factories of the North or of Europe. President Lincoln knew that the South now depended on her trade with Europe to supply her with guns, ammunition, war supplies, and even some food. Without these things, the South did not have a chance of winning the war.

In order to stop the South's trade

Map Study: The United States during the Civil War

Free states
Slave states
Border states
Territories

with Europe, President Lincoln sent Union ships to block all the South's major seaports. Such a plan is called a **blockade.** The blockade did hurt the South. A few ships managed to fool the North and slip through, but most Southern ships were stopped.

The Merrimac and the Monitor

The Southern navy had very few ships compared to the Northern navy. The South badly needed to break the blockade which was preventing her from getting important supplies. Since she did not have as many ships, she must come up with a wise plan and at least one powerful ship!

The Confederates raised an old ship that the Union had sunk. This ship was named the *Merrimac.* As you can imagine, there was much work to be done before the *Merrimac* could sail. How could an old, sunken ship be fixed to be better and stronger than the Union's ships?

The Confederates covered the *Merrimac* with iron plates. Cannon balls and gun shells would simply bounce off these thick plates. Guns were fitted on

The battle between the North's *Monitor* (right) and the South's *Merrimac* (left) was probably the strangest-looking navy battle that ever took place.

each side of the ship. A sharp piece of iron was fitted to the boat's bow. With this, the *Merrimac* could ram into the sides of the Union's ships.

At this time, all Union and Confederate ships were made of wood. It would be simple for an **ironclad** ship to destroy wooden ones without receiving any harm itself. The *Merrimac's* first battle was a tremendous success. Within a short time, she destroyed two of the best ships in the Union navy.

However, the South did not know that the Union was also building an ironclad ship. It was named the *Monitor.*

Soon afterwards, the South's *Merrimac* met the North's *Monitor* in battle. And what a strange-looking battle that

must have been! People have described the *Merrimac* as looking like an upside-down bathtub, while the *Monitor* has been described as looking like a cheese-box on a raft. These two ships shot at each other and tried to ram each other. But neither could do any better than dent the sides of the other. The battle was a draw. Neither side won.

Even so, the battle did have an important result. It proved the value of ironclad ships to the navy. Gradually, the wooden ships of the world became outdated. From then on, ships were built with iron and steel.

The Emancipation Proclamation

The question of what he should do with the slaves bothered President Lin-

204

coln. If he set them free, what would happen to them after the war was over? They had no homes to live in nor jobs to make a living. Very few had any education. How could they get jobs in order to buy homes, food, and clothing? How could a nation, already weak from war, help them?

Yet as the war dragged on, President Lincoln felt he could weaken the South and shorten the war by setting the slaves free. *He made an announcement that on January 1, 1863, all slaves would be considered free in any states that were fighting against the North.* This is known as the **Emancipation Proclamation.** To **emancipate** means to set free. A **proclamation** is an important statement.

There are several things that the Emancipation Proclamation did not do. It could not really free the slaves until the North won the war. It did *not* free any slaves who were owned in states that were not fighting against the Union. After the war, an *amendment* or change would be added to our Constitution giving all slaves in the United States and her territories their freedom.

However, the Emancipation Proclamation did have one immediate result. For many people, it changed the reason for fighting the Civil War. Before, the Union army was fighting to keep our country from dividing. Now the Union army was also fighting to free the slaves.

Before, England had thoughts of helping the South become a separate country. However, England was against slavery. She had no wish to help the South continue slavery. So, the Eman-

Lincoln reads a copy of the Emancipation Proclamation to members of his cabinet. Lincoln said about the Proclamation, "If my name ever goes into history, it will be for this act, and my whole soul is in it."

cipation Proclamation ended the chance of England's helping the South.

A Divided Country— Its Military Leaders

Ulysses S. Grant, Union General

All through his life, Grant was a very determined person. Once he made up his mind to do something, he tried his best to succeed. In 1864, President Lincoln made Grant the commander of all Union armies. His determination to win did lead the Union to victory.

In victory, he proved himself to be a gentleman, being generous and forgiving to those he had defeated.

Robert E. Lee, Confederate General

The thought of war greatly troubled Robert E. Lee. He loved the United States and could not bear the thought of its dividing. He hated slavery and had even set his own slaves free.

Why then did he become the general of the Confederate Army? He loved his home state of Virginia. When Virginia left the Union, he felt it was his duty to follow his state, for he could not stand the thought of fighting against his own state. Lee became the most amazing general in the whole Civil War.

The Battles

During the Civil War, many different battles were fought. *At first, the war did not go well for the North.* During the first two years, the North lost more battles than it won. The fighting so far had only been in the South. The Confederates fought hard to keep the North from sweeping over the South.

Then the Confederates decided to fight in the North. General Robert E. Lee marched 70,000 men from Virginia to Pennsylvania. There, the South lost the three-day **Battle of Gettysburg.** (The battle of Gettysburg *was the turning point of the war.*) Sadly, General Lee marched his men back to Virginia.

General Lee would have been even sadder if he had known that on that same day, the fourth of July, 1863, General Grant had defeated and taken over Vicksburg, Mississippi.

Ulysses S. Grant   Robert E. Lee

Abraham Lincoln delivering the Gettysburg Address.

Why was the **Battle of Vicksburg** so important? Vicksburg was an important city on the Mississippi River. The Mississippi River divided the Confederate states. *By gaining control of Vicksburg, the Union army was also winning control of the Mississippi River.* No longer could the Confederates on one side of the river send supplies to Confederates on the other side. The South was cut in two, yet she would not give up.

The Gettysburg Address

The Battle of Gettysburg took a terrible toll on both the Northern and Southern armies. Thousands of men died in this one battle. After the battle, Gettysburg became a great cemetery. A special ceremony was held to honor the men who had been killed at Gettysburg. Many famous men were scheduled to speak, including President Lincoln.

The main speaker at Gettysburg on November 19, 1863, was a famous orator [speaker] named Edward Everett. He gave an address which lasted two hours. He held the audience spellbound as he described in flowery language the events of the recent battle. Then came the President's turn to speak. But instead of a long speech, Lincoln spoke for less than three minutes. He spoke ten simple, direct sentences, and then sat down. But those ten sentences—now known as the Gettysburg Address—make up one of the most famous and familiar speeches in American his-

During Sherman's march to the sea, Northern soldiers destroyed everything in sight. Here they are seen destroying some railroad tracks.

tory. Edward Everett's long speech has been forgotten, but everyone is familiar with the Gettysburg Address.

In the speech, Lincoln quoted a historical document. He borrowed Thomas Jefferson's words in the Declaration of Independence when he said that "all men are created equal." To Abraham Lincoln, that was the most important part of the Declaration. He believed that the secret to America's greatness was the idea that all men are created equal in worth to God. That is why Lincoln quoted it in the Gettysburg Address. He reminded everyone that America still believed that all men are created equal. Lincoln wanted to honor those men who had given their lives so that all men—blacks and whites, Northerners and Southerners— could be free. Lincoln's words challenged the people then, and still challenge us today, to be willing to die for our country. Our Constitution, which promises freedom and equality under the law to all Americans, must be preserved, no matter what the cost.

Sherman's March to the Sea

Everyone was tired of fighting. General Grant made plans which he hoped would hasten the end of the war. He chose **General William T. Sherman** to carry out this plan. This time, Grant's plan included capturing Atlanta, Georgia, which was a very important city to the Confederates. From there, he wanted Sherman to march to Savannah, Georgia, on the Atlantic coast.

Sherman carried out his orders. Knowing that the only way to make the South surrender was to discourage her even further, he gave orders for his Union troops to burn or destroy everything they found, including homes, barns, animals, food, and crops. *The South could not possibly keep fighting much longer after such destruction.*

The Surrender at Appomattox

Meanwhile, General Grant had been fighting General Lee to capture **Richmond,** Virginia. Richmond had been the capital of the Confederate States just as Washington, D.C., is the capital of the United States.

After many months of hard fighting, the Union troops surrounded the Confederate army. The Confederates had been beaten in too many places. General Lee knew there was nothing else his troops could do. *He told General Grant that he would surrender.*

On April 9, 1865, Lee met Grant in a farmhouse in the town of **Appomattox, Virginia.** It was here that Grant wrote very generous terms of surrender. Like President Lincoln, Grant was glad the fighting was coming to an end. He had

After four years of courageous fighting, General Lee surrendered to General Grant at Appomatox, Virginia. The Civil War had at last come to an end.

no wish to hurt the South further.

In his terms of surrender, Grant wrote that there would be no prisoners of war. General Grant did not take away all the horses from the Confederate soldiers, for he realized that the Southern farmers would need these animals to help plant crops for a now starving South.

The officers of the Confederate army were allowed to keep their guns. General Lee was allowed to keep his sword.

When Lee read the terms of surrender that Grant had written, he said gratefully, "You have been very generous to the South."

Now that the Confederate army had surrendered, Grant ordered that food be taken to the starving Confederate soldiers.

Results of the War

The soldiers began returning to their homes. Peace had come after four years of bitter fighting, but the fighting had not been in vain. The war settled two important problems: *(1) No state could leave the Union, and (2) there would be no more slavery in the United States.*

Plans for Peace

There were people in the North who felt bitter against the South. They said that because the South had begun the war, it should be punished.

Great Plans for Peace

Just before the war had ended, President Lincoln was elected for the second time as President of the United States. He made it clear that he looked forward to the time when our nation would be whole again. *He did not intend to hate or punish the South.*

He spoke these words to our nation: "With malice [hate] toward none, with charity [love] for all." He then asked the people "to bind up the nation's wounds; to care for him who shall have borne the battle, and for his widow, and orphan—to do all which may achieve...a just and lasting peace."

Did you notice that in Lincoln's speech, he did not say, "only the North" or "only the South." Instead, he referred to "all." Yes, President Lincoln was making great plans to bring peace again to our whole country. Unfortunately, he never lived to carry out his plans.

Our Nation Mourns

The Civil War had been over for only five days. A very tired but happy President Lincoln took his wife to see a play at Ford's Theatre in Washington, D.C.

Abraham Lincoln was killed by John Wilkes Booth, a half-crazed actor who blamed the President for the Civil War.

he died the next morning. Our whole nation mourned the death of this great man. *Even the South was beginning to realize the friend they had in President Lincoln.*

A Bitter Peace

Andrew Johnson *became President in Lincoln's place.* Although he wanted to carry out Abraham Lincoln's wishes, there were many men in Congress who felt nothing but bitterness toward the South. These men were able to make Congress strong enough to stop President Johnson's plans. As a result, for several years Congress passed laws that punished the South. In return, the South grew bitter.

While they were watching the play, a half-crazed actor named **John Wilkes Booth** slipped through the theater to where the President sat watching the play and shot Lincoln, probably because he blamed Lincoln for the Civil War.

Men carried the President to a house across the street from the theater, where

Fortunately, with the passing of time, the bitterness and hatred caused by the Civil War was forgotten. Once again, the men from the North and the South were willing to stand side by side to help their country.

People Worth Knowing More About

Abraham Lincoln—the Man Who Saved the Union

Many people consider Abraham Lincoln to be the greatest President this country has ever had. He is truly one of the great men of all time. And he is a good example to show that America is a land of freedom and opportunity.

Abraham Lincoln was born in 1809 in Kentucky, but his family soon moved to Indiana. There Abe grew to be a strong boy who helped his father farm. Because he was so busy farming, he had little chance to go to school. But Abe didn't want to be ignorant. He read what few books he could get his hands on. He especially enjoyed reading the Bible, *Pilgrim's Progress,* and a biography of George Washington. Abe grew very wise. Men would come from all around to swap stories with young Abe at the general store. When a war with the Indians started, the men chose Abraham Lincoln as their leader. He won their respect for his bravery in the war.

Once as a young man Lincoln traveled down the Mississippi River to New Orleans. He enjoyed himself there, but he saw something which deeply disturbed him. He saw men, women, and children being sold like animals at an auction. This was the first time he had seen what slavery was, and from that time on he wanted to do something for those poor people.

Mr. Lincoln decided to move to Illinois to seek a better life. That is one of the great things about America: if you are not satisfied with the job you are doing, you are free to move anywhere you want and try your hand at any job you choose. That is what Lincoln did in Illinois; after several years of study, he became a lawyer. Soon he had built up a successful practice. People liked Abe. He was honest and kind-hearted. People called him "Honest Abe."

Lincoln was bothered by the trouble in the country. He saw hatred and conflict over the slavery issue. He knew that sooner or later America would have to reach a decision: either America would accept slavery or America would reject it. He quoted a Bible verse to prove his point: "'A house divided against itself cannot stand.' I believe this government cannot endure permanently half slave and half free. I do not expect the Union to be dissolved—I do not expect the house to fall—but I do expect it will cease to be divided. It will become all one thing, or all the other."

Lincoln hoped that by becoming President he could keep

the Union from falling apart. When the Southern states withdrew from the Union, it hurt him deeply. He saw that war was the only way to bring the country back together again. And before he died he did see his beloved country re-united.

Because America is a free country, Lincoln was able to overcome his poverty and become President. Being the son of a poor farmer did not stop him. Not being able to go to college did not stop him. This was America; he was free to work toward his goals. And because he was from the common people, he understood and loved the common people. The American people were saddened when he died; they have loved and honored him ever since because he fought to save the Union. He has also helped many young people to reach for high goals in their lives. Because of the example of Abraham Lincoln, many boys even today would like to some day become President of the United States of America.

Facts to Remember

1. What was America often called during the Civil War period? _____

2. Why did the North reject slavery? _____

_____

_____

3. What were the South's two main crops? _____

4. Who invented the cotton gin? _____

5. Why was the cotton gin such a help to Southern farmers? _____

_____

6. What two states were brought into the Union under the terms of the Missouri Compromise? _____

   Which was slave and which was free? _____

   _____

7. Who was elected President in 1860?_____

8. Why did the South dislike Lincoln? _____

   _____

9. What was the first state to leave the Union? _____

   What other six states left the Union not long after that? _____

   _____

   What did these states call themselves? _____

   _____

10. Who was elected President of the Confederacy? _____

    _____

11. What were the Northern soldiers called?_____

12. What were the Southern soldiers called? _____

13. At what fort did the Civil War begin? _____

14. How many states made up the Confederacy?_____

    How many states stayed with the Union? _____

15. What did the North set up against the South to weaken it? _____

16. What was the name of the first Southern ironclad? _____

    What was the name of the first Northern ironclad? _____

    Which ship won the battle when they fought each other? _____

214

17. What document issued by Lincoln freed the slaves? _____

18. What important effect did the Emancipation Proclamation have on the Civil War? _____

_____

19. Who was the leader of the Union army? _____

20. Who was the leader of the Southern army? _____

21. What battle was the turning point of the war? _____

22. What battle put the Mississippi River under Northern control? _____

_____

23. What Union general led a destructive march to the sea? _____

_____

24. What city served as the capital of the Confederacy? _____

_____

25. What was the site of Lee's surrender to Grant? _____

26. What two things did the Civil War make certain? _____

_____

_____

27. Who shot and killed President Lincoln? _____

_____

28. Who became President after Lincoln's death? _____

_____

New Frontiers

Rebuilding the South

After the Civil War, much of the South was desolate. Many farms had been ruined. Worst of all, millions of slaves had been freed who had no jobs, no property, no homes, no education.

Two men spent their lives trying to improve conditions for the blacks in the South. The first was **Booker T. Washington.** Booker grew up with a deep love of learning. As a boy, he taught himself to read by using an old, battered copy of Webster's Blue-backed Speller. Booker was tremendously excited when he heard that a teacher was coming to his town to teach the children. That first day at school was one of the greatest days of Booker's life.

Booker continued to learn. When he was fifteen, he left home to go to a school named Hampton Institute. It was there that Booker learned to love the Bible. He also learned many skills.

In 1881, a town named Tuskegee in

Alabama asked Booker T. Washington to teach school there. Washington was thrilled. His own school building, his own books, his own students! But when Washington reached Tuskegee, he received a shock. There was no building. There were no books. And there were just a handful of students. So Washington went to work to build a school. He worked harder than he ever had before in his life, but he didn't mind, because he knew that his hard work was worthwhile. "Nothing ever comes to one,

that is worth having, except as a result of hard work," he said.

The Tuskegee school started out in a leaky, ramshackle old building. But it grew rapidly. More and more students came to be taught by Booker T. Washington. Washington wanted to teach his students that they should work hard to support themselves. He and his students worked to plant a garden at the school. They used the crops for food and sold whatever was left over to get money for books. When more buildings were needed, Booker taught the students to make bricks and build their own buildings. Extra bricks were sold to get money. The school, which came to be known as Tuskegee Institute, prospered and grew. It still provides excellent training for men and women.

In 1896 Booker T. Washington was looking for a good chemistry teacher for his school. He wrote a letter to a man who had just gotten a degree from Iowa State College and invited him to come down to Tuskegee for a lifetime of "hard, hard work." The man's name was **George Washington Carver,** and he was not at all afraid of hard work. He had been born a slave, but his masters were very kind. They let him read and study all he wanted. He was fascinated by nature, and he taught himself all about the plants of the

Booker T. Washington, the great educator who founded Tuskegee Institute.

forest. His knowledge of trees and plants amazed his teachers in college. He decided that he could put his knowledge to good use at Tuskegee, so he accepted Washington's invitation to teach there.

George Washington Carver amazed the world with his accomplishments. It seemed that he was a genius who could do anything with plants. He studied the chemistry of plants very thoroughly and knew what could be done with them. For example, he found 118 uses for the sweet potato. He made flour, starch, paste, vinegar, ink, rubber, chocolate, dyes—all from sweet potatoes! From the peanut he made over 285 products, including milk, butter, cheese, candy, coffee, shaving lotion, lard, soap, shampoo, and ink! One time Carver served a delicious meal to a group of visitors. After the meal, the guests complimented Carver on his cooking. Only then did Carver reveal that all the food in the meal had been made from peanuts!

George Washington Carver's knowledge of plants helped rebuild farms in the South.

But we do not remember Carver simply because he stayed in his laboratory and did amazing tricks with peanuts and sweet potatoes. He did far more valuable work when he helped poor farmers in the South become prosperous. For years, cotton was practically the only crop planted by Southern farmers. But cotton wears out the soil and makes the soil unable to grow crops. Carver found crops which

New Words

1. **reservation**—a piece of land which the United States has set aside for the Indians
2. **transcontinental**—crossing the continent; from one coast to the other
3. **stampede**—a confused running-around by a frightened group of cattle
4. **graze**—to feed on grass

New Names

5. **Booker T. Washington**—the great educator who built Tuskegee Institute
6. **George Washington Carver**—the scientist whose work with plants helped Southern crops
7. **Cyrus McCormick**—inventor of the mechanical reaper

helped the soil, and he traveled around the South convincing farmers to plant them. He encouraged farmers to plant peanuts, which nourished and enriched the soil instead of wearing it out. He urged farmers to grow soybeans, which today is one of the most profitable crops a farmer can grow. Years and years of growing cotton had exhausted the soil and had made Southern farmers poor. George Washington Carver encouraged farmers to diversify their crops and helped the South get on the road back to prosperity.

The Last Frontier

After the end of the Civil War, Americans once again began to feel the urge to move West. Many Northerners found that they could not find a job when they got back from the war. Many Southerners came home to find that their farms and cities had been destroyed in the fighting. So Northerners and Southerners alike began to look to the West, where there was still plenty of free land waiting for them. And because America is a free country, no one stopped these people from leaving their homes to look for a better life. Before long, wagons were once again rumbling over the western trails.

This was to be the last great westward movement. These were to be the last pioneers to point their horses westward. It was a period of cowboys and Indians and farmers, each trying to gain control of the West. It was a period of great danger and great excitement.

We have seen that the "West" kept moving over as settlers moved into a region. By the year 1900, settlers had pushed the West all the way to the Pacific Ocean, and what was once called the West became known as the Midwest. From ocean to ocean, all regions became settled, and modern America began to take shape.

Over one hundred years had passed since Daniel Boone led many of the first pioneers into Kentucky. Since then,

8. **Union Pacific and Central Pacific**—the two railroads which built the transcontinental railroad
9. **Homestead Act**—a law which promised 160 acres of land to each settler in the West

New Places
10. **Promontory Point, Utah**—the place where the transcontinental railroad was completed

New Dates
11. 1862—the Homestead Act passed
12. 1869—the transcontinental railroad completed
13. 1889—the Oklahoma land rush
14. 1890—the "end of the frontier"
15. 1924—Congress passed a law which made all Indians citizens of the United States

there had been a continual movement of pioneers traveling westward. Bit by bit, the frontier was shrinking. By the middle of the 1800's, California and Oregon had already begun settlement. The Great Plains and the area around the Rocky Mountains remained the last frontier to settle.

Many soldiers returning home from the Civil War had heard stories of the West. Eager to forget the hardships of the war and make a new way of living for themselves, thousands decided to travel West. Thousands of pioneer families joined them. Together they headed for the last frontier.

The Indians of the West

As the pioneers moved westward, the Indians were usually forced to move, too. There was plenty of land to be developed and used. The Indians could not understand that America's way of life was rapidly changing.

Our government gave the Indians the Great Plains for their own land.

To many Indians, the Great Plains was home. Huge herds of buffalo roamed through this country. Next to his horse, the buffalo was the most important animal in the Indian's life. The buffalo provided the Indians with meat to eat. The buffalo skins were used to make clothing and tepees. Even the

The buffalo provided Indians with food, shelter, and clothing.

bones were used to make tools. There was no other animal that could provide these Indians with food, shelter, and clothing.

Pioneers decided to build settlements on the Great Plains, too. Little by little, the Indians watched land that they considered theirs being taken away. Many could not understand that their way of life would have to change as the United States grew. Then the white men began to kill off the buffalo herds. Men came from the East to hunt the buffalo only for its hides or skin. These hides would be sold back East. And then there were men who came just to shoot the buffalo for sport. There came to be fewer and fewer buffalo.

"The white man has broken his promise to us. We will not be forced to move again. The white man must be sent back to live on his own land," the Indians said as they decided to fight for what they believed was theirs.

Many were the Indian raids that followed. Settlements were burned and men, women, and children were killed.

Indian wars followed. There was cruelty on both sides. This is a sad part in our country's history. The Indians had many false religions which influenced their way of life and which made it hard for the Indians and the white men to get along. Yet few white men tried earnestly to teach the Indians Christianity. Neither side tried to understand the other. Each side fought for what they believed was theirs.

Finally, the United States government sent soldiers to the West to fight the Indians. One by one, the Indian tribes were defeated and forced to move onto **reservations.** A reservation is a piece of land which the United States has set aside for the Indians. Here they were promised protection.

In 1924, our government passed a law which made the Indians citizens of the United States. Happily, since that time, there has been a greater understanding and friendship between the white man and the Indian.

A Gold Spike for a Railroad

"What? California and Oregon become states some day? Impossible! They are too far from the East."

That was how some people felt in the early part of the 1800's. However, the coming of the railroad changed people's minds. Little by little, railroads were improved. Men began to dream of a railroad that could connect the East with the West. Soon, plans were made to build our country's first **transcontinental** railroad.

Union Pacific railroad workers are seen here spanning a river in Wyoming. They were about 150 miles short of their goal when this picture was taken.

A transcontinental railroad would be a long, difficult job. The track would not only have to be laid across prairies and plains, but also around and up and down mountains. Two railroad companies would work on this tremendous job: the **Union Pacific Company** and the **Central Pacific Company**. Work was begun in 1862, during the Civil War.

The Union Pacific began work in Omaha, Nebraska. A railroad had already been built this far from the East. The Union Pacific workers built their tracks westward from Omaha.

The Central Pacific began work in Sacramento, California, and built their tracks toward the East. Somewhere in the middle, these two railroad companies would meet and join to form our first transcontinental railroad.

Building the transcontinental railroad was not an easy job. It took seven years of hard work to take the railroad across rugged mountains, through deep valleys, and across miles of endless plains.

Many years of hard work went into this job. There were no stores along the way to buy supplies and food for the twenty thousand workers. As far as the new tracks were finished, trains would carry the needed supplies to the workers. Buffalo were shot for fresh meat.

The workers did not have an easy job. Summer days were hot and the

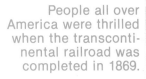

People all over America were thrilled when the transcontinental railroad was completed in 1869.

winter days cold. Indians often attacked the working men.

Day by day, the two sets of tracks came closer and closer to joining each other. The two railroad companies raced each other to see which company would finish the most miles of tracks. Finally on May 10, 1869, a Union Pacific locomotive traveling west met a Central Pacific locomotive traveling east. The place where the two railroads met was **Promontory Point, Utah.**

But the great railroad was not finished yet. The last long nail, or spike, needed to be driven into the rails at their meeting place. An ordinary spike could not be used for such a great event. Amidst the sound of cheers and the blows of sledge hammers, a gold spike was driven into the last rail.

This transcontinental railroad brought tremendous changes to our country: (1) It helped to settle the West. Settlers began traveling West in trains rather than in the slow wagons. (2) The East was brought closer to the West. People from the East could visit people who had moved West. Farmers and businessmen from the West could send their products back East by train to sell them. In return they could buy supplies from the East.

The American Cowboy

Even before the transcontinental railroad was built, the Great Plains became an ideal place to raise beef cattle. By the time of the Civil War, many ranchers from Texas were raising large herds of half-wild cattle called longhorns. One look at their picture and you will see how these cattle got their name. Over the next few years, ranches spread to other parts of the Great Plains including Wyoming, Montana, Colorado, Nebraska, and Kansas.

In those days, there were no fences to control the cattle. They roamed where they pleased. Often, a herd was made up of a thousand or more cows. The rancher needed help in looking after a herd this size. The men whom the rancher hired to take care of his cattle were the American cowboys.

In this picture, cowboys are roping cattle and taking them to be branded.

The cowboy practically lived with the cattle, making sure they had food, water, and protection. Since there were no fences to keep one rancher's cattle from mixing with the cattle from another ranch, the cattle were branded with a hot iron. The brand burned a special mark onto the cow's or calf's hide. Every ranch had its own special brand, different from any other ranch. During the spring, the cowboys would round up all the new calves for branding.

The Long Drive

After the Civil War, beef was scarce in the East but plentiful in the West. How could a rancher get his cattle over the great distance to the East? The coming of the transcontinental railroad provided the answer. But you must remember that there was not a railroad in every city or even every state. Most ranchers had to move their herds over several hundred miles to the nearest railroad that would handle cattle. Such a town with a railroad was called a cow town.

The three or four months' journey to a cow town was called the long drive. Since the rancher had his ranch to look after, he usually hired many cowboys for the long, hard job. During the long drive, there were always dangers to

look out for—Indian attacks, a wild animal, or a storm. Any one of these, or even a sudden noise, could cause a **stampede** in which the cattle would wildly run.

At night the cowboys would take turns keeping watch over the herd. To soothe the tired animals and prevent stampedes, the cowboys often sang soft songs, such as:

Whoopee ti yi yo, git along, little dogies;
It's your misfortune and none of my own.
Whoopee ti yi yo, git along, little dogies;
For you know Wyoming will be your new
   home.

Even though the cowboy was devoted to his work, you can be sure he was glad to reach the cow town. Here,

The long drive to a cow town often took them three or four months.

A sudden noise or flash of lightning could start a stampede. It was the cowboy's job to slow the cattle down and keep them from running off.

the cattle were sold and placed on the train. Then the cowboy was paid for the work he had just accomplished.

The Cowboy and the Farmer Disagree

By this time, many families were moving West to buy land and build farms. The cowboy was used to letting his herd roam the open range for grass to eat. As farms were built, the farmers planted fields of wheat and corn. You can imagine the trouble that arose when the cowboy's herd of cattle spied a young green cornfield or wheatfield. Of course, the cattle preferred young ten-

der wheat and corn to the grass they could eat every day on the Plains.

The angry farmer would not stand to see his crops trampled and ruined. When there were few farms, this was easy to correct. All the cowboys had to do was drive their herd where there were no farms. But as the West became more settled, this became impossible.

You must realize that the cowboy did not own the land over which he drove his cattle. Neither did he pay for using it. The United States government owned this land and had begun selling it to farmers. Since the farmers were now the owners of this land, they had a right to keep the roaming cattle from destroying their crops. The farmers began putting barbed-wire fences around their farms.

For a time, the farmer and the cowboy fought. Slowly, the cowboy realized that if he was going to succeed in raising cattle, he must buy his own farm and fence in large pastures for his cattle to **graze.**

The Homestead Act

In 1862, our government passed the **Homestead Act.** This was a law which said that any family that settled in certain areas of the West could receive 160 acres of land. To keep this land for his own, the head of the family had to live on that land and farm it for five years.

This sounds like a good offer, but there were several problems with it. At the time the law was passed, the Civil War was going on. Families were concerned with the problems of the war. There were also still problems with the Indians in the West. Many men did not want to risk the lives of their families for a free farm. There was also another problem. Many people wondered how they could farm in the West because of the hot, dry summers of the Great Plains. What crops could survive this weather?

When the Civil War was over, many people were willing to try. By this time, the Indians were being placed on reservations. New methods of farming with less water made it possible to grow some crops. And many soldiers, returned home from the war, restless and eager for a change.

As the years passed, there was less and less land for the government to give away in the West, for more and more people settled in the West as a result of the Homestead Act. As the government made land available for settlement, there would be a great land rush. People would line up in wagons and on horses, waiting to claim their 160 acres that the government would give them.

The Oklahoma Land Rush

Originally, the government had given the territory known as Oklahoma to the Indians. But once again the Indians were moved and a date was set aside for the settlers to claim land in Oklahoma. The year was 1889.

The day came for the great Oklahoma Land Rush. Many thousands of people were lined up along the borders of Oklahoma. Some were in carriages, some in wagons, and some in trains. Some were on horseback, and some were on foot.

Soldiers guarded the borders. No one could move over the border until a signal was given. At last at noon, the signal was given. The eager settlers began the scramble to find some land that they could call their own. You can see why this was called a "land rush." Before the day was over, most of the land in the Oklahoma Territory was claimed.

In 1890, it was announced that there was no more frontier land left in the United States. There were still large, unsettled areas, and there were still some homesteads to be given away, but there was no longer a clear line drawn between an unsettled area and a settled area. That meant that there was no more frontier land left in the United States.

This photograph was taken at the very instant when the borders of Oklahoma were opened. Many thousands of people joined in the Oklahoma Land Rush.

A homesteader and his wife and children stand in front of their house, which was built of bricks cut from the tough, sun-baked prairie sod.

People Worth Knowing More About

This painting shows the first public demonstration of Cyrus McCormick's reaper.

Cyrus McCormick

Thousands of people moved to the West to homestead. Most farmers planted wheat. The plains filled up with wheat so fast that it was hard to find workers to harvest it all.

Once again an ingenious American came up with the solution to a knotty problem. Cyrus McCormick was a Virginian who liked to tinker around with mechanical devices. One of his projects was a mechanical reaper which his father had tried unsuccessfully to build. Cyrus studied his father's designs and made improvements on them. In 1831, Cyrus invited his neighbors to watch the first demonstration of his mechanical reaper. He hitched horses to the reaper, climbed aboard, and headed into a wheatfield. The reaper cut down the wheat neatly and evenly. It would have taken several men hours and hours to cut down the wheat in that field; Cyrus McCormick did it by himself in a brief time.

McCormick set up a factory for producing reapers in Chicago, near the plains. Farmers everywhere ordered McCormick reapers. Cyrus McCormick became a wealthy man, and his ingenuity helped make farming easier and more efficient.

Facts to Remember

1. Who founded and built Tuskegee Institute in Alabama? _____

   _____

2. Who was a famous scientist who found many uses for the peanut and the sweet potato? _____

3. What crop which Carver urged farmers to plant has become very profitable?

   _____

4. By the middle of the 1800's, what was the last frontier which remained to be settled? _____

5. What region did the United States promise to give to the Indians as their home? _____

6. What animal provided the Indians with food, shelter, and clothing? _____

   _____

7. Where were Indians put when white men began to settle the Great Plains? ___

   _____

8. What is a transcontinental railroad? _____

   _____

9. Which two railroad companies built the transcontinental railroad? _____

_____

10. When and where was the transcontinental railroad finished? _____

_____

11. What two changes were brought about by the transcontinental railroad? ____

_____

_____

12. What was the cowboy's main job? _____

13. Why were cattle branded? _____

14. What was the purpose of the long drive? _____

_____

15. Why did the cowboys sing to their cattle? _____

16. What was the disagreement between cowboys and farmers? _____

_____

_____

17. What law promised 160 acres of land to anyone who would farm the land for

five years? _____

18. What territory—originally promised to the Indians—was thrown open to set-

tlers in 1889? _____

19. When was the announcement made that there was no more frontier land left

in the United States? _____

20. Who invented the first successful mechanical reaper? _____

_____

An Age of Progress

Our Nation Grows

During the last part of the nineteenth century, our country saw great progress in many areas, and the population of our country grew rapidly. In 1870, there were thirty-eight million Americans; by 1916, there were almost one-hundred million Americans. The population almost tripled in forty-six years!

Where did all these new Americans come from? Some of them were born here, but most of them were immigrants.

An **immigrant** *is a person who leaves his own country to make his home in another country.* The United States is truly a country made up of immigrants. From the days of early colonization, people had come to America from Europe for freedom of religion, freedom to work and own land, and freedom from oppressive governments.

As the years passed, the reasons for

The Metropolitan Museum of Art, Gift of Lyman G. Bloomingdale, 1901.

immigrants coming to America grew. Immigrants came for the freedoms that America had to offer—the freedom of speech, press, and religion. Some came from poor families where they faced starvation. Many came because they could not own their own homes, businesses, or farms in their old homeland, but in America, if they worked hard, they could. Along with all of these

hopes, they wanted an education for their children. This may have been impossible in their old homeland, but in the United States, every child could have a good education.

These new Americans came from many different countries. For the first time, people came from Italy, Poland, Russia, Austria-Hungary, China, and Japan.

America was not an easy beginning for these new Americans. Few knew how to speak English. They had few possessions and very little money. But most had a big desire to work and build for themselves a home in a new and free country. By their work and determination, they helped build an even stronger America.

Spreading the Gospel

The nineteenth century was an age of progress in all areas of life. Christianity, too, made progress in this period by being spread to people throughout our country and throughout the world.

In almost every covered wagon which traveled westward was a Bible. The Bible molded the lives of many frontier families, and most of the pioneers were godly people. But religion was also im-

Millions of immigrants came to America to find freedom and a better life.

portant in the East. During the last half of the nineteenth century (and in the early days of the twentieth) great revivals swept America's large cities. These revivals were so successful that they reminded people of the Great Awakening. **Charles Finney** (1792–1875) was one of America's greatest revival preachers. Finney was a lawyer who became an evangelist. He had great influence in his day; usually, the buildings could not hold the crowds that came to hear him preach. He also brought revival to London, England.

Dwight L. Moody (1837–1899) *came after Finney as America's most famous evangelist.* Moody was a shoe salesman from Massachusetts who came to know Christ and was stirred by an urgent desire to share the gospel with as many people as possible. His historic revival services in America and England drew thousands upon thousands of people. He also founded Moody Bible Institute in Chicago.

In the early 1900's another evangelist captured America's attention. **Billy Sunday** (1863–1935) had been a famous baseball star for several years before his conversion at the Pacific Garden Mission in Chicago. Sunday's energetic and flamboyant preaching drew great crowds. Some people came because they were concerned about their souls; some people came simply because they were curious. But no matter why they came, before they left they would hear the gospel presented in a clear and

New Words

1. **immigrant**—a person who leaves his own country to make his home in another country
2. **pony express**—a mail service which used fast horses to carry the mail from St. Louis to Sacramento
3. **telegraph**—a device which sends messages over a wire
4. **Morse code**—a series of dots and dashes representing letters and numbers, used to send messages over the telegraph
5. **assembly line**—a fast method of making a product; each man stays in one place and has one specific job to do
6. **glider**—an aircraft which has no engine

New Names

7. **Charles Finney**—one of America's greatest revival preachers

8. **D. L. Moody**—a famous revival preacher and the founder of Moody Bible Institute
9. **Billy Sunday**—a baseball star who became a famous evangelist
10. **Adoniram Judson**—one of the first American missionaries
11. **Andrew Carnegie**—the man who built the steel industry in America
12. **John D. Rockefeller**—the man who organized the oil industry
13. **Sir Henry Bessemer**—the man who developed a quick method of making steel from iron
14. **Robert Fulton**—the man who developed the first successful steamboat
15. *Clermont*—Fulton's first steamboat
16. **Samuel Morse**—the man who invented the telegraph

Dwight L. Moody

Billy Sunday was a converted baseball player who received nationwide attention for his fiery preaching. His meetings attracted huge crowds.

simple style. And many were saved.

These evangelists did much to mold and shape American life. When Finney, Moody, or Sunday would hold a meeting in a town, the town would experience a genuine change. Saloons and theaters would close. Businessmen found that people became more honest and came in to pay their bills.

Changes took place in other lands as

17. **Alexander Graham Bell**—the man who invented the telephone
18. **Thomas A. Watson**—Bell's assistant
19. **Thomas Edison**—the man who invented the light bulb, the phonograph, and many other things
20. **Henry Ford**—the man who built the Model T, an assembly-line car which most people could afford
21. **Orville and Wilbur Wright**—the brothers who built and flew the first successful airplane
22. **Robert Goddard**—the man who built the first successful liquid-fueled rocket

New Places
23. **Menlo Park, New Jersey**—the location of Thomas Edison's laboratory, where he did most of his experiments
24. **Kitty Hawk, North Carolina**—the place where the Wright brothers made their first successful flights

New Dates
25. **1807**—Fulton made the first voyage in the *Clermont*
26. **1844**—Morse sent the first message over the telegraph
27. **1861**—the telegraph connected the East with the West for the first time
28. **1876**—Bell built his first telephone
29. **1884**—France gave the Statue of Liberty to America
30. **1903**—the Wright brothers made the first airplane flight
31. **1915**—the first coast-to-coast telephone call was made
32. **1926**—Goddard flew the first successful liquid-fueled rocket

well, for missionaries began to go out from America in large numbers during this period. *One of the first missionaries was* **Adoniram Judson** (1788–1850), *who spent many years preaching to the people of India.* Other men and women followed in his footsteps and sought to take the gospel "to the uttermost part of the earth."

The nineteenth century was a time when people took Christianity seriously. They responded in large numbers to the preaching of evangelists. Many of those who responded desired to obey the Bible and to let the Bible change their lives and their society. They showed their love for others by sending out missionaries to other lands. So great were the advances made by Christianity during this time that one history writer called the nineteenth century "the greatest century which Christianity had thus far known."

Steel and Oil: Ingredients for Success

The nineteenth century was a time of great prosperity and growth in industry. **Industry** *is the manufacturing business, the kind of work that has factories for making things. Two main products allowed American industry to grow rapidly: steel and oil.* The leaders of these two industries became giants in American history. Their names were **Andrew Carnegie** and **John D. Rockefeller.**

Andrew Carnegie Sees the Future of Steel

For many years iron had been the chief metal used by industry. But there were problems with iron: it was heavy, it was expensive, it was brittle (that is, easily breakable). Around 1856, an

Andrew Carnegie made millions of dollars in the steel industry, then used most of his fortune to help his fellow man.

234

Englishman named **Sir Henry Bessemer** developed a method of turning iron ore into steel, a metal which is just as strong as iron but is much lighter and more flexible. The man who brought the steel industry to America was Andrew Carnegie.

Andrew Carnegie was an immigrant. In 1848, when he was a boy of thirteen, his family came to America from Scotland to find a better life. Andrew's father got a job in a mill factory and soon secured a position for his son as well. At first, Andrew was paid $1.25 a week. But Andrew was an able and willing worker, and he soon moved on to better jobs. He became a messenger boy, then a telegraph operator, then a railroad clerk, and finally a railroad supervisor. As he earned more money, he used it wisely. He got involved in iron factories and prospered. But when he saw Bessemer make steel from iron, Carnegie became a steel man at heart. He converted all his factories to steel production. People thought he was being foolish, but he disagreed. "The age of iron is over; the age of steel is here," he said. "All the railroads will want steel rails because their old iron rails break too easily. Bridges will be built of steel, and ships and tall buildings and many other things that we don't even know about yet. The future is in steel."

Carnegie was right. The steel industry became a huge success, and Carnegie's steel company was the most successful of all. After many years, Carnegie was very wealthy. But he felt it was wrong for rich men to use their money selfishly. The best thing to do with money is to give it away for worthy causes. "The man who dies rich dies disgraced," said Carnegie, who spent the last years of his life giving away his fortune. He loved good church music, and he donated over 7,000 pipe organs to churches. He paid for schools and colleges. As a boy, he had loved to read, and he wanted all boys and girls to have books to read. So he began building libraries in towns throughout America. Eventually Carnegie paid for the construction of over 3,000 public libraries. By the time of his death in 1919, Carnegie—who had once earned $1.25 a week—had given away over $350,000,000.

John D. Rockefeller Organizes the Oil Industry

Early farmers and settlers in Pennsylvania were often bothered by a sticky black liquid which muddied their streams. Then they heard from the Indians that the gooey substance had magical powers, so they bottled up the black liquid and sold it as medicine.

The substance was oil. Soon people discovered that oil made a good fuel, and people flocked to Pennsylvania to pump oil out of the ground. Dozens and dozens of small petroleum companies were established.

John D. Rockefeller (1839–1937) decided that the oil industry could get off the ground only if someone organized it. He began to unite small companies into one big company. The results were lower prices for oil and better service to the consumer. *Rockefeller called his company Standard Oil. He became the first billionaire in history, and was for many years the richest man in the whole world.*

But Rockefeller, like Carnegie, believed that his money was useful only when it was given to help others. He created the Rockefeller Foundation, an organization which handled the huge task of giving away all that money. Rockefeller lived to be ninety-eight years old, and he gave away over $530,000,000 during his lifetime.

Both Andrew Carnegie and John D. Rockefeller were born poor. But because America is a land of freedom, both were free to work hard and to be rewarded for their work. As a result of their labor, both became wealthy. Through their efforts, American industry grew and prospered. And through

John D. Rockefeller, leader of the oil industry, was for many years the richest man in the world.

their generosity the lives of millions have been improved in many different ways.

Inventions: New Ways to Do Things

At one time or another, each of us has been an inventor. God has given each of us minds through which we are able to think of better or faster ways of getting jobs done. Since the creation of man, there have been inventions.

However, a good invention is never really finished. Someone else is bound to improve upon a good idea. For example, look at pictures of the first cars and planes. Can you imagine yourself still riding around in those early models instead of the modern ones? Aren't you glad that other inventors have continued to make improvements upon them? People will continue to invent new ways to improve the car and plane as well as every other important invention. This is called *progress*—moving forward to improve our way of life.

The First Successful Steamboat

By the beginning of the 1800's, the steam engine was being used to run machines in factories. The steam engine, run by burning wood and coal, interested several Americans who wondered if steam could also be used to make boats move.

Several men attempted to build a steamboat but were unsuccessful. Although most people laughed at the idea, **Robert Fulton** felt sure he could succeed. He was not successful at first, but he was willing to be patient and try again.

In 1807, just thirty-one years after America became a nation, Fulton's steamboat was completed in a New York shipyard. He named his boat the *Clermont.* Would the *Clermont* work? The only way to find out was to give it a trial run.

When the day arrived, crowds of people gathered on the river banks to watch. Many laughed and made fun of the *Clermont* before they even had a chance to see if it worked. Some people became frightened as smoke and sparks began to pour from the *Clermont's* smokestack. Nearly everyone was surprised when the *Clermont's* paddle wheels began turning and the *Clermont* began splashing its way up the river.

Before the steamboat, man had only sailboats and boats rowed by men to carry them up and down the river. Sailboats had depended upon the wind. It could take a sailboat several days to make the same trip that a steamboat could make in a day. Few people laughed at the steamboat now.

Men began working to improve the steamboat. Within a few years, steamboats replaced the sailboats in carrying manufactured goods and passengers up

Robert Fulton's *Clermont* was the first successful steamboat.

and down large rivers. Soon, steamboats were even traveling across the oceans.

The Telegraph—
Messages Sent by Electricity

People were now living all over the United States. How they wished they had a faster way of communicating with their loved ones who had moved or whom they had left behind! People tried many different ways of making communication faster. One of these was called the **pony express.** The pony express was a mail route which opened in 1860 and lasted only nineteen months. The route stretched from St. Joseph, Missouri, to Sacramento, California. The mail was carried by boys or young men who were small and light and who were not afraid of riding through Indian country alone. The mail carrier would ride a pony as fast as he could for a fifteen-mile stretch. Then he would stop at a way station to switch to a fresh pony and be on his way again in less than two minutes. The rider would cover from 75 to 100 miles in a day. A letter sent by pony express could travel from coast to coast in ten days. But the pony express was expensive (it cost $5.00 to send a letter) and very dangerous. Men continued to look for a faster means of communication.

Being a pony express rider was a dangerous job. This rider is being chased by a group of hostile Indians. The mail for the pony express was carried in the leather pouches on the sides of the saddle.

Steamboats and railroads speeded up communication somewhat, but there were some men who felt there had to be a faster way. One of these was a Christian man named **Samuel Morse.** He believed that messages could be sent over long distances through a wire by electricity.

In the 1840's, electricity was still new and exciting. Samuel Morse set about drawing plans for his invention. Then he began building what was called the **telegraph.** The biggest problem that he ran into was lack of money. An invention may make a person wealthy, but the invention has to be built and proved before someone will become interested in buying it.

Samuel Morse needed money to finish his experiments. Most of all, he needed money to spread telegraph lines over long distances in order to prove that his experiment worked. Morse was a poor man with a family to support. He often went without food himself so that he could work a little longer on his experiments.

Morse knew that his invention would greatly benefit our country. If he had the money to prove it would work, important messages could be sent from city to city in a matter of seconds instead of days. Knowing this, he decided to ask the United States Congress for money to prove his experiment.

Morse demonstrated his first telegraph in 1837. The first telegraph looked like this.

Samuel F. B. Morse was the inventor of the telegraph.

At first, Congress said no. Several years passed. Morse became discouraged, but he would not give up. Again, he asked Congress for the money, and this time, Congress voted yes. Thirty thousand dollars was given to build a telegraph line from Washington, D.C., to Baltimore, Maryland. The distance between the two cities is about forty miles.

Morse knew he could not send words over his telegraph wire. Instead, he figured out a code of short and long dots and dashes to be clicked over the telegraph wire. By this system of dots and dashes, known as the **Morse code,** the letters of the alphabet and numbers can be tapped over the telegraph wires.

In May of 1844, the telegraph was ready to test. Morse was at a telegraph set in Washington, D.C., while another man was at a telegraph set in Baltimore. A message was written down to send over the telegraph. This was the message: "What hath God wrought!" Morse tapped out this message on his telegraph set. Within seconds, the man waiting in Baltimore heard the message on his telegraph set. He then sent back the message he had just heard to Morse in Washington.

Samuel Morse's telegraph was a great success. Telegraph wires were run from pole to pole, from city to city, from state to state, until finally, in 1861, a telegraph wire stretched from the East Coast to the West Coast of the United States.

When the transcontinental railroad was completed, it was the telegraph that sent the message of the railroad's success to cities across the United States. Now, newspapers in cities that were hundreds and even thousands of miles apart could print the nation's news the same day that it happened, thanks to the telegraph. People who were moving West no longer felt out of touch with those in the East. *The telegraph had brought the East and the West together.*

Talking over a Wire— the Telephone

Alexander Graham Bell sailed to America from Scotland when he was a young man. He loved America and the opportunities he had as an American. Bell was a teacher of students who were *deaf* and *mute*. This means that they could neither hear nor speak. Usually, these students could not talk because they had never heard words or sounds.

Bell was a very good and patient teacher who did his best to teach the deaf how to talk. He once made the comment, "If I can make a deaf-mute talk, I can make iron talk." The idea and plans for a telephone were already developing in his mind.

As we have found out from other inventors, inventing something worthwhile can be costly. Bell was not a wealthy man, either, but fortunately, he was offered help. The fathers of two of his students offered him money to help continue his work.

Now Bell was able to hire a helper, **Thomas A. Watson,** to help him with his work on the telephone. Watson became Bell's close friend as well as a hard worker.

In March, 1876, Bell was in his attic workshop. Watson was in a distant room that was connected to Bell's only by a wire. Suddenly Bell said, "Mr.

Watson, come here, I want you!'' Excitedly, Mr. Watson came running. The telephone worked! He had heard Bell's voice over the telephone!

Americans were slow to realize the importance of Alexander Graham Bell's invention. They thought of the telephone more as a toy than as an important invention that could change their way of living.

In 1876, a world's fair was held in Philadelphia, Pennsylvania, to celebrate our country's one hundredth birthday. Our country had changed greatly since the Declaration of Independence had been written. Since new inventions had an important place in that change, many new inventions were shown at the world's fair, one of which was the telephone.

Important men came from many different countries to judge the inventions.

The American judges wanted to pass by Bell's invention, but the emperor of Brazil was too interested to pass by. He picked up the receiver and Bell talked to him from the other end.

''It talks!'' said the excited emperor.

That interested an English scientist. ''This is the most wonderful thing in America!'' he said.

Americans finally began to see the telephone's usefulness. One year later, the first Bell Telephone Company came into being.

In 1915, another important telephone conversation took place between Bell and his friend, Watson. Again Bell said, ''Mr. Watson, come here, I want you!'' But Bell was joking this time. You see, Alexander Graham Bell was speaking in New York. Mr. Watson was in San Francisco, California! *It was the first coast-to-coast telephone conversation.*

Alexander Graham Bell was very proud to become a citizen of the United States in 1882. What do you think he wanted to be remembered for the most? If you said ''the telephone,'' you are wrong. He wanted to be remembered first of all as a teacher of the deaf, for he greatly loved his students and did all that was within his power to help them.

Alexander Graham Bell is shown here speaking into his most famous invention, the telephone.

A Man of Many Inventions— Thomas Edison

There is hardly an American whose daily life is not affected by the work of **Thomas Alva Edison.** How many times have you used electric lights today? Has your teacher ever used a science movie to help your class learn science? Perhaps your family has a favorite album of hymns that you like to play on your record player. If your dad works in an office, he may use machines that have been developed from Edison's ideas.

Edison was so interested in inventing that he built a large invention factory at **Menlo Park, New Jersey.** Here, Edison worked both day and night, stopping only for naps.

The electric light, motion pictures, the phonograph, and office machinery are a few of Thomas Edison's inventions. He was truly a man of many inventions. How many? He designed over a thousand. There is only space to tell you about two here. To learn more, you might read a biography of Thomas Edison's life.

The most fascinating invention to Edison was the phonograph. If you saw Edison's phonograph, you probably would not recognize it as a phonograph, for it looks nothing like the phonograph or record player of today. It was not even run by electricity. The first phonograph actually recorded a person's voice. The person spoke into a mouthpiece and at the same time, turned a handle. This recorded the person's voice. Adjustments were then made, and the handle was turned again. This time, as the handle was turned, the recorded sound could be heard. The machine talked!

At first, even Edison's workers did not believe that such a strange-looking machine could talk. As his workers watched, Edison thought of what he would say. Then he put his mouth down

Thomas Edison was a tireless worker. He would perform hundreds of experiments until he had found the solution to his problem.

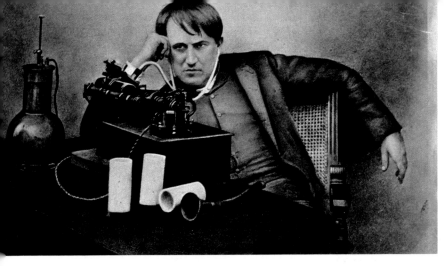

Thomas Edison invented the phonograph in 1877.

to the mouthpiece and began turning the handle. "Mary had a little lamb; its fleece was white as snow....," he said and finished the nursery rhyme. His workers waited as he adjusted the machine. Then he began turning the handle again.

In Edison's voice, the machine repeated, "Mary had a little lamb...." The workers were amazed! Then laughter and cheers filled the room. Edison himself was very pleased. This invention would make him famous.

As in all of Edison's inventions, he was never through with his phonograph. He worked day and night to make an even better one. Imagine Edison's delight when the President of the United States asked him to come to the White House to demonstrate the phonograph.

Something to Think About

Edison was never content to put one of his successful inventions aside. He always worked to improve his inventions. Many people called him a "genius." To that remark, Edison replied, "Genius is one percent inspiration and ninety-nine percent perspiration." He meant that having a good idea was only a small part of being successful. Hard work to make that good idea work is the largest part.

Perhaps you have a hobby at home or a subject in school in which you do very well. Do not be content with your work because it is already good. Work hard to make it even better.

Something to Think About

Did Thomas Edison ever fail? The answer is "yes," but he never became a failure! Failures may have slowed his inventions down, but he chose to learn from his mistakes. Once he was working on a special battery. Each one of the 8,000 tests he made on this battery failed.

"Aren't you discouraged?" asked his friends, as they wondered why he wouldn't give up.

"Discouraged?" he asked. "Why I've made progress! I have found out 8,000 things that won't work!" And with that, he went back to work.

Each one of us has tried and failed in something, but that does not make us failures either. Let's work to make our failures become progress, and in time, we will become successful.

After Edison finished his work on the phonograph, he worked on the electric light bulb. The idea of an electric light bulb was not a new one. Several different men besides Edison had been trying to invent one. Edison himself had the same problem they had. Many men had invented unsuccessful bulbs which would burn out in only a minute or two.

After two years of experimenting, Edison invented a successful bulb. When he turned the light on, he watched excitedly as it kept burning hour after hour. That first successful light bulb burned for forty hours. Then Edison and his workers kept working to make light bulbs that would burn even longer.

Edison's success with the light bulb gradually changed America's way of life. People had parades as electric lights lit up their streets. Soon stores and other buildings in big cities wanted electric lights too. Gradually, electric lights spread to homes throughout America.

To the end of his life, Edison worked on improving both his and other people's inventions. For example, he worked to improve the telephone. His ideas inspired other men to invent. As a result, today we can enjoy a better life because someone would not give up.

The First Cars

Today nearly every American family owns a car, but this was not always true. When the car, or as it was first called, "the horseless carriage" was invented, it was so expensive that only the very wealthy could afford to buy one. At that time, each car was made completely by hand. You can imagine how long it took to build one car.

Fortunately, a man named **Henry Ford** was interested in building cars. Henry Ford did not invent the car. While he was only a boy, a few people already owned cars. *Ford's dream was to make an inexpensive car that nearly every American family would be able to afford.*

While the first cars were costly, they were not very dependable. They were run by steam engines or electricity. Sometimes they would go and some-times they would not go. A little later, the gasoline engine was invented. "Why could the gasoline engine not run a car?" Henry Ford asked himself. To answer this, he first had to learn how to build a gasoline engine.

After he built the gasoline engine, he had to build the body of a car in which to put his engine. It had four bicycle wheels for tires. The car itself was shaped like a box. Instead of a steering wheel, there was a stick. At last the car was finished. There was only one thing left to do. He must try it out. His first car with a gasoline engine ran successfully, but like the rest, it was completely made by hand. It would still be expensive to buy. The year was 1896.

Henry Ford knew his work was not finished. He built other cars, making improvements on each one. In 1903, the Ford Motor Company began, yet it was still only the wealthy that could afford to buy cars. Ford was determined to find a way of building a car for a low price. Finally, he found a way.

Ford built the Model T by developing a method which we call the **assembly line.** On an assembly line, each worker has his own special job to do. The worker becomes very skilled in this job and can work quickly. To make his work even faster, the car comes to the worker on a moving belt. The belt

This picture shows Henry Ford wheeling out the first car he ever built.

This is part of Ford's Model T assembly line. Here, the Model T's are nearing completion. Using this efficient method, Ford produced 15 million Model T's.

moves at just the right speed to allow the worker to finish his job. Then the belt moves the unfinished car on to the next worker who has another job to do. This keeps on until the car is completed at the end of the assembly line.

By hand, it had taken many days to assemble one car. With the assembly line, one car could be completely assembled in one hour! *Because it took less time to build cars, cars could be made at a much cheaper price—a price most American families could afford.*

The Model T was a very good car and sold for a reasonable price. By 1914, there were more than a million Model T Fords on the roads. And the number kept growing and growing.

Ford's dream did come true. He may not have been the inventor of the car itself, but he was the first to use the idea of the assembly line to build cars. By using the assembly line, Henry Ford made his own reasonably priced car that most Americans could afford to buy.

Soon other factories were using Ford's idea to create other kinds of goods faster and cheaper. Because this good idea was put to work, Americans began enjoying a better and more modern way of life.

The Wright Brothers
Pop! Whirr—.
Off flew the toy "helicopter" as its

two young owners watched in delight. The year was 1878.

"What?" you ask. "Helicopters were not invented until the 1900's. How could children be playing with toy helicopters in 1878?"

These toys did not look much like the helicopters we see today. They were made from a piece of bamboo, cork, and paper. They were propelled by rubber bands. After the rubber band was twisted tightly and let go, the "helicopter" flew straight up.

The two boys were brothers, named **Wilbur and Orville Wright.** At the time, Wilbur was eleven years old and Orville was seven.

"Let's do it again," cried Orville.

Again and again they sent their prized "helicopter" into the air until it broke, but they were only saddened for a moment.

"Let's make another one!" Wilbur suggested.

"A bigger and better one!" nodded Orville.

They experimented by making several of their own helicopters, but they found out that the bigger they made their helicopters, the less they would fly. The two disappointed brothers wondered why.

Some men who were also interested in flying were also asking themselves a question. Would it ever be possible for a man to fly? Men had flown in balloons, but a balloon is not the same as a flying machine. Some men had tried to fly by strapping wings to their arms. Some had built strange-looking machines. But all had failed.

After the Wright brothers grew up, they became the owners of a bicycle shop, but they were still interested in flying. Their bicycle shop soon became a place for experimenting and finding the answers to their questions.

Several men had experimented with

The Wright Brothers—Orville (left) and Wilbur (right)—built and flew the first successful airplane.

gliders. The Wright brothers decided to build their own. This took several years of work. When they were finished, with the advice of the United States Weather Bureau, they decided to test their glider at **Kitty Hawk, North Carolina.** Here there were sandy beaches to give their glider a soft landing and good ocean winds to help it fly.

Their glider was successful, but the brothers were not satisfied. They must build a better one. They built a second and then a third glider. The third flew more than 600 feet. Again and again they tried their third glider until they had made almost one thousand flights. This was the best glider any man had ever made.

Now they were ready to build something even better! This time it would not be a glider. *It would be a plane run with an engine.* Men had been successful in building gliders before the Wright brothers, but no one had ever been successful in building a plane run by an engine. This kind of plane is called an airplane.

By that time, gasoline engines were already being built for cars, but they were not light enough to be carried by a plane. The brothers had to build their own light gasoline engine. They also had to build special propellers for their plane.

A historic moment: this photograph was taken just as the Wrights' airplane rose from the ground. It was the first time man had flown.

It took them almost a year to build their first airplane. *On December 17, 1903, they were ready to test it.* Orville was to test it. He warmed up the engine. The airplane started forward, slowly lifting itself into the air. *That first airplane ride lasted twelve seconds. Orville had flown 120 feet.*

The brothers made two more flights during that same day. Wilbur made the third flight. It lasted 59 seconds. He flew 852 feet!

These three flights were the first to be controlled by a man through the use of an engine. It was a tremendous step forward for the progress of America. Wouldn't you think that all the newspaper reporters of America would have been eager to write the story of the Wright brothers' flight? The next day, only a very few newspapers in our whole nation carried the story. Why? They just could not believe that man could really fly! They thought the story was a joke.

The Wright brothers would not give up. They continued their work on the airplane and made improvements. By 1908, people finally became interested in the airplane.

Although Wilbur died in 1912, Orville lived until 1948. During his life, he had seen great improvements that other men had made on the airplane. By the time of Orville's death, large airline companies had been formed. Some men were even beginning to talk about flying to the moon. Most Americans at that time said flying to the moon was a silly joke. What do you think Orville Wright thought about such a flight?

Robert H. Goddard and the Rocket

Even when **Robert Goddard** was a boy, he dreamed of one day sending an object high into space. At that time, men were having enough trouble experimenting with an airplane. To most people at that time, the idea of an airplane was foolish enough. The thought of sending a rocket into outer space seemed ridiculous.

When Robert was a boy, people laughed at his dream, but when he graduated from college, Robert began work on making his dream come true. People continually made cruel jokes of his efforts. Although he was hurt by these jokes, he would not give up his experiments.

He began work on a rocket that would burn liquid fuel. He used a combination of gasoline and liquid oxygen. This was a new idea. Liquid oxygen is highly explosive and very dangerous. Goddard and his workers were very careful.

In 1926, Goddard launched the first

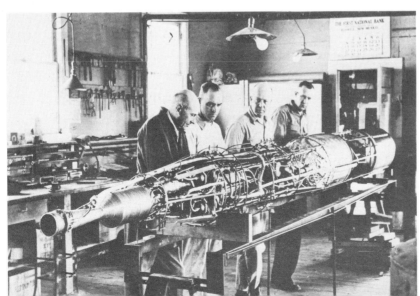

Robert Goddard (at the far left) is shown working on one of his rockets.

successful liquid-fuel rocket ever built. In the following years, he built bigger and better rockets. For many years to come, people would not realize the importance of his work. Goddard himself realized he probably would never live long enough to build a rocket big and fine enough to fly to the moon. It often took years of work to make one improvement on the rocket. Goddard realized there were many improvements to be made.

Goddard must have realized that other scientists would follow in his steps, as indeed they did. As a result, we have seen astronauts as well as rockets sent to the moon.

Facts to Remember

1. What is an immigrant? _____

_____

2. Why did so many immigrants come to America? _____

_____

3. What countries did many nineteenth-century immigrants come from? _____

_____

4. Who was one of the first evangelists to hold large city-wide revivals? _____

_____

5. What evangelist who came after Finney drew huge crowds to his revivals and

founded a famous Bible institute in Chicago? _____

6. What famous evangelist of the early 1900's was once a baseball star? _____

_____

7. Who was one of the first American missionaries? _____

8. What two products helped American industry grow? _____

_____

9. Who built the steel industry in America? _____

10. Who developed a method for making steel from iron? _____

11. Where was oil first discovered in America? _____

12. Who organized the oil industry and made it prosper? _____

_____

13. What did Rockefeller call his oil company? _____

14. What did both Carnegie and Rockefeller do with their money as they grew

    older? _____

15. Who developed the first successful steamboat? _____

16. What did Fulton name his steamboat? _____

17. What mail service was introduced in 1860 to speed up the mail? _____

_____

18. The pony express carried the mail between what two cities? _____

_____

19. How long did it take to get a letter across the country using the pony express?

_____

20. What man invented the telegraph? _____

21. Who gave Morse the money that he needed to continue his work? _____

_____

22. What are the dots and dashes called that are used to send messages over the

    telegraph? _____

23. How did the telegraph bring the East and West together?_____

_____

24. Before he invented the telephone, what did Alexander Graham Bell do? _____

_____

25. Who was Bell's assistant? _____

26. What were the first words spoken over the telephone? _____

_____

27. When did people really start to take notice of Bell's telephone? _____

_____

28. What happened in 1915? _____

29. Why did the book not mention all of Edison's inventions? _____

_____

30. What are among Edison's most famous inventions? _____

_____

31. What were the first words recorded by the phonograph? _____

_____

32. Where was Edison's laboratory? _____

33. Did Henry Ford invent the automobile? _____

Why is he so important in automotive history? _____

_____

34. What was the name of Ford's most popular car? _____

35. Why was the Model T so cheap? _____

_____

36. Where did the Wright brothers go to test their gliders and make their flights?

_____

37. When did the first airplane flight take place? _____

Who was the pilot? _____

How long was the flight? _____

38. Who developed the first successful liquid-fueled rocket? _____

_____

39. What did Goddard use to make his liquid fuel? _____

_____

40. When did Goddard's rocket make its first flight? _____

Beyond Our Boundaries

Until the end of the Civil War, the United States was interested only in its growth from coast to coast. In the next few years, the last frontier would come to an end. What would happen then?

Alaska

England, France, and Spain were not the only countries to have a part in the history of America. When the thirteen colonies won their independence from England, Alaska was owned by Russia. At that time, Alaska was called **Russian America.** The Russians were interested in the furs and the fish they could find in Alaska.

In 1867, after the Civil War, our country's Secretary of State, **William H. Seward,** received a visitor from the Russian government. During that visit, it became evident that Russia was willing to sell Russian America. The price would be $7,200,000. Was the United States interested?

This picture shows the Panama Canal being built. The building of the canal was one of the most ambitious projects ever undertaken by America.

Most Americans thought of Russian America as a worthless land of ice and snow. "What good would such a land be to us?" many Americans asked one another.

Of course, these people had never been to Alaska. In southeast Alaska, there is rich farmland. There is also beauty in its rivers and mountains. *At that time, no one knew of the great riches in gold and natural resources*

such as coal and petroleum that would one day be found there. These riches would make seven million dollars seem a very small price.

Seward urged our government to buy Russian America. He knew the wealth of valuable furs that could be trapped there. The purchase would also open the way for a large and profitable fishing industry. Besides, Russian America was an enormous piece of land.

At last our government accepted the offer, although many Americans made fun of it. They called Russian America "Seward's folly" and **"Seward's icebox."**

The name "Russian America" was

BROTHER JONATHAN GOES INTO THE ICE BUSINESS.

Brother Jonathan.— Wal, that ar is a purty big lump of ice; but guess I'll be able to use it. Jest give it to Bill Seward, and here's yer money for it."

Many people thought that America was making a mistake when it bought Alaska. In this cartoon, America is shown paying $7,200,000 to Russia for "Russian America"—pictured as a useless chunk of ice.

255

Map Study: Alaska

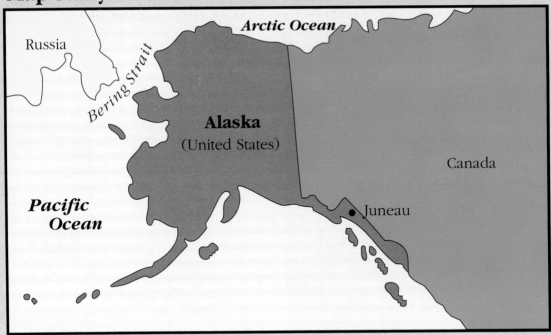

changed to Alaska. Fishing and furs soon proved to be very valuable. *In the year 1896, gold was discovered.* Alaska soon paid for itself many times. No longer could Americans make fun of the purchase of Alaska.

Alaska did not become a state when it was purchased. It became a **territory** of the United States. As a territory, the people who lived in Alaska could not vote in our elections or choose their own governor. Instead, the President of

New Words

1. **territory**—an area of land which the United States owns and controls, but which has not yet become a state
2. **canal**—a man-made waterway

New Names

3. **Russian America**—the name for Alaska when Russia owned it
4. **William H. Seward**—the Secretary of State who arranged the purchase of Alaska
5. **Seward's Icebox**—a name given to Alaska by those who believed that Alaska was a worthless, frozen land
6. **Captain James Cook**—the discoverer of Hawaii
7. **The** *Maine*—the American battleship which blew up in Cuba, the event which led to the Spanish-American War
8. **George Dewey**—the American admiral who won a great victory in a naval battle at the Philippines
9. **Theodore Roosevelt**—the leader of a group of soldiers named the Rough Riders; later President of the United States
10. **William Gorgas**—an army doctor who fought diseases caused by mosquitoes in Cuba and later in the Panama Canal Zone.

After studying the map, answer the questions below.

1. What country is west, across the Bering Strait?

   _____

2. Which ocean is north of Alaska?

   _____

3. Which ocean is south?

   _____

4. What country would you have to go through if you drove to Alaska from the United States?

   _____

the United States appointed a governor for Alaska. The governor could then tell our government what Alaska needed.

The people of Alaska wanted Alaska to become a state, but this did not happen until much later. *It was not until 1959 that Alaska was admitted as our forty-ninth state.*

Why did it take so long for Alaska to become a state? You must remember that a great distance separated the

New Places

11. **the Philippines, Guam, Puerto Rico**—territories obtained by the United States in the Spanish-American War

12. **San Juan Hill**—the place where the only major land battle was fought during the Spanish-American War

13. **Isthmus of Panama**—the thin strip of land which connects North and South America; the place where the Panama Canal was built

New Dates

14. **1867**—the United States purchased Alaska from Russia

15. **1878**—the French started to build a canal in Panama, but failed to complete it

16. **1896**—gold was discovered in Alaska

17. **1898**—Hawaii became a U.S. territory; the Spanish-American War was fought

18. **1902**—the French sold their rights to build a canal in Panama to the United States

19. **1914**—the Panama Canal was opened

20. **1959**—Alaska and Hawaii entered the Union as the forty-ninth and fiftieth states

21. **1978**—a treaty was signed which will return the canal to the country of Panama

Americans who think of Alaska only as a land of ice and snow have never seen Alaska.

United States from Alaska. From the time it was purchased until 1942, there were no roads connecting Alaska to the United States. The huge land of Canada lay between Alaska and the United States.

Today, Alaska is very important to our country. Its natural resources such as coal, oil, and natural gas supply a need for our energy. Alaska is also important to the defense of our country. Both navy and air bases were built there to watch constantly and alert our country if an enemy tries to attack.

Hawaii— Our Fiftieth State

When people talk about Hawaii, they usually mean the group of eight islands that are called the Hawaiian Islands. The largest island is named Hawaii, from which the islands get their group name. *This beautiful group of islands in the Pacific Ocean is more than 2,000 miles away from the coast of California.* How then did Hawaii become our fiftieth state? To answer that question, we must go back in time about 200 years.

Hawaii was discovered in 1778 by the English explorer, **Captain James Cook.** For the next forty years, English and American explorers, adventurers, trappers, and whalers stopped at the Hawaiian Islands for food and supplies on their way to and from China. These visitors had a deep influence on the Hawaiian people, who had for years been worshiping false gods. Contact with people who believed in the one true God made the Hawaiian people want to find out more about God.

In 1820 Christian missionaries began arriving in the Hawaiian Islands from America. The people were ready for the

Captain James Cook discovered Hawaii in 1778.

Alaska was the forty-ninth state; Hawaii was the fiftieth. Both entered the Union in 1959. These stamps were issued by the government to honor the two states.

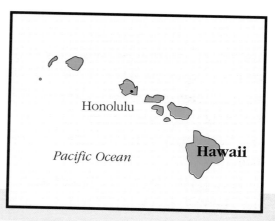

Map Study

Hawaii

After studying the map, answer the questions below.

1. How many islands are there?

   _____

2. In what ocean are they located?

   _____

3. In what direction would you have to fly to get back to the United States mainland? (You may have to look at a bigger map.)

   _____

message of salvation, and many Hawaiians accepted Christ. Many Christian churches and schools were started.

Other Americans came to Hawaii, also. Among them were men who began to raise large fields of pineapple and sugar cane. The Americans hired islanders to work their fields. Most of the crops were sold to the United States. Soon the islanders began to depend on their trade with the United States.

As the years passed, the Americans who were living in Hawaii wanted the islands to become a part of the United States. At first when they asked, they were refused. *In 1898, the United States Congress voted to make Hawaii a United States Territory.* Hawaii's rule was similar to Alaska's. And like the people of Alaska, the people of Hawaii wanted Hawaii to become a state. *It was not until 1959 that the United States Congress voted to accept Hawaii as our fiftieth state.*

The Spanish-American War

You will remember that in the years following Columbus's discovery of America, the Spanish gained control of a large part of the New World. Then other European countries began to build colonies in the New World. As these colonies grew more powerful, they took Spain's colonies away from her.

The island of Cuba is located ninety miles south of Florida. It was one of Spain's last possessions in the New World. Though Spain struggled to keep Cuba, the people of Cuba constantly fought for their independence.

The Cubans fought hard, but they could not win. In an effort to stop the fighting, the Spanish sometimes treated the Cubans cruelly. The people of the United States grew sympathetic toward the Cubans. It was their wish that the people of all countries could be free and independent as they were.

There were some Americans that owned businesses in Cuba. They were in danger of having their businesses ruined by the fighting.

"Remember the **Maine***"*

Our government sent the United States battleship *Maine,* on a peaceful trip to Cuba to protect Americans living there. All went well until a great explosion sank the Maine. Most of her sailors were killed or drowned.

Who blew up the *Maine?* Even today, no one knows the answer to that question. At the time, people of the United States blamed the Spanish, but the Spanish said they did not do it. Not be-

The destruction of the battleship *Maine* angered Americans and led to the Spanish-American War.

lieving them, the angry Americans wanted our country to go to war against Spain. "Remember the *Maine*" was their cry.

On April 25, 1898, our government declared war on Spain. The purpose of the United States entering this war was to set Cuba free from Spain.

Since the only way to Cuba for both the United States and Spain was by water, the navies of both countries were very important. The United States set out to destroy the Spanish navy; so when the war began, **Admiral George Dewey** of the United States Navy was sent to the **Philippine Islands.** Although these islands are in the Pacific Ocean, not far from China, but very far from Cuba, they also belonged to Spain. *Admiral Dewey sailed into a bay of the*

Philippine Islands where a fleet of Spanish ships were docked. There the United States Navy destroyed the Spanish ships without receiving harm to our own ships.

The Rough Riders

Meanwhile, Americans were fighting the Spanish in Cuba and in the seas nearby. A group of American men known as the Rough Riders was headed by **Theodore Roosevelt,** who would one day become President of the United States. The Rough Riders played an important part in winning the most important land battle fought in the Spanish-American War, the Battle of **San Juan Hill.** This battle hastened the end of the war.

Teddy Roosevelt led the Rough Riders up San Juan Hill.

The entire war lasted only three months. It was the shortest war the United States has ever fought.

Results of the Spanish-American War

As a result of the Spanish-American War, Spain gave Cuba her freedom. And the United States received these islands that had previously belonged to Spain: (1) the **Philippines** in the Pacific Ocean; (2) **Guam** in the Pacific Ocean; and (3) **Puerto Rico,** an island near Cuba. In return for these islands, the United States paid Spain twenty million dollars.

During the years after the war, the United States tried to help the people of these islands by building hospitals and schools. Many missionaries from America went to the Philippine Islands. Americans helped the people of the Philippines to learn how to govern themselves. Since then the Philippine Islands have become independent. The people of Puerto Rico and Guam now govern themselves but are also considered citizens of the United States.

In return, these islands provided us with more trade and places for extra military bases that might be needed to protect the United States and other free countries of the world from being attacked.

Spain, which once owned a great wealth in American possessions, now owned none. *Perhaps the most important result of the war to our country is that other countries now saw us as one of the "world powers," for we now had a part in distant lands.*

The Panama Canal

The North American continent is connected to the South American continent by a narrow strip of land called the **Isthmus of Panama.** This thin strip of land is about 480 miles long and from about 30 to 120 miles wide. On one side of Panama is the Pacific Ocean. On the other side is the Atlantic.

Centuries ago when Balboa first discovered the Pacific Ocean, he thought how wonderful it would be if only there were a place for ships to sail through this narrow strip of land from one ocean to another. Instead, *ships had to travel thousands of extra miles around South America to cross from one ocean to the other.*

*As time passed, men talked about building a **canal** across the narrow strip*

Map Study: The Panama Canal

of land that would connect the two oceans. However, no work was ever begun, because the problems would be too great. Even in the late 1800's, it would have taken millions of dollars to build a canal. Very few countries were willing to risk such a large amount of money. But every country agreed that such a canal would save ships going from ocean to ocean thousands of miles of travel.

In 1878, the French were the first to attempt to build a canal, but they ran into problems and had to stop.

It took the Spanish-American War for the United States to realize how important a canal would be to our country's safety. During the war, a United States battleship was ordered to sail from California to Cuba. The ship began the long trip around the South American continent and finally reached Cuba sixty-eight days later. By then, the war was nearly over. It would have taken less than half the time if a canal had been built.

Fortunately, the United States won the war anyway, but what if a battleship were urgently needed to go from one ocean to the other in the future? *In 1902, the French sold their rights to build a canal to the United States.*

Building the canal kept 40,000 people busy for ten years. *When the Panama*

Teddy Roosevelt tries out the controls of one of the giant machines which were used to construct the Panama Canal.

Building the Panama Canal was a monumental task. Construction of the canal took more than four years.

Canal opened in 1914, all nations not at war with the United States were allowed to use the canal. Since the United States had bought the right to build this canal, since the United States first had the approval of the people of Panama to build this canal, and since the United States had paid over three hundred million dollars to build this Panama Canal, the United States now had the right to control the canal from its enemies.

Although the United States controlled the canal, the people of Panama have always regarded the ten mile piece of land on which the canal is built as part of their country. With the passing of years, the people of Panama grew restless. They began to demand that the United States give the country of Panama more control over the canal. Even though the United States broke no law by building the canal in Panama and had every legal right to keep the canal, the United States graciously agreed to give the canal to Panama.

In 1978, a treaty was voted upon by the United States government. By this treaty or promise, the United States will give the ownership of the Panama Canal to the country of Panama by the year 2000. According to the treaty, the United States will always have the right to defend the canal in case of war or trouble. However, the fact that this important canal is being placed in the hands of a small, weak country might tempt an enemy—Russia, for example—to take over Panama and thereby gain control of the canal. Many Americans felt that we should have kept the canal to make sure that it remained in safe hands.

Over 13,000 ships use the Panama Canal each year. Each ship, whether it is American or foreign, has to pay a *toll* to pass through the canal. This toll, figured by the size of the ship, usually amounts to $5,000 or more. If this price sounds high, you must take into consideration not only the cost of building the canal, but also the enormous cost of keeping it repaired and operating. And for the country who owns the ship, the toll is much cheaper than the price of sailing a large ship an extra 8,000 miles around the tip of South America.

The time it takes for a ship to travel through the Panama Canal is usually about eight hours. Compare that with the weeks it would take to sail around South America. The Panama Canal is quite a short cut! *The Panama Canal is truly one of the greatest American building achievements of the twentieth century.*

People Worth Knowing More About

Colonel William Gorgas

Colonel William Gorgas

During the Spanish-American War, more men died from malaria and yellow fever than were killed in battle. Panama had the same problems as Cuba—its warm, moist air was an excellent place for mosquitoes to grow, and mosquitoes carry malaria and yellow fever.

Colonel William Gorgas, who had been successful in Cuba in destroying the mosquitoes which carried the two diseases, was now sent to Panama, where he was successful again. Gorgas helped to save the lives of both the canal builders and the people who lived in Panama.

A large, modern ship is seen here traveling through the Panama Canal.

Map Study: Beyond Our Boundaries

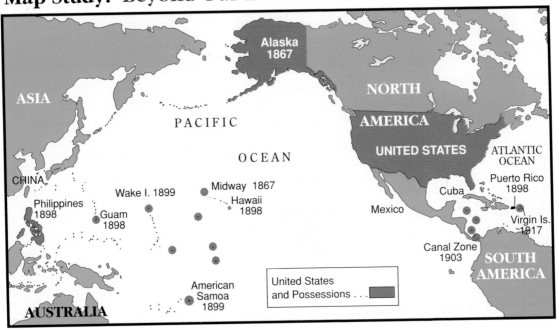

Facts to Remember

1. Who owned Alaska before the United States bought it? _____

   What was Alaska called in those days? _____

2. How much did the United States pay for Alaska? _____

3. What happened in 1896 which convinced everyone that Alaska was a valuable territory? _____

4. How does a territory differ from a state? _____

   _____

5. When did Alaska enter the Union? _____

   Why did it take so long for Alaska to become a state? _____

   _____

6. How far is it from California to Hawaii? _____

7. Who discovered Hawaii? _____

8. What happened in 1898 which made Americans angry and which led to the
   Spanish-American War? _____

   _____

9. Which American admiral defeated the Spanish fleet? _____
   Where did his great victory take place? _____

10. What was the name of the group of American soldiers led by Theodore
    Roosevelt? _____
    What battle did they fight in? _____

11. Who won the Spanish-American War? _____
    How long did the war last? _____

12. Which territories did the United States receive as a result of the Spanish-
    American War? _____

    _____

13. What is a canal? _____

14. What country was the first to try to build a canal across the Isthmus of
    Panama? _____

15. When did the United States obtain the rights to build the canal? _____
    When did the canal open? _____

16. In 1978, what did the United States promise to do with the Panama Canal?

    _____

    _____

17. How did William Gorgas help the men who built the Panama Canal? _____

    _____

The World Wars

While the United States was finishing the building of the Panama Canal, there were problems in Europe that kept growing. Many of Europe's people had turned away from God, and this led to terrible troubles. The people of the United States were saddened over Europe's troubles, but they saw no need to become alarmed. The United States seemed so far away from Europe. If war did break out in Europe, how could the United States be threatened?

One of the results of forgetting God was the wrong kind of nationalism. **Nationalism** *is the sense of loyalty to one's country.* If you love your country, you will want to be proud of its growth and of its accomplishments. Nationalism is natural and is good. But there were some leaders in Europe who twisted it into a selfish meaning. Such leaders tried to convince their people that their country should grow so big and so powerful that it could gain con-

trol of all the countries in the world. If you stop to think about it, there is no room for freedom or democracy in this twisted form of nationalism. There is only room for a dictator. *A* **dictator** *is a person who rules other people by force, not allowing them any freedom.* This kind of dictator would want you to believe that the only race of people worth caring about are those from his own race. If he is German, he would say the only people worth caring about are Germans. If he is Japanese, he would say the only people worth caring about are Japanese. Perhaps you already see the danger in such thinking. Certainly, such thinking is against our Christian beliefs, for we know that our Lord cares for everyone.

This twisted, evil kind of nationalism and its selfish desires to control others and become powerful, made other countries fearful. Other countries had no desire to be controlled by a dictator; so they began building up their armies.

World War I

Kaiser Wilhelm II, the ruler of Germany in 1914, wanted Germany to control more land. England had the greatest navy in the world, but the German ruler also wanted to gain control of the seas. With this in mind, he began building up Germany's army and navy.

With Germany building up her army and navy, other countries became fearful. They decided to form *alliances* against Germany. *An* **alliance** *is a promise between two or more countries to fight together against their enemies in time of war.*

The countries that sided against Germany were called the Allied Powers or the **Allies**. Those countries that sided with Germany were called the **Central Powers**. The few countries that decided not to take any side were called **neutral nations**.

European countries were preparing themselves for war. The only thing they lacked was an excuse to begin a war. The excuse came on June 28, 1914.

Archduke Ferdinand, the man who was to one day rule over Austria-Hungary, was visiting the small country of Bosnia with his wife. At that time, Bosnia was controlled by Austria-Hungary. The control of Bosnia was causing ill will between Austria-Hungary and the small country of Serbia, which also wanted to influence Bosnia. (Today, Bosnia and Serbia do not exist. They are part of one country— Yugoslavia.) As the archduke and his wife rode by in an open car, a Serbian teenager shot them both to death.

The country of Serbia was sorry for what this boy did, but Austria-Hungary blamed everyone in Serbia. Germany's ruler seemed eager for an excuse to begin war, and he told Austria-Hungary that it could count on Germany's help if it went to war against Serbia.

Austria-Hungary declared war on tiny Serbia. Meanwhile, Russia told Serbia that the Russians would help

Serbia. This angered the Germans, who then declared war on Russia. Since France promised to help Russia, Germany declared war on France, too.

One by one, the countries of Europe declared war on one another. Soon England declared war on Germany. One Englishman said, "The lamps are going out all over Europe." Indeed, gloomy days were ahead for all of Europe.

Woodrow Wilson *was President of the United States at that time.* Most Americans felt that the United States should stay out of the war in Europe. For the first three years of war, Presi-

The angry youth who murdered Francis Ferdinand and his wife did not know that his actions would plunge the world into war.

New Words

1. **nationalism**—the love for one's own country
2. **dictator**—a person who rules other people by force, not allowing them any freedom
3. **alliance**—a promise between two or more countries to fight together against their enemies in time of war
4. **U-boat**—another name for a submarine
5. **communism**—a form of government which steals businesses, homes, and land from people and claims to own them
6. **fascism**—a form of government which lets people keep their private property but takes away their freedoms
7. **Nazi government**—the government which claimed that it was more important than the people of Germany; that certain peoples (such as Jews) are inferior; and that the leader could do no wrong
8. **truce**—an agreement to stop fighting

New Names

9. **Wilhelm II**—the leader of Germany during World War I

10. **Francis Ferdinand**—the man whose death caused the outbreak of World War I
11. **Woodrow Wilson**—the President of the United States during World War I
12. **Lusitania**—a passenger ship sunk by the Germans; the death of American passengers on the ship eventually led to America's entry into the war
13. **Zimmermann Note**—a treacherous note which made Americans angry at Germany and led to the American declaration of war on Germany
14. **Veterans Day**—the day on which World War I ended; the day on which we honor all Americans who have fought for their country
15. **League of Nations**—an organization that was formed after World War I to try to preserve world peace
16. **Great Depression**—a period between the world wars when millions of Americans had no jobs and America's economy slowed down
17. **Joseph Stalin**—the Communist dictator of Russia

Woodrow Wilson was President of the United States during World War I.

dent Wilson kept our country neutral, which meant we would not take sides.

German U-Boats

Germany's powerful army was successful in defeating several countries. The Germans had to think of a different plan for defeating England. Since England is an island, she depended on ships to bring her food and supplies. Germany knew that if she could destroy England's ships, she could starve the people of England into giving up.

With this plan in mind, the Germans began to use **U-boats** (under-water boats). Today, we call them subma-

18. **Benito Mussolini**—the Fascist dictator of Italy
19. **Adolf Hitler**—the Nazi dictator of Germany
20. **Tojo**—the military dictator of Japan
21. **Franklin D. Roosevelt**—the President of the United States during World War II
22. **Axis Powers**—Germany, Italy, and Japan
23. **Allies**—Great Britain, Russia, China, the United States
24. **United Nations**—the organization which was established after World War II to keep war from breaking out
25. **Harry S. Truman**—the man who became President when Franklin D. Roosevelt died

New Places

26. **Geneva, Switzerland**—the city where the League of Nations met
27. **Poland**—the country where World War II started
28. **Pearl Harbor**—the American navy yard which was bombed by the Japanese
29. **Berlin**—a city which was divided into two parts by a Communist wall

30. **Korea**—an Asian country where UN forces fought Communist troops

New Dates

31. **1914**—World War I began; Francis Ferdinand assassinated
32. **1915**—the *Lusitania* was sunk
33. **1917**—the United States entered World War I
34. **1918**—World War I ended
35. **1939**—Germany and Russia invaded Poland; World War II began
36. **1941**—Germany defeated France; the Japanese bombed Pearl Harbor; the United States entered World War II; Germany attacked Russia
37. **1943**—Italy surrendered to the Allies
38. **1945**—Germany surrendered; the United States dropped two atomic bombs on Japan; Japan surrendered, bringing World War II to a close; the United Nations was formed
39. **1950**—the Korean War began
40. **1975**—the Vietnam War ended

During World War I, the Germans used U-boats to destroy any ships that might be carrying food or supplies to England.

rines. This is a type of warship that moves under the water where it cannot be seen. The submarine is able to fire torpedoes through the water at an enemy ship. Upon hitting the ship, the torpedo explodes, destroying the enemy ship.

The Germans used the U-boats to destroy any ships that could be carrying food or supplies to England. The United States claimed to be neutral, but she continued to send ships to England. As a result, the Germans began sinking United States ships sailing in the waters around England.

The Sinking of the Lusitania

In May, 1915, an English passenger liner, the *Lusitania,* left New York on

its way to England. As it neared England, a German U-boat, without any warning, sent a torpedo into the side of the *Lusitania*. The ship sank quickly. Over a thousand men, women, and children lost their lives. Over one hundred of those killed were Americans.

Americans became very angry. Although there was talk of war, the United States decided to stay neutral.

The United States Enters World War I

In 1917, a German letter was discovered, asking Mexico to enter the war on the German side. This letter was called the **Zimmermann Note.** If Mexico was willing to help, Germany promised to give Mexico land from the

Americans became very angry when a German U-boat sank the *Lusitania,* an English passenger liner.

states of New Mexico, Texas, and Arizona. In other words, *Germany was promising Mexico part of the United States if Germany won the war!* Although Mexico did not help Germany, you can imagine how angry Americans became at the German threat to break up and divide the United States.

It was plain to see that the German ruler would stop at nothing. If the German ruler won in Europe, he would go after America. Our country was being threatened. Those who loved the United States realized we had no other choice but to enter the war.

In April, 1917, the United States declared war on Germany. President Wilson read a war message in which he said, "**The world must be made safe for democracy.**" The United States joined the Allies.

In France, the French cheered the American soldiers as French bands played "The Star-Spangled Banner." The coming of the American troops gave a new hope to the Allies of Europe.

And so the Germans met a brand new, fresh army. The German army had begun to weaken. With American help, the French and British began beating back the Germans. No battle was easy. Each day, each country fighting lost hundreds of lives. These

For the first time in history, battles took place in the air as the recently-invented airplane became a deadly weapon of war.

People everywhere were joyful when the war ended. Parades and celebrations were held in many cities.

men felt that their countries were worth fighting for.

The fighting was long and hard, but finally the Central Powers surrendered. *It was agreed that on* **November 11, 1918,** *all fighting would stop.* On that date, World War I came to an end. (Today, November 11 is celebrated as **Veterans Day,** honoring all those who have fought for our country in any war.)

The League of Nations

You will remember that when the United States entered the war, President Wilson said that "the world must be made safe for democracy." With this in mind, Wilson suggested that a **League of Nations** be formed. In his plan, all the countries who joined the League of Nations would promise not

to make war on any other nation that was a member of the League.

A League of Nations was formed. The building for the League of Nations was built in **Geneva, Switzerland.** Although sixty countries joined, the United States refused to become a part of it. The people of the United States were afraid that joining the League of Nations would involve the United States in other wars between the countries of Europe rather than keeping us out of war.

President Wilson was disappointed that his own country did not join the League, but the people of the United States were happy that the war was over. We had been the added strength the Allies needed to win the war. The Americans who had fought in Europe were coming back home to their families. Americans wanted to do their best to forget about war.

Between the World Wars

The Roaring Twenties

By the beginning of 1920, most Americans turned their thoughts from war to happier times. *Factories stopped making war supplies and began making products that would change the style of living in America.* In a few years a housewife did not have to wash her clothes in a tub on a scrub board anymore. She could buy a washing machine. Later, toasters, vacuum cleaners, and refrigerators were a few more products a family could choose to buy to make their lives a little easier.

The invention of the radio gave Americans another product to buy. In the evenings, many American families sat quietly around their radios listening to news, music, and programs. The radio was exciting, but everyone had to listen quietly. The first radios made a crackling sound, which sometimes made it difficult to hear the program.

For the first time, many families were able to enjoy beautiful music and interesting programs on the radio. They could now hear the latest news even while it was happening. They could all listen to the President and other leaders

Listeners had to strain their ears to hear the weak signals from the early radios. Loud static also made listening difficult.

give speeches, no matter where they lived.

The first President to give his inaugural address over the radio was **Calvin Coolidge**, in 1925. Families gathered around the radio heard the new President talk about America's history and America's future. "Because of what America is and what America has done," President Coolidge said, "a firmer courage, a higher hope, aspires the heart of all humanity." Then he gave Americans a challenge to learn from their history. "We can not continue these brilliant successes in the future," he said, "unless we continue to learn from the past."

The radio also brought the gospel message to many people who could not or would not go to church, as many great preachers spread the message of salvation over the airwaves.

Automobiles were becoming more and more popular. Special highways were being built for automobile traffic. These roads amazed the people of the 1920's. How surprised these people would have been if they could have looked ahead to see the modern, wide highways of today. And how surprised they would have been if they could have seen those highways filled with millions upon millions of cars, in every size, shape and color!

It became a tradition for the whole family to go for a drive in the country on Sunday afternoons. And it became much easier to visit grandparents and other relatives who lived in a different part of the country.

During the 1920's, business was excellent. Factories made more and more products. More workers were hired to make more products. So carefree were the years of the 1920's, that they came to be known as the "Roaring Twenties."

The Great Depression

In October, 1929, hard times came to our country. The banks ran out of money, and people did not have money to buy things. Factories closed down.

There were no new jobs. Without jobs, how could people make a living?

As weeks turned into months, people began to go hungry. There was no money to buy food. In our own United States, people began to stand in bread lines to be given enough bread and soup to keep from starving. Even though prices dropped very low, people still could not afford to buy food, clothes, or factory goods. People began to lose their homes because they could not pay their bills.

These sad years in our country became known as the **Great Depression**. *It lasted for about ten years* (1929–1940). Millions of United States citizens suffered. Their spirits were good, though, and families and individuals worked together to make the best of what they had. People who went through these years look back on them as a time when God helped in special ways when all else seemed to fail.

The government began working to see how it could end the Great Depression. President Franklin D. Roosevelt thought of a way to create jobs through projects such as building highways, dams, and bridges. The men who worked on these projects were paid by the government. But the government was just as poor as everyone else. Where did the money come from to pay

During the Great Depression, many people in the United States had to stand in bread lines to keep from starving.

these men? In a risky move, the government began to spend more money than it had. If you go into a store and try to spend more money than you have, you'll eventually get into trouble! The government got into trouble, too. It saw that printing so much money was causing the value of the dollar to go down. This has troubled the American economy ever since. Though the government helped people temporarily during the Depression, some of the policies set up then have caused serious problems that are still with us today.

Sometimes it seemed as though the Great Depression would never end, although by the late 1930's things were improving a little. Men found jobs again and earned money to buy food, clothes, and other products. But only

when America went to war again did the last traces of the Great Depression disappear.

Plans for Peace That Failed

Peace-loving countries remembered World War I with horror. The United States, Great Britain, France, Italy, and Japan decided on a plan to reduce or cut back on the number of weapons and the size of the armed forces that a country has. They agreed that no new battleships were to be built for ten years.

Immediately, the United States, England, and France began to cut back on their weapons. They felt sure of peace. They did not realize that Italy and Japan had no thought of keeping their promise. *While the United States was making her navy smaller and less powerful, Japan was secretly making hers stronger.*

To make matters worse, Germany began to build an even stronger navy and army than she had during World War I. *Secretly, Germany's factories began making war materials again with plans to build new and powerful bombs with planes to carry them.*

The World between the Wars

The United States was not the only country to suffer from the Great Depression. The war-torn countries of Europe knew nothing but hunger and poverty as they worked to rebuild their cities after World War I.

It is only natural that people would want to pull themselves out of the hard times they were experiencing. Unfortunately, the people of Russia, Germany, and Italy began listening to men who wanted to become more powerful, even if it was through war. Eager to see better times, many people believed the promises of these men to make their country powerful.

New forms of government came to power. Germany and Italy were taken over by dictators.

Japan, which had been ruled by an emperor for years, began to be ruled more and more by its military forces.

Let's take a look at the changes that took place in Russia, Italy, Germany, and Japan. Then perhaps you will see why there was another world war.

Russia—Communism

Just before the end of World War I, the Communist party took over control of Russia. In a free country such as ours, people can own their own businesses, homes, and land. When **communism** takes over a country, the government steals these things from the people and claims to own them. The people *must* work for the communist government or suffer great losses. Although the people in Russia can vote, their vote does not affect the government. Usually they have only one candidate to vote for—the Communist candidate!

In Russia, the Communist party allows no freedom of speech, press, or religion. It is a Communist goal to control other countries. The Communists believe that when communism takes control of the world, Christianity will disappear. By 1924, **Joseph Stalin** had become the Communist dictator in Russia. In 1939, he made an agreement with Adolph Hitler, who was then the dictator of Germany. He promised to help Germany if there was another war.

Benito Mussolini (left) was the Fascist dictator of Italy; Adolph Hitler (right) was the Nazi dictator of Germany.

Italy—Fascism

After World War I, Russia's Communist party said Russia would gain control of other countries. The people of Italy feared that communists would take over Italy. A man named **Benito Mussolini** promised the Italians he would save them from communism. The people believed him and let him become their leader.

It was true that Mussolini hated communism, but Mussolini himself became a harsh dictator. He allowed no other government party in Italy but his, which was called **the Fascist party.**

Although the people owned their own property, they could not do with their property as they thought best, and thus they lost their freedoms. Anyone who dared to disobey Mussolini was killed or put into prison. *The people who had feared communism found themselves trapped by something that was almost as bad.*

The Italians listened as Mussolini told them that Italy would become powerful. He began building one of the strongest armies in Europe.

Germany—National Socialism

After World War I, the German people were poor and discouraged from war. They wanted a leader who could lead them out from under their problems. The **National Socialist,** or **Nazi** form of government promised to make Germany a powerful nation, free from problems. Hearing these promises, many German people became eager to follow the National Socialist leader, **Adolph Hitler.** In doing so, *they gave up their freedom and came under the rule of one of the cruelest dictators the world has ever known.*

Like communism, National Socialism is against freedom. Nazism teaches (1) that the leader and the government of a country are all-powerful and are more important than the people of that country; (2) that all people are *not* equal in worth, but some groups of people (such as Jews) are inferior; and (3) that the leader can do no wrong. Everyone in Germany was forced to obey the harsh National Socialist laws. No one could even disagree. Those who complained were put into jails or killed.

The Nazi leader, Adolph Hitler, expected everyone to be loyal to him. He hated anyone that was loyal to someone else. Hitler hated Jewish people and blamed the problems of Germany on them. One of the most horrible things that Hitler did was to kill millions of people, including several million Jews, God's special people.

Hitler tried to make the German people think that Germans were superior to other peoples of the world.

"The Germans should conquer and rule the world," Hitler told his people. With this in mind, Hitler built a powerful army, navy, and air force.

Japan—Militarism

Before and during World War II, **Hirohito** was the emperor or the ruler of Japan. Japan had a very powerful army and navy. The *military* leaders—especially a general named **Tojo**— became more powerful than the emperor. The emperor had no choice but to go along with the military leaders' wishes.

The plan of Japan's military leaders was to conquer and rule Asia. As early as 1931, Japan began attacking China.

The Attacks Begin

The government leaders of Russia, Italy, Germany, and Japan each gained powerful control over the people of their country. Although each ruler represented a different kind of government, each was the same in its selfish desires to gain control of other countries, thus becoming powerful in the world's eyes.

Germany began attacking the small, weak countries of Europe. Italy attacked the tiny country of Ethiopia on the continent of Africa. Japan attacked China. Russia watched and waited. With all this happening, could there possibly not be another world war?

What was the reaction of the rest of the world? They criticized these countries for attacking others, but they did nothing to stop them. They told themselves that Germany would stop soon on her own. And China and Ethiopia seemed so far away that the people of Europe were not concerned. Everyone else was tired of fighting, and they had no wish to begin another war.

This delighted Hitler. With each new country he conquered, he told the world, "I am satisfied now. I will stop." Then suddenly his army would conquer another country.

With the coming of the 1940's, there were German people who did not trust Hitler; there were Russians who hated communism; there were Italians who disagreed with Mussolini; and there were Japanese who disliked the idea of war. Yet each group of people was powerless to stop the plans of its government.

Once again, the lights were beginning to go out all over Europe.

World War II

Germany Conquers

By 1939, Hitler's army had taken over the small countries of Austria and Czechoslovakia. Now Hitler demanded that **Poland** give up a piece of her land to Germany. Poland refused. Troubled by Hitler's desire to conquer, *England and France both warned Hitler that if he attacked Poland, they would help Poland.*

Meanwhile, Germany and Russia made a secret agreement to divide Poland once it was conquered. The Germans then invaded Poland. *England and France kept their word and declared war on Germany. This was the beginning of World War II.* Next, the Russian army marched into Poland. With two powerful armies attacking

Franklin D. Roosevelt was President during the Great Depression and World War II.

Poland, there was little that England and France could do. In less than three weeks, Poland was defeated and divided between her enemies, Germany and Russia. Another light had been snuffed out in Europe.

In April, 1940, Germany attacked and defeated Norway and Denmark. In May, Germany defeated the three small countries of Belgium, the Netherlands, and Luxembourg. From there, Germany entered France and defeated her.

The free countries of the world were alarmed when France fell under German rule. Now, Great Britain was the only free country left in Europe not occupied by Germany. Great Britain begged the United States for help.

This airplane factory —producing hundreds of bombers for the war—shows why Roosevelt called America the "great arsenal of democracy."

"The Great Arsenal of Democracy"

At that time, **Franklin D. Roosevelt** was President of the United States. The defeat of France shocked the American people. The cries for "peace at any price" began to die out. Our country's factories began to make war supplies and our armed forces began to build up our navy, army, marines, and air force. Although we still had not entered the war, we had to be prepared in case of an attack. Many guns and war supplies were either sold or loaned to Great Britain and other countries struggling against the enemies. Because of this, President Roosevelt called the United States "the great arsenal of democracy."

Germany Attacks England

Since England is an island surrounded by water, Germany could not send its armies marching into her, but Hitler could send his airplanes to drop bombs over England. The Battle of Britain began.

For three months, German planes dropped bombs on England. Each day, Hitler expected England to give up, but the people of England fought hard. England's air force was finally able to beat back the Germans. Though the war was far from over, the United States was relieved. Great Britain had not been conquered.

Russia Is Surprised

Since both Hitler and Mussolini hated communism, perhaps you have wondered why Russia was fighting on Germany's side. Do you suppose Communist Russia could trust a dictator who hated communism? For that matter, do you suppose anyone could have trusted Hitler?

Hitler had been planning a surprise attack on Russia. If Russia was defeated, Hitler could then force Russia to provide Germany with food and supplies. Russian people could be forced to make war supplies for Germany.

In June, 1941, Germany attacked Russia. The Russian armies were surprised, but the Russian people pulled together and fought hard. Joseph Stalin, Russia's dictator, now turned and asked for help from England and the United States. Because Russia was now willing to fight against Nazism, England agreed to help.

However, *it was the cold Russian winter that helped Russia most of all.* It was now December. The German soldiers had no warm winter clothing. Their food froze. Their trucks and tanks froze. Slowly but surely, the Russian army beat the Germans back.

Three Wars in One

Although our attention has been on the fighting in Europe, we must remember that there was fighting on three continents—Europe, Africa, and Asia. Germany's Hitler led the war to conquer Europe; Italy's Mussolini led the war to conquer and control the riches found in Africa; and Japan's military leaders set out to conquer Asia and the islands in the Pacific.

These three leaders were alike in their selfish goals. *Together, Germany, Italy, and Japan were known as the* **Axis powers.**

Those countries who struggled against them were called the Allied Powers, or **Allies.** *At that time, the three most powerful Allies were Great Britain, Russia, and China. The United States would soon join the Allies.*

If you look at a world map and find the three continents of Europe, Africa, and Asia, you will see how spread out World War II was. This war involved more of the world than World War I had.

Yet this one big war was really three smaller wars—one in Europe, one in Africa, and one in Asia and the surrounding islands. It became clear to the Allies that all three enemies would have to be defeated if World War II was to come to an end.

The United States Enters World War II

On one of the beautiful islands of Hawaii, there is an important United States navy base called **Pearl Harbor.** Now that airplanes had been improved and were used for war as well as peace, it was important that the Hawaiian

The United States was totally unprepared for the bombing of Pearl Harbor.

Islands be protected. If an enemy took control of Hawaii, it would not be long before the West Coast of the United States would be in danger of enemy air attacks.

You will remember that Japan wanted to control Asia and the islands in the Pacific. *"The power of the United States Navy must be destroyed,"* *the Japanese military leaders told each other.* "If Pearl Harbor is destroyed, it would be too hard for the Americans to bring other ships to the Pacific Ocean. Besides," the Japanese boasted, "Americans would rather give up than fight."

To trick the Americans, Japan sent men to Washington, D.C., to talk about making peace. Meanwhile, the Japanese secretly prepared to attack. There would be a gigantic air raid on Pearl Harbor.

Without any warning, on Sunday morning, December 7, 1941, nearly 200 Japanese planes flew over Pearl Harbor. They quickly destroyed the American planes sitting on the airfields. Eight battleships had been part of our Pacific navy. Seven of them were either sunk or badly damaged. Over 2,000 American men were killed.

Later on that day, Americans who were listening to their radios were shocked to hear their programs interrupted by an emergency news report—"Pearl Harbor has been bombed."

Now Americans realized how serious this war had become. "Peace at any price" would most likely cost them their freedom. Instead of peace, they now cried for war. *On December 8, 1941, we declared war on Japan. Soon afterwards, Germany and Italy declared war on the United States.*

Victory Comes at Last

More battles were fought during World War II than can possibly be described here. The United States had joined the Allies. The Allies had before them a gigantic job of defeating three powerful enemies—Italy, Germany, and Japan. Different battles were fought in different places of the world at the same time. American men fought in the Pacific Ocean, China, the Mediterranean Sea, Africa, Europe, and the Atlantic Ocean.

In 1943, after fighting in North Africa, Italy surrendered to the Allies.

Next, the Allies turned their strongest attention upon Europe. Many Allies fought to free France. Soon afterwards, the Allies were attacking the country of Germany. *Germany was forced to surrender on May 7, 1945. This is called V-E Day (Victory in Europe Day).*

Japan remained the only enemy for the Allies to defeat. She had learned since Pearl Harbor that Americans were hard, courageous fighters. Although the United States Navy in the Pacific was almost destroyed by the attack on Pearl Harbor, within a year our navy was repaired and built back up again.

The Japanese had suffered much loss during the war, but they refused to surrender. The military leaders of Japan seemed to care little about the thousands of their own people who were being killed in each battle and air raid

A World War II bombing mission

upon their cities as well as the thousands who died fighting against them. Yet the Allies knew that Japan must surrender or freedom in the countries of Asia would still be in danger.

The United States had to make a hard decision. The powerful and very destructive atomic bomb had been invented. Should it be used to bring the war in Japan to a quick end? The decision was made. *On August 6, 1945, an atomic bomb was dropped over the Japanese city of Hiroshima. A few days later, another bomb was dropped on Nagasaki. Both cities were destroyed.* **The Japanese quickly surrendered**. World War II had come to an end.

All wars are cruel. World War II was perhaps the cruelest war the world had ever known. One of the cruelest things that happened was not fully discovered until after the war. The Allied soldiers found prison camps (called concentration camps) where men, women, and children had been penned up with very little food. In Germany and other lands held by Hitler, millions of people had been heartlessly massacred. Included in these numbers were several million Jewish people.

Again, America had been blessed. No enemies had fought in and destroyed our cities, as had happened in other parts of the world. The soldiers of other

A Japanese aircraft carrier being bombed by American planes.

countries had to return to a poor and war-torn country. Those from America returned to peaceful homes and a powerful nation. Once again, the United States left the war as the most powerful nation in the world.

The war had done much to help Americans feel united for their country. Everyone wanted to do his or her part. Even the women, who could not fight, went to work in factories to help make weapons and supplies for the soldiers. Americans knew that they were fighting for a good, just cause, and their spirit throughout the war years was one of unity and patriotism.

After the World Wars

The United Nations

As World War II was coming to an end, many Americans hoped for a lasting peace. Yet many had hoped for this at the close of World War I. What was there to prevent the coming of a third war? You will remember that at the closing of World War I, President Woodrow Wilson planned a League of Nations wherein the countries of the world could talk out their problems peacefully. Although the League of Nations was formed, the people of the United States did not want to become a part of it. They were afraid that being a member of the League would force them to fight in other countries' wars. Many of them also realized that not

every country in the world can be trusted, even if it promises to be friendly.

President Franklin Roosevelt began to dream of another world organization made up of nations that would work together to settle their problems. This organization would be called the **United Nations,** or the UN.

Franklin Roosevelt died before the United Nations came into being and before World War II came to an end. If the President of the United States dies

These soldiers are preparing to land on the beach and fight a battle.

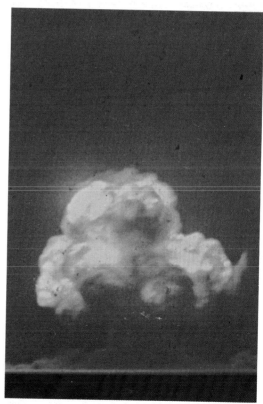

The atom bomb brought a quick end to World War II.

while he is still in office, the vice president takes his place. Vice president **Harry S. Truman** took Roosevelt's place.

Before he died, President Roosevelt wrote a speech telling how the United Nations could help people by using "scientific" methods. "We must cultivate the science of human relations," he wrote, "the ability of all people, of all kinds, to live together and work together, in the same world, at peace." Science can bring us wonderful things, but peace comes from a kind of understanding that science can never bring. Roosevelt did not understand this, and neither did many people around the world.

In 1945, men from many different countries held a meeting in San Francisco, California, to make important decisions about forming the United Nations. The United States was the first nation to join the UN. Other nations quickly followed. By the end of that first meeting in San Francisco, fifty nations had joined the UN. Later a building was built for the UN in New York City.

The UN meets in these headquarters in New York City. The UN has failed to bring about world peace.

been fought around the world! Over one billion people have become slaves under communism, and more than forty million people have been executed by the communists. The United Nations has not been able to preserve the rights of these people.

Each member nation of the UN is supposed to share in the expenses of the United Nations, but many do not do their part. Most of the money to support the United Nations has come from the United States. When countries have needed protection, most of the soldiers have been Americans.

Since the United States gives the United Nations so much financial (money) support and does most of the fighting that is needed when member countries are in trouble, you would think that the United States would have

The Failure of the United Nations

The United Nations has failed in its dream of ending wars. Since its charter was signed, over seventy-five wars have a great deal of say in how the United Nations is run. This is not true. More than half the UN member nations have a population smaller than that of New York City, and yet their vote counts just as much as the vote of the United States. The country that really has the most say is Russia. This is because Russia has ways of forcing all the countries of Eastern Europe to vote the way Russia wants. Other countries that are controlled by communism, such as Cuba, many of the countries in South America and Central America, and many of the African nations, are also very careful to follow the leading of Russia.

The United Nations has failed to end wars and bring about world peace, and many people think it has helped to spread communism.

Communism Becomes a Greater Problem

Although World War II defeated nazism in Germany, fascism in Italy, and militarism in Japan, it did not defeat communism in Russia.

You will remember that Russia was willing to work together with Germany until Germany attacked her. It was only then that Russia decided to join the Allies. Although Russia supposedly fought with us to free Europe from Nazi rule, it soon became clear that she meant to control the small, helpless countries in which the Nazis were just defeated.

The Communists spread their influence from Europe into Asia. Communists took control of China. Once again, the people of freedom-loving countries became fearful.

Berlin Is Divided

Berlin is the biggest city in Germany. However, after World War II, it was divided into two parts. West Berlin became free and independent. East Berlin fell under Communist Russia's rule.

The people of East Berlin have no freedom, and many of them tried to escape to the freedom of West Berlin. In

The Berlin Wall has become a symbol of communism. Communism does not allow men to be free.

289

These marines are fighting a battle against North Koreans. Most of the UN forces in Korea were made up of Americans.

1961 the Communists built a wall that divides the city in two. The wall is guarded so that few have a chance to escape. The Berlin Wall has become a dark and frightening symbol of communism.

The Korean War

The small country of **Korea** is located in Asia. *At the end of World War II, Korea was divided into two parts.* The northern half was placed under the control of Russia. The southern half was under the control of the United States.

In South Korea, the people were allowed to hold elections. They set up a democratic government. In North Korea, the Russians set up a communist government. The United Nations again

failed in that it was able to do nothing to protect the rights of these people against Communist invaders.

The Communists had made it clear that it is their desire to gain control of other countries. Now the Communists wanted South Korea as well as North Korea. *In 1950, Communist North Korea invaded South Korea.* The UN ordered North Korea to stop fighting, but North Korea would not obey.

The United Nations sent an army to South Korea. Although men from the United States made up most of this army, fifteen other nations also sent troops to help South Korea. This was called the Korean War. After three years of fighting, a **truce** or agreement to stop fighting was signed. In this agreement, North Korea was to remain under Communist control and South Korea was to be free.

Communism and Democracy

Since the end of World War II, communism and democracy have remained bitter enemies. The aims of these two kinds of governments are completely opposite:

- The Communists believe that the people exist to help the government, while the democracies believe that the government exists to help the people.
- The Communist Party allows its people no freedom of choice, while a democracy abounds in freedom.
- The Communist Party wants to take control of as much of the world as it can, while a democracy believes that each country has the right to choose its government.
- The Communist leaders use brutal force in ruling their people; they use horrible torture tactics, such as slave labor camps, imprisonment, etc.
- The Communist leaders are atheistic (they do not believe in God). They teach the children there is no God.

The differences between the two kinds of government have caused many arguments and wars. The United States left World War II as the strongest nation in the world, but Russia was not far behind us.

The Communists have bragged that they will one day control the United States. Many Americans believe that if we are to protect our own country, we must help others in their fight against communism. This led to fighting in **Vietnam** which ended in 1975, with the Communists taking over that country. Democratic countries have formed alliances, promising to help each other in case of a Communist attack. The free countries of the world want to do their part to make the world safe for democracy.

The Communists have overthrown many governments and forced their control upon the people. In 1959 Fidel Castro did this in Cuba, which is just 90 miles off the coast of Florida. Many South and Central American countries have been taken over by communism. Many countries in Africa are now controlled by the Communists. The Communists have continued to push ahead in their goal to rule the world. The future of the world does look grim for lovers of democracy. We should be thankful to live in a country like the United States where we still have many freedoms. We should daily pray for our national leaders that we "may lead a quiet and peaceable life in all godliness and honesty" (I Timothy 2:2). As Christians we know there can never be true worldwide peace until Jesus Christ comes again.

Facts to Remember

1. What is nationalism? _____

   _____

   How did some men twist nationalism and make it a bad thing? _____

   _____

2. What is a dictator? _____

   _____

3. Who was Germany's leader in 1914? _____

4. What are *alliances*? _____

   _____

5. What happened on June 28, 1914 that caused World War I to begin? _____

   _____

6. Who was President during World War I? _____

7. What did the Germans use which made them victorious on the seas? _____

   _____

8. The sinking of what ship in 1915 by the Germans made the Americans very

   angry? _____

9. What note caused America to enter World War I? _____

   Why did the note make Americans so angry? _____

   _____

10. Who won World War I? _____

    When did the fighting stop? _____

11. What was formed after World War I in an effort to keep war from breaking out again? _____

12. Name two products which changed the lives and habits of millions of Americans during the 1920's. _____

13. What are the years of the 1920's called? _____

14. What caused the Great Depression? _____

_____

What did the government do to try to end the Depression? _____

_____

Was this a wise policy? _____

15. What two countries began to build up their armed forces after World War I?

_____

16. What happens when communism takes over a country? _____

_____

17. Who was the Communist dictator of Russia?_____

18. Who was the Fascist dictator of Italy?_____

19. How are people treated under Fascism? _____

_____

20. Who was the Nazi dictator of Germany? _____

21. What three things did Nazism teach? _____

_____

22. What general built up a powerful military dictatorship in Japan? _____

23. The invasion of what country started World War II? _____

24. What countries did Germany defeat during the first years of the war? _____

_____

25. Who was President during World War II? _____

26. On what three continents was World War II fought? _____

_____

27. Who made up the Axis powers? _____

_____

28. Who were the Allies? _____

_____

29. What caused the United States to enter World War II? _____

_____

30. When did the fighting in Africa stop? _____

31. When did the fighting in Europe stop? _____

32. What caused the Japanese to surrender? _____

_____

33. What was formed after World War II to preserve world peace? _____

Has it succeeded in that task? _____

34. What city was divided when the Communists built a wall there? _____

35. What event in 1950 started the Korean War? _____

_____

36. Who fought the North Koreans in the Korean War? _____

Where did most of the soldiers fighting the North Koreans come from?_____

_____

37. What is a truce? _____

_____

38. How long did the Korean War last?_____

39. Name three ways in which communism and democracy differ. _____

_____

_____

_____

40. What war ended in 1975 with a Communist victory?_____

Today's Efforts, Tomorrow's Challenges

The United States is continuously working for progress. Progress means moving ahead. If we are to stay a powerful nation to which the other nations of the world look for an example of democracy, we cannot stand still.

Science has played an important part in the progress of our nation. Man, through the study of science, is continuously at work to make improvements. Let's look at how science has helped our nation in the twentieth century to make both progress and history.

Medicine

Thousands of Americans work each day in the research of diseases and the development of medicines, so that the people of the United States and of the world can live longer and healthier lives.

Polio

Although no one likes to go to the doctor, you can be very thankful you have the opportunity to get **immunized** against polio. In the early 1950's, this terrible disease was rapidly increasing in the United States, with no way to stop it from crippling or even killing children and young adults. Then **Dr. Jonas Salk** successfully developed and tested a **vaccine** to prevent polio. As soon as the vaccine was put into use, the cases of polio began to drop. As a result, today polio is no longer a dreaded disease for those who go to their doctor to get immunized.

Steps Forward

Since the 1950's, many steps have been taken to reduce the number of diseases. People learned that they could prevent many diseases themselves by taking better care of themselves, eating the right foods, getting the proper rest, and seeing their doctors regularly.

Medicines have also been developed to prevent certain diseases. Once every parent could expect his child at some time to come down with measles or mumps. Today, there are vaccines to prevent these illnesses. And thanks to other medical advances, some dreadful diseases such as tuberculosis and scarlet fever are rarely heard of today.

Surgery has taken giant steps forward. Modern equipment and scientific research have made it possible to save many lives through specialized surgery.

Of course, medicine still has a long way to go. Scientists and doctors are still working on ways to cure or prevent such medical problems as heart disease, cancer, and even the common cold.

Space

In 1957, Russia surprised the world by announcing that it was the first country to *launch* a *satellite* into space. This

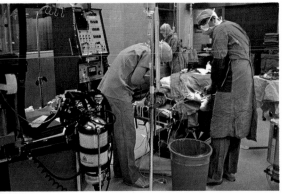

Surgery has taken giant steps forward. The top picture shows surgeons and their equipment in the early days of this century; below it is a photograph of a modern surgery ward.

The Russian *Sputnik I* was the first man-made satellite launched into orbit.

satellite, called *Sputnik I,* circled the earth, sending back information to the Russians. *This started a "space race" between Russia and the United States,* for many Americans were afraid that Russia was becoming stronger than we were. A few months later, in 1958, the United States sent its first satellite, named *Explorer I,* into space.

John Glenn, seen here getting into his space capsule, was the first American to orbit the earth. This trip in 1962 took him five hours. He circled the earth three times.

Alan Shepard became the first American to go into outer space. This photo shows his spacecraft lifting off the launch pad.

In 1961, Russia was the first country to send a man into space. That same year, **Alan B. Shepard, Jr.,** became the first American to go into outer space. In 1962, **John Glenn** became the first American to *orbit* or circle the earth. Russians call a man who has been sent into space a **cosmonaut.** The people of the United States call their spacemen **astronauts.**

New Words

1. **immunize**—to make a person safe from certain diseases
2. **vaccine**—a substance which is put into the body so that the body will build up the ability to fight off a disease
3. **cosmonaut**—the Russian name for a man who has been shot into space
4. **astronaut**—the American name for a man who has been shot into space
5. **blizzard**—a heavy snowstorm with a very strong wind
6. **solar energy**—energy which comes from the sun
7. **nuclear energy**—the energy released when atoms are split

New Names

8. **Dr. Jonas Salk**—the man who developed the polio vaccine during the 1950's
9. *Sputnik I*—Russia's first successful satellite
10. *Explorer I*—America's first successful satellite
11. **Alan Shepard**—the first American to travel into outer space

During the 1960's, both Russia and the United States continued their space race, sending many flights into space. The United States now expressed a new desire in their space program—to land a man on the moon by the end of the 1960's. This was called the Apollo Program.

During Christmas 1968, many Americans watched a wonderful event. The

The earth looked like this to the astronauts on the Apollo 8 mission.

Apollo 8 astronauts were circling the moon. As Americans sat in their homes watching this event on their television sets, they saw and heard the astronauts read the first ten verses of Genesis, beginning with "In the beginning God created the heaven and the earth," and ending with "And God called the dry land Earth; and the gathering together of the waters called he Seas: and God saw that it was good."

Then they heard the astronauts say,

And from the crew of Apollo 8, we close with good night, good luck, and Merry Christmas, and God bless all of you—all of you on the good earth.

Once again Americans gave witness to the entire world of the courage and faith that have been a part of our heritage since our nation was founded.

There were many Apollo flights.

In 1969, the dreams of many Americans came true when two American astronauts from **Apollo 11** *successfully landed and walked on the moon.* These

12. **John Glenn**—the first American to orbit the earth
13. **Apollo 11**—the space mission which made the first landing on the moon
14. **Neil Armstrong**—the first human being who ever set foot on the moon

New Dates

15. 1957—*Sputnik I,* Russia's first satellite, was launched into space
16. 1958—*Explorer I,* America's first satellite, was launched into space

17. 1961—Russia sent the first man into space; later that year, Alan Shepard became the first American to go into space
18. 1962—John Glenn became the first American to orbit the earth
19. 1969—Neil Armstrong became the first man to set foot on the moon
20. 1971—the "moon rover" was used for the first time
21. 1972—America's moon program ended
22. 1973—Skylab was launched into orbit

men were **Neil Armstrong** and Edwin Aldrin, Jr. When Armstrong took his first steps on the moon, he spoke these famous words: **"That's one small step for man, one giant leap for mankind."** Of course, that giant leap was progress, for never before had man walked on the moon.

There were other moon flights. In all, twelve astronauts walked on the moon. In December, 1972, the moon program was over. But the space program continues. In May, 1973, the first Skylab was launched. This spaceship was so large that it had bedrooms and workshops for the many astronauts it was able to carry. Through the use of Skylabs, it has been proven that man can live and work in space for several months.

You may be asking, "How did these space flights help our country? What

The lunar rover was designed to drive over the surface of the moon.

did they do to help me?" To answer these questions, we must go back to the years when men experimented with satellites.

Before any man could be sent into space, important information had to be learned. To do this, high-powered rockets had to be developed that could carry a satellite beyond the earth's atmosphere. This was done and many sat-

Satellites help us in our everyday lives. At the left, a Telstar communications satellite is being prepared for launching. At the right, a Tiros weather satellite is seen in orbit around the earth.

ellites were sent into space. Each of the satellites had special instruments to do special jobs. Today, satellites still do important work for us, such as

...telling the weather.

The United States launches weather satellites that are able to send back pictures and information that help weathermen predict the weather with fewer mistakes. This is especially helpful when harmful storms such as hurricanes develop. Now, thanks to weather satellites, people can be warned ahead of time of most disastrous storms.

...defending our country.

Other satellites have been developed and are being used to warn the United States if enemy *missiles* are launched against us anywhere in the world. These are called military satellites. Although we hope we will never need them, these

Many hospitals are now using special equipment made of space-age materials to save lives. This cradle warmer, designed to keep a very sick newborn baby warm, is one such piece of equipment.

satellites could help us if an enemy tried to attack our country.

...communicating over long distances.

Imagine sitting in your home in the United States and watching a television news program live from London, England, or other cities all over the world! This is possible through satellites which are developed to send pictures all over the world or even from outer space. Imagine the world's wonder, when on July 20, 1969, a satellite sent pictures of man's first walk on the moon to people watching television here on earth! Then in 1971, people watched again as American astronauts used a special car called "the moon rover" or "moon buggy" built especially for the moon, to drive over the surface of the moon.

Thanks to satellites developed for communications, we are better informed of what is happening in the world around us.

Space Age Man-Made Materials

Spacecrafts have to be built out of materials that will hold up under temperatures of extreme heat and cold. Astronauts' space suits have to be made out of special materials to protect the men who will wear them. It took many years of study to develop and improve these materials. Many different kinds of plastics have been developed, some of which you probably already use in your home.

These and other man-made materials, developed through space research, can be found in many places besides the home.

Many places of sports and recreation have benefited by space age research. One of these is the Silverdome in Pontiac, Michigan. The Silverdome is a large, year-round, all-purpose stadium. To keep out the cold winter weather of Michigan, the stadium was built with a roof. This roof is very special. It is made from the same material that was developed for astronauts' space suits!

Think for a moment how strong the material for an astronaut's suit must be. It must also be lightweight, it cannot shrink or stretch, and it must be flame resistant. This same material is also weather resistant. All of these qualities in the space suit material can be found in the Silverdome's roof!

Of course, there are hundreds of other ways space research has helped our country. Without realizing it, the research of the space age has touched and affected nearly every citizen of the United States. And scientists are still at work to find ways to develop the ideas learned in space research to produce progress for our nation and a better way of life for us.

Energy

As our nation has continued to grow stronger, so has our need for energy continued to grow. In fact, a nation's growth and its increasing need for energy seem to go hand in hand. For example, a poorer country where the people have few cars and little electricity has a smaller demand for energy than a growing country where nearly every family has at least one car and nearly all homes have electricity.

Energy is important because it keeps our country moving. Perhaps you have been in a bad storm when the electricity went off. Until the electricity came back

The Silverdome in Pontiac, Michigan, has a roof made of the same material that was used to make spacesuits.

Solar energy (energy from the sun) is a good source of power. This elementary school in Atlanta, Georgia, gets all of its power from the sun. The panels on the roof of the school are collecting sunlight, which is then converted to electrical energy. Solar panels are being used more and more on schools, office buildings, and homes.

on, you had to depend on candles. If the storm was a **blizzard,** you were fortunate if you had a fireplace or a wood-burning stove to keep you warm. If the electricity was off long enough, the food in your refrigerator began to get warm. The food in the freezer began to thaw and there was no electric stove to prepare your dinner. If you have ever been in a situation like this, you must have been very happy when the electricity came back on in your house.

Now think what it would be like if our whole nation suddenly lacked the energy to make electricity and there were no fuels to run our motor vehicles. We would be forced to live as they did in colonial days when each family had

to care for itself and supply its own needs. The progress we have made in the last two centuries would be gone.

The United States produces and uses more energy than any other country in the world. Because of the great demand for energy to run our factories, warm our homes, heat and refrigerate our food, and provide us with means of transportation and communication, Americans keep working on new and better ways of producing energy.

Our natural resources are those we get from nature. *A few of our natural resources are water, coal, oil, and natural gas.* Water is a resource that most often replenishes itself. When we have a hot summer, we sometimes have to use our water sparingly, but when we have a few days of rain, the water is usually replenished.

Some natural resources cannot be replenished. When they are used up, they will be gone. Coal, oil, and natural gas are resources that cannot be replaced. Scientists are developing new and better ways to find and use these natural resources, and they are always looking for new ideas as well. One new idea is **nuclear energy**, and its possibilities for providing our needs are very great.

Solar energy (energy from the sun) is just one of the ways that scientists are experimenting with to provide us with energy. Perhaps you have already seen or at least heard of solar houses. As long as there is a sun in the sky, solar energy is available to us, but we must first learn good methods of using it.

As Americans work together in their free country, they are finding more and more ways to use God's gifts to benefit mankind.

Thankful to Be Americans

We Americans have many things to be thankful to God for.

We have a land rich in natural resources and a free society in which people can work to earn their own living and to bring us food, minerals, timber, and sources of energy.

We have people who are constantly inventing better tools, machines, and labor-saving devices, and we have people who are creating new books, music, and art for us to enjoy.

We have more comforts and conveniences than people in any other part of the world. When people come to America from other countries, they are often amazed at our cars, our washing machines, our television sets and refrigerators. In many countries, these things are scarce, and even those who are rich enough to afford them may have to wait many years to get them.

But better than all this, we have a country based on the dream of liberty and justice for all, the belief that all men are created equal and given the rights to life, liberty, and the pursuit of happiness.

We have a representative form of government based on the consent of the governed.

We have free churches that are granted their God-given right to conduct worship services without interference from the government.

America has been greatly blessed by God throughout its history. We have much to be thankful for. We have much to be prayerful about, too. We know that no country can continue to be great without God's continued blessing.

As Americans, we should pray daily that God will continue to bless our country. As Christians, we should do our part to live right lives according to the teachings of the Bible and to help other people in America and throughout the world to learn the message of the Bible.

As students in school, we can learn more and more about our country's founding and growth. We can learn about America's great men and women and try to be like them. We can learn to love our country and to want to do our part to keep America great. We can learn to express our knowledge and feelings about America, as one fifth-grade boy did in the following patriotic speech:

What Made America Great?

What made America great? That question is everywhere. I know the answer. Freedom and prayer made America great.

Men like George Washington fought to make America free. Those men under George Washington were brave men. They walked through ice and snow. They were not forced to do it. They did it for their country. Most of them died. Then there were men like Patrick Henry who said those famous words, "Give me liberty or give me death!"

And let's not forget prayer. George Washington prayed. He prayed to God to give his country freedom. Most of all the men who helped make our country great were men of prayer.

I love America because she is the greatest country in the whole world. When I grow up, I will do all I can to keep America free. I may not be able to do great things like George Washington or Patrick Henry, but I can do little things that may count as great things to our country. Schools like my Christian school make America great, too. I hope that America keeps the name of "The land of the free and the home of the brave."

—*Alan Stone*

The Pilgrims were thankful, and they had very little by today's standards. How much more thankful should we be for the way God has blessed America. Let us be thankful and prayerful and always willing to do our part to keep America a land abounding with liberty and justice for all.

Facts to Remember

1. What does *immunize* mean? _____

_____

What is a *vaccine*? _____

_____

_____

2. What dreaded disease was conquered in the 1950's? _____

   Who found the vaccine for this disease? _____

3. What are some other diseases that can now be cured, thanks to modern

   science? _____

   _____

4. What was the first country to launch a satellite into space? _____

   What was the name of the satellite, and when was it launched? _____

   _____

5. What was the name of America's first satellite, and when was it launched? __

   _____

6. When did the first man travel into space? _____

   What country was he from? _____

7. Who was the first American in space? _____

   What year did he make his flight? _____

8. Who was the first American to orbit the earth? _____

9. What do the Russians call a man who has been into space? _____

   What is the American name for such a man? _____

10. On which Apollo mission did the astronauts read from Genesis? _____

11. When did men first land on the moon? _____

   Which Apollo mission achieved this goal? _____

Who was the first man to set foot on the moon? _____

12. When did America's moon program end? _____

13. What was Skylab? _____

    When was it launched? _____

14. How do weather satellites help us? _____

    _____

    _____

15. How do satellites help us defend our country? _____

    _____

16. How do satellites aid communciation? _____

    _____

17. What was the moon rover designed to do? _____

    _____

    When was it first used? _____

18. What are three good sources of energy for our country? _____

    _____

19. Name six things for which we as Americans should be thankful. ____

    _____

    _____

    _____

    _____

    _____

Document Memorization

Because patriotic documents constitute such a large part of the framework of American history, students are not fully aware of their great heritage unless they learn the contents of these masterpieces. Elementary students are in the peak of their ability to memorize, and they will easily learn the documents in this section if just two or three minutes a day are set aside for class recitation. Students should also learn the states and capitals and the Presidents of the United States. The suggested number of weeks to spend on each document or list is given.

The American's Creed *(4 weeks)*

I believe in the United States of America as a government of the people, by the people, for the people, whose just powers are derived from the consent of the governed; a democracy in a republic; a sovereign Nation of many sovereign States; a perfect Union, one and inseparable; established upon those principles of freedom, equality, justice and humanity for which American patriots sacrificed their lives and fortunes.

I therefore believe it is my duty to my country to love it, to support its Constitution, to obey its laws, to respect its flag, and to defend it against all enemies.

—William Tyler Page

The Declaration of Independence *(6 weeks)*

In Congress, July 4, 1776

When, in the course of human events, it becomes necessary for one people to dissolve the political bands which have connected them with another, and to assume, among the powers of the earth, the separate and equal station to which the laws of nature and of nature's God entitle them, a decent respect to the opinions of mankind requires that they should declare the causes which impel them to the separation.

We hold these truths to be self-evident:—That all men are created equal; that they are endowed by their Creator with certain unalienable rights; that among these are life, liberty, and the pursuit of happiness. That, to secure these rights, governments are instituted among men, deriving their just powers from the consent of the governed; that, whenever any form of government becomes destructive of these ends, it is the right of the people to alter or to abolish it, and to institute a new government, laying its foundation on such principles, and organizing its powers in such form, as to them shall seem most likely to effect their safety and happiness. Prudence, indeed, will dictate that governments long established should not be changed for light and transient causes; and, accordingly, all experience hath shown that mankind are more disposed to suffer, while evils are sufferable, than to right themselves by abolishing the forms to which they are accustomed. But, when a long train of abuses and usurpations, pursuing invariably the same object, evinces a design to reduce them under absolute despotism, it is their right, it is their duty, to throw off such government, and to provide new guards for their future security. . . .

Preamble to the Constitution *(2 weeks)*

We the people of the United States, in order to form a more perfect Union, establish justice, insure domestic tranquillity, provide for the common defense, promote the general welfare, and secure the blessings of liberty to ourselves and our posterity, do ordain and establish this Constitution for the United States of America.

First Amendment to the Constitution *(2 weeks)*
(Article One to the Bill of Rights)

Congress shall make no law respecting an establishment of religion, or prohibiting the free exercise thereof; or abridging the freedom of speech, or of the press; or the right of the people peaceably to assemble, and to petition the government for a redress of grievances.

The Rights of Americans *(2 weeks)*

1. The right to worship God in one's own way.
2. The right to free speech and press.
3. The right to petition for grievances—in fair and honest judgment.
4. The right to privacy in our homes.
5. The right to own private property.

6. The right to own, keep, and bear arms.

7. The right to move about freely at home or abroad.

8. The right to habeas corpus—without excessive bail.

9. The right to trial by jury—innocent until proven guilty.

10. The right to free elections and personal secret ballots.

11. The right to the service of government as a protector and referee.

12. The right to freedom from arbitrary government regulation and control.

13. The right to work in callings and localities of our choice.

14. The right to bargain for goods and services in a free market.

15. The right to contract about our affairs.

16. The right to go into business, compete, and make a profit.

Lincoln's Gettysburg Address *(6 weeks)*

Fourscore and seven years ago our fathers brought forth upon this continent a new nation, conceived in liberty, and dedicated to the proposition that all men are created equal.

Now we are engaged in a great civil war, testing whether that nation, or any nation so conceived and so dedicated, can long endure. We are met on a great battlefield of that war. We have come to dedicate a portion of that field as a final resting place for those who here gave their lives that that nation might live. It is altogether fitting and proper that we should do this.

But, in a larger sense, we cannot dedicate—we cannot consecrate—we cannot hallow—this ground. The brave men, living and dead, who struggled here, have consecrated it far above our poor power to add or detract. The world will little note nor long remember what we say here, but it can never forget what they did here. It is for us, the living, rather, to be dedicated here to the unfinished work which they who fought here have thus far so nobly advanced. It is rather for us to be here dedicated to the great task remaining before us—that from these honored dead we take increased devotion to that cause for which they gave the last full measure of devotion; that we here highly resolve that these dead shall not have died in vain; that this nation, under God, shall have a new birth of freedom; and that government of the people, by the people, for the people, shall not perish from the earth.

Facts about the Presidents *(6 weeks)*

(Memorize Presidents in Order)

NO.	NAME	BORN/DIED	YEARS IN OFFICE	STATE
1	George Washington	1732 1799	1789–1797	Va.
2	John Adams	1735 1826	1797–1801	Mass.
3	Thomas Jefferson	1743 1826	1801–1809	Va.
4	James Madison	1751 1836	1809–1817	Va.
5	James Monroe	1758 1831	1817–1825	Va.
6	John Quincy Adams	1767 1848	1825–1829	Mass.
7	Andrew Jackson	1767 1845	1829–1837	Tenn.
8	Martin Van Buren	1782 1862	1837-1841	N.Y.
9	William Henry Harrison	1773 1841	1841	Ohio
10	John Tyler	1790 1862	1841–1845	Va.
11	James K. Polk	1795 1849	1845–1849	Tenn.
12	Zachary Taylor	1784 1850	1849–1850	La.
13	Millard Fillmore	1800 1874	1850–1853	N.Y.
14	Franklin Pierce	1804 1869	1853–1857	N.H.
15	James Buchanan	1791 1868	1857–1861	Pa.
16	Abraham Lincoln	1809 1865	1861–1865	Ill.
17	Andrew Johnson	1808 1875	1865–1869	Tenn.
18	Ulysses S. Grant	1822 1885	1869–1877	Ill.
19	Rutherford B. Hayes	1822 1893	1877–1881	Ohio
20	James A. Garfield	1831 1881	1881	Ohio
21	Chester A. Arthur	1830 1886	1881–1885	N.Y.
22	Grover Cleveland	1837 1908	1885–1889	N.Y.
23	Benjamin Harrison	1833 1901	1889–1893	Ind.
24	Grover Cleveland	1837 1908	1893–1897	N.Y.
25	William McKinley	1843 1901	1897–1901	Ohio
26	Theodore Roosevelt	1858 1919	1901–1909	N.Y.
27	William Howard Taft	1857 1930	1909–1913	Ohio
28	Woodrow Wilson	1856 1924	1913–1921	N.J.
29	Warren G. Harding	1865 1923	1921–1923	Ohio
30	Calvin Coolidge	1872 1933	1923–1929	Mass.
31	Herbert Hoover	1874 1964	1929–1933	Calif.
32	Franklin D. Roosevelt	1882 1945	1933–1945	N.Y.
33	Harry S. Truman	1884 1972	1945–1953	Mo.
34	Dwight D. Eisenhower	1890 1969	1953–1961	N.Y.
35	John F. Kennedy	1917 1963	1961–1963	Mass.
36	Lyndon B. Johnson	1908 1973	1963–1969	Texas
37	Richard M. Nixon	1913	1969–1974	Calif.
38	Gerald R. Ford	1913	1974–1977	Mich.
39	James E. Carter	1924	1977–1981	Ga.
40	Ronald Reagan	1911	1981–1989	Calif.
41	George Bush	1924	1989–	Texas

Facts about the States *(6 weeks)*

(Memorize States and Capitals)

NAME	CAPITAL	STANDARD ABBREVIATION	TWO-LETTER ABBREVIATION*	DATE OF ADMISSION TO UNION	NUMBER IN ORDER OF ADMISSION
Alabama	Montgomery	Ala.	AL	1819	22
Alaska	Juneau	Alaska	AK	1959	49
Arizona	Phoenix	Ariz.	AZ	1912	48
Arkansas	Little Rock	Ark.	AR	1836	25
California	Sacramento	Calif.	CA	1850	31
Colorado	Denver	Colo.	CO	1876	38
Connecticut	Hartford	Conn.	CT	1788	5
Delaware	Dover	Del.	DE	1787	1
Florida	Tallahassee	Fla.	FL	1845	27
Georgia	Atlanta	Ga.	GA	1788	4
Hawaii	Honolulu	Hawaii	HI	1959	50
Idaho	Boise	Idaho	ID	1890	43
Illinois	Springfield	Ill.	IL	1818	21
Indiana	Indianapolis	Ind.	IN	1816	19
Iowa	Des Moines	Iowa	IA	1846	29
Kansas	Topeka	Kans.	KS	1861	34
Kentucky	Frankfort	Ky.	KY	1792	15
Louisiana	Baton Rouge	La.	LA	1812	18
Maine	Augusta	Maine	ME	1820	23
Maryland	Annapolis	Md.	MD	1788	7
Massachusetts	Boston	Mass.	MA	1788	6
Michigan	Lansing	Mich.	MI	1837	26
Minnesota	St. Paul	Minn.	MN	1858	32
Mississippi	Jackson	Miss.	MS	1817	20
Missouri	Jefferson City	Mo.	MO	1821	24
Montana	Helena	Mont.	MT	1889	41
Nebraska	Lincoln	Nebr.	NE	1867	37
Nevada	Carson City	Nev.	NV	1864	36
New Hampshire	Concord	N. H.	NH	1788	9
New Jersey	Trenton	N. J.	NJ	1787	3
New Mexico	Santa Fe	N. Mex.	NM	1912	47
New York	Albany	N. Y.	NY	1788	11
North Carolina	Raleigh	N. C.	NC	1789	12
North Dakota	Bismarck	N. Dak.	ND	1889	39
Ohio	Columbus	Ohio	OH	1803	17
Oklahoma	Oklahoma City	Okla.	OK	1907	46
Oregon	Salem·	Oreg.	OR	1859	33
Pennsylvania	Harrisburg	Pa.	PA	1787	2

*To be used only with ZIP code.

NAME	CAPITAL	STANDARD ABBREVIATION	TWO-LETTER ABBREVIATION*	DATE OF ADMISSION TO UNION	NUMBER IN ORDER OF ADMISSION
Rhode Island	Providence	R. I.	RI	1790	13
South Carolina	Columbia	S. C.	SC	1788	8
South Dakota	Pierre	S. Dak.	SD	1889	40
Tennessee	Nashville	Tenn.	TN	1796	16
Texas	Austin	Tex.	TX	1845	28
Utah	Salt Lake City	Utah	UT	1896	45
Vermont	Montpelier	Vt.	VT	1791	14
Virginia	Richmond	Va.	VA	1788	10
Washington	Olympia	Wash.	WA	1889	42
West Virginia	Charleston	W. Va.	WV	1863	35
Wisconsin	Madison	Wis.	WI	1848	30
Wyoming	Cheyenne	Wyo.	WY	1890	44
District of Columbia	Washington	D. C.	DC	1791	••

*To be used only with ZIP code.

Acknowledgments

Cover photos: Roger Williams—The Bettmann Archive; Signing U.S. Constitution, Lincoln—The Granger Collection, New York; Shuttle *Columbia*—Hank Morgan/Science Source/Photo Researchers, Inc.

The Bettmann Archive, Inc.: 12, 14, 24, 26, 30, 38, 40 all, 44, 45, 46, 49 top right and bottom right, 53, 54, 56 left, 58, 59, 62, 64, 68, 70, 72, 75, 82 top, 83, 87, 89, 92, 98 top, 99 bottom, 101 bottom, 103 right and bottom left, 104 right, 105, 134, 145, 152, 154, 159 top, 175 bottom, 178 bottom, 180, 182, 186, 187, 190, 191, 197 bottom, 201 both, 204, 208, 222 both, 223, 224, 225, 227 top left and bottom, 234, 236, 238, 239 top, 243, 245, 246, 248, 254, 255 bottom, 261 bottom, 270, 272, 273 bottom, 297 top left

Brown Brothers: 265 top

Christopher Dock Mennonite High School: 111

Culver Pictures: 84, 103 top left, 115 right, 118 right, 130, 198

Art Resource, N.Y.: 35 (Jim Tuten), 39 bottom right (Breitenbach), 42 top, 147 bottom, 156 left, 196, 220

ERDA: 303

FPG: 287 left (Photoworld), 297 bottom left (Lee Balterman)

The Granger Collection, N.Y.: 28, 110 top, 142, 143, 171 bottom, 174, 200, 205, 206 both, 216, 217 bottom, 218, 231 bottom, 233 right, 237, 239 left, 241 242, 247, 249, 258 bottom, 263, 268, 274, 275, 277, 279

Historical Pictures Service, Chicago: 34, 39 top left, top right, bottom left, center right, center left, 42, 51, 56 right, 61, 82 bottom, 85, 91, 93, 95, 101 top, 102, 107, 114, 118 left, 121, 125, 129 right, 132, 135, 136, 168 bottom, 183, 207, 209, 221, 227 top right

Los Alamos Scientific Laboratory: 287 right

Courtesy McDonnell Douglas: 282

NASA: 296, 299

New York Historical Society: 48

Photo Researchers (Van Bucher): 104 left

ROLOC: 32, 36, 98 bottom, 110 bottom, 138, 139, 144, 146, 147 top, 148, 150, 151, 153, 155, 156 right, 157, 159 bottom, 164, 168 top, 170, 171 top and middle, 178 top, 211, 258 top, 259 both, 261 top, 264 both, 265 bottom, 271, 273 top, 281, 284, 285, 286, 288, 289, 290

ROLOC/NASA: 298 both, 300 all, 301

St. Louis Art Museum: 193

Silverdome, Detroit: 302

State Historical Society of Wisconsin: 128

Stock Boston (Milton Feinberg): 71

Tass from Sovfoto: 297 right

314

myessential body wear. com !801